The Foreign Policy of Churchill's Peacetime
Administration 1951–1955

The Foreign Policy of Churchill's Peacetime Administration 1951-1955

Edited by John W. Young

1988
LEICESTER UNIVERSITY PRESS

First published in 1988 by Leicester University Press

Designed by Douglas Martin
Filmset in Linotron 101 Palatino
Printed and bound in Great Britain by
Billing and Sons Ltd, Worcester

British Library Cataloguing in Publication Data

The foreign policy of Churchill's peacetime
administration 1951–1955.
1. Great Britain. Foreign relations.
Policies, 1951–1955 of government
I. Young, John W. (John Wilson)
327.41

ISBN 0–7185–1264–2

Contents

List of Maps

Abbreviations

AIOC	Anglo-Iranian Oil Company
ANZUS	Australian-New Zealand-United States alliance
CIA	American Central Intelligence Agency
ECSC	European Coal and Steel Community
EDC	European Defence Community
EPC	European Political Community
EPU	European Payments Union
FRUS	Foreign Relations of the United States
GATT	General Agreement on Tariffs and Trade
NATO	North Atlantic Treaty Organization
NSC	American National Security Council
OEEC	Organization for European Economic Co-operation
PRO	Public Record Office
	References are to documents at the Public Record Office, Kew, unless otherwise stated
ADM	Admiralty
BT	Board of Trade
CAB	Cabinet
CMD	Command Papers, Houses of Parliament
COS	Chiefs of Staff
CRO	Commonwealth Relations Office
DEFE	Defence
DO	Dominions Office
FO	Foreign Office

RAF   Royal Air Force
SANF   South African Naval Force
SEATO   South-East Asia Treaty Organization
SPC   Schuman Plan Committee
TCC   NATO Temporary Control Committee
UNC   United Nations Command in Korea
WEU   West European Union

HC Deb. 5s *Debates, House of Commons*
HL Deb. 5s *Debates, House of Lords*
PREM   *Prime Minister's Office*
WFIS   *Whitman File, International Series, Eisenhower Library, Abilene*

Notes on Contributors

Anthony Adamthwaite was Foundation Professor of History at Loughborough University and now teaches at the University of Salford. His publications include *France and the Coming of the Second World War, 1936–1939* (1977), *The Making of the Second World War* (1979), and *The Lost Peace: International Relations in Europe, 1918–1939* (1980).

G.R. Berridge has been Lecturer in Politics at the University of Leicester since 1978 and his principal publications include *Economic Power in Anglo–South African Diplomacy* (1981), *The Politics of the South African Run: European Shipping and Pretoria* (1987), and *International Politics: States Power and Conflict since 1945* (1987). He was also co-editor of *Diplomacy at the U.N.* (1985).

Peter Boyle (M.A. Glasgow University, Ph.D. U.C.L.A.) is a Lecturer in American History at the University of Nottingham. He has published several articles on relations between Britain, the United States and the Soviet Union in the years 1945–55.

Peter Lowe is a Senior Lecturer in History at Manchester University. Previous books include *Great Britain and Japan, 1911–15* (1969), *Great Britain and the Origins of the Pacific War* (1977), *Britain in the Far East: a Survey, 1819 to the Present* (1981), and *The Origins of the Korean War* (1986). He is currently preparing a comparative study of British policy in East Asia, c.1948–53.

Ritchie Ovendale is a Reader in the Department of International Politics, University College of Wales, Aberystwyth. He has written *'Appeasement' and the English Speaking World: Britain, the United States, the Dominions, and the Policy of 'Appeasement', 1937–1939* (1975), *The Origins of the Arab–Israeli Wars* (1984) and *The English-Speaking Alliance: Britain, the United States, the Dominions and the Cold War 1945–51* (1985), and has edited *The Foreign Policy of the British Labour Governments, 1945–1951* (1984).

Brian Holden Reid is Lecturer in War Studies at King's College, London, and Resident Historian at the British Army Staff College, Camberley. From 1984 to 1987 he was editor of the Royal United Services Institute *Journal*, and he is author of *J.F.C. Fuller: Military Thinker* (1987).

J.E. Spence has been Professor of Politics at Leicester since 1973 and was the University's Pro-Vice-Chancellor 1981-5. His publications include *Republic under Pressure: a Study of South African Foreign Policy* (1965), *Lesotho – the Politics of Independence* (1968), and *The Strategic Significance of Southern Africa* (1970). He was editor of the *British Journal of International Studies* from 1975 to 1981.

Geoffrey Warner is Professor of European Humanities at the Open University. He is author of *Pierre Laval and the Eclipse of France* (1968) and of numerous articles on international history.

John Young is Lecturer in International History at the London School of Economics and author of *Britain, France and the Unity of Europe 1945–51* (1984).

Preface

THIS BOOK presents a number of essays from leading inter-national historians, highlighting some of the more significant issues in British foriegn policy during the Conservative government of 1951–5. These were the years of a potential 'thaw' in the Cold War following the death of Stalin, of the resolution of the Korean conflict in the Far East, and of the build-up to the Suez crisis with Egypt in 1956. Too often, of course, the foreign policy of the immediate post-war governments is viewed in the light of Suez. Churchill's peacetime government may indeed have failed to adjust to the country's underlying weaknesses, but the period also saw some successes for British policy-makers and the country remained the 'third power' in world politics. Dwarfed now by her two wartime allies, America and Russia, Britain none the less had an important role in resolving such problems as the Korean War, the Indochina conflict and German rearmament; Anthony Eden, though dogged by ill health, brought his negotiating skills to bear on a number of diplomatic crises, with particular success in 1954; and the ageing Churchill was still able to make his unique mark on the 'special relationship' with Washington and the question of detente with Moscow. By drawing together studies on these and other major issues it is hoped to stimulate more debate about this key period of post-war foreign policy.

On behalf of all the contributors I would like to thank the staff of all the archives consulted in writing the book, particularly those at the Public Record Office, Kew. Copyright material from the Public Record Office appears by permission of Her Majesty's Stationery Office. I also wish to thank Peter Boulton and the staff at Leicester University Press for their patience and diligence in bringing the book to publication.

John W. Young
July 1987

Introduction: The Foreign Office and Policy-making

Anthony Adamthwaite

IT IS generally agreed that the 1945–51 Labour governments coped well with the retreat from power and that the period was 'among the most successful in the history of British external policy'.[1] By contrast, the 1951–5 Churchill government has won few tributes. Even discounting the retrospective blight cast by the 1956 Suez crisis, Britain's greatest post-war humiliation, the fact remains that the second Churchill Cabinet's lasting achievement was small. The descent from power continued apace. Against Foreign Secretary Anthony Eden's negotiating triumphs on Indochina, German rearmament and Trieste in 1954 must be set the withdrawal from the Suez Canal zone, Britain's Middle East bastion. Within a year the new Foreign Secretary, Harold Macmillan, complained of 'Eden's chickens coming home to roost'.[2] Why, despite sharing the same objectives as Labour governments, did the second Churchill administration accomplish less? The explanation lies largely in the interaction of three elements: Britain's want of power to solve her problems; the uneasy Churchill–Eden partnership; the deficiencies of the government machine.

The 'decline of Britain' debate can all too easily distort assessments of the second Churchill government. Blanket assertions that post-war governments put grandeur before decline and encouraged debilitating myths are misleading in the context of the early 1950s. The literature often assumes that the abandonment of pretensions to world power would have enabled leaders to focus resources on internal growth and so escape rapid decline. However, this essay argues that the only realistic option at the time was the gradual reduction of overseas commitments while seeking a reduced world role. This was the strategy which Clement Attlee and Ernest Bevin had successfully pursued. The same strategy might well have worked for Conservative leaders but never received a fair trial. Prime Minister Winston Churchill opposed any withdrawals and quarrelled with Eden on a number of issues. Their bitchy and acrimonious partnership contrasted sadly with the solid and harmonious Attlee–Bevin relationship. Furthermore, institutional weaknesses ensured that policy-making was badly fragmented and ill defined.

A full assessment of the Churchill government's foreign policy is hampered by the limitations of the sources. At first sight this may seem surprising. In one sense there is a formidable array of primary sources – public and private papers, Hansard, memoirs, periodicals, newspapers, films and oral history. Nevertheless, the foreign policy-making record has important lacunae. Despite the stacks of Public Record Office material many questions remain unanswered and may never be satisfactorily resolved. The greatest obstacle lies in the inequality of available sources – a mountainous mass on some issues; extremely fragmentary or non-existent on others. Some gaps are decreed by Whitehall: intelligence files and other papers deemed sensitive are locked away.[3] Exceptionally the 'weeders' have left clues and a jigsaw puzzle can be pieced together but usually there are missing pieces. Other gaps in the record will never be filled. Changes in Foreign Office working methods make it difficult to discover the whys and wherefores of decisions. Before the Second World War consultation within the Office and with other government departments was mostly by correspondence; during the war much more was done orally, and this became the norm. The urgency of post-war issues ensured that they were handled in *ad hoc* or informal meetings which often went unminuted. The sheer volume of incoming papers (in 1913, 68,000; in 1953, 586,000), the inevitable decline in the standards of filing, the mass of unrecorded telephone conversations, make it 'quite impossible for anybody to unravel with any accuracy from the archives the detailed history of events'.[4]

Record-keeping procedures may conceal as much as they reveal. Cabinet minutes were designed not so much as a record of proceedings but as instructions for action to departments. The Secretary was 'under instructions to avoid . . . recording the opinions expressed by particular ministers'.[5] In 1953 Macmillan, then Minister of Housing, complained that the minutes might mislead:

> Historians reading this fifty or a hundred years hence will get
> a totally false picture. They will be filled with admiration and

surprise to find that the Cabinet were so intellectually disciplined that they argued each issue methodically and logically through to a set of neat and precise conclusions. It isn't like that at all.[6]

In the words of the anonymous verse:

Now that the Cabinet's gone to dinner
The Secretary stays and gets thinner and thinner
Racking his brains to record and report
What he thinks that they think they ought to have thought.

The multiplicity of problems crowding Eden's desk would have disheartened most Foreign Secretaries. The job, Eden remarked, 'had killed Bevin and destroyed Morrison and now he understood why'.[7] The Cold War was at its height dividing East and West by political and ideological conflict; Germany and Austria were dismembered and occupied with no sign of peace treaties; in Iran, Prime Minister Mossadeq had nationalized the oil industry and thrown out the Anglo-Iranian oil company; the Egyptian government had denounced the 1936 treaty with Britain which allowed the stationing of British forces in the Suez Canal Zone until 1956, and early in 1952 the whole of the strategic reserve was sent to Egypt to deal with terrorism in the Canal Zone; whilst in Korea a full-scale war raged between North and South with Chinese communists helping the North Koreans while the South was supported by United Nations forces; and in Indochina, France fought Viet Minh nationalists aided by Communist China. Britain had her own colonial wars – from 1950 the emergency in Malaya and in 1952 the Mau Mau rebellion in Kenya. Nearer home Italy and Yugoslavia clashed over their claims to the city of Trieste.

For Eden and his advisers these challenges were dwarfed by the fundamental problem of how to sustain a world role with diminishing resources in a harsh and swiftly changing environment. Britain was a captive of circumstance. The 1939–45 conflict confirmed that she was not a great power from her intrinsic strength. In 1945 a war-weary and bankrupt country was eclipsed by two superpowers, the United States and the Soviet Union. After six years of peace, rationing remained and in January 1952 the meat ration was even reduced. 'We are in a balance of payments crisis worse than 1949, and in many ways worse even than 1947', 'Rab' Butler, Chancellor of the

Exchequer, warned in October 1951.[8] A year later he repeated the warning:

> We were all agreed when we took office that the defence programme which we inherited was beyond the nation's means. It was based on assumptions about American aid and the strength of our economy which have since been proved false . . . We are attempting to do too much . . . Anything more than the current level of expenditure means moving towards a war economy with radical revision of our social and economic policies.[9]

Britain's predicament was pinpointed by John Colville, Churchill's private secretary, in June 1952:

> It is foolish to continue living with illusions . . . the facts are stark. At the moment we are just paying our way. A trade recession in America will break us; the competition of German metallurgical industries and the industrialisation of countries which were once the market for our industrial products will ruin our trade sooner or later . . . What can we do? Increasing productivity is only a palliative in the face of foreign competition. We cannot till sufficient soil to feed 50 million people. We cannot emigrate fast enough to meet the danger, even if we were willing to face the consequent abdication of our position as a great power . . . Lord Cherwell sees hope in the union of the English Speaking World . . . But now England, and Europe, distrust, dislike and despise the United States. Some pin their faith on the development of the Empire as a great economic unit . . . We have left it too late.[10]

Britain patently lacked the military and economic strength to retain all her world interests. Since 1945 the United States and the Soviet Union had grown more powerful both in absolute terms and in relation to other major powers. In relative terms Britain's military strength continued to decline. The nuclear umbrella gained by the testing of an atom bomb in 1952 gave a brief illusion of strength. However, she was clearly a poor third in the thermonuclear stakes. In 1952 the United States exploded a hydrogen bomb, followed a year later by the Soviet Union. Britain did not catch up until 1957. The revolution in nuclear war represented by the hydrogen bomb underlined Britain's weakness. Limited resources, as Macmillan recognized when he became Minister of Defence, in 1954, meant that 'we really cannot fight any war *except* a nuclear war. It is quite impossible to arm our forces with two *sets* of weapons – conventional and unconventional.'[11] The hydrogen bomb also hit at Britain's Middle East primacy. The Canal Zone could be destroyed virtually at a blow. Sir Ivone Kirkpatrick, Permanent Under-Secretary of State at the Foreign Office, minuted in 1954:

> I do not believe that in this atomic age we shall have either the wish or the ability to reactivate the base. We will be sufficiently occupied struggling for survival . . . the power and numbers of these frightful weapons will be so great that the chances of our wanting to conduct a campaign in the Middle East will be less than it is today.[12]

The missile race proved beyond Britain's means and by 1958 her missile programme was running into serious financial difficulties.

Britain's influence was also eroded by major changes in the Empire and Commonwealth. The grant of independence to India and Pakistan in 1947 was the crucial event in post-war overseas policy. In 1945 Britain's world power had been perceived as resting not on the United Kingdom alone but on the Empire-Commonwealth. India, 'the jewel', had been the centrepiece of Britain's east of Suez domination. The Indian army enabled control to be exercised over the whole area on the trade route from Malta to the Far East and Australia. Although India and Pakistan joined the Commonwealth Britain lost military control of the sub-continent. Before 1939 Britain's relationship to the Commonwealth countries was still largely a maternal one. British ambassadors in foreign countries normally looked after the interests of the Dominions as well. Only Canada had a separate foreign service of any size. Commonwealth countries habitually looked first to Britain in all circumstances, irrespective of their geographical position. This was no longer true in the early 1950s. The 'old Dominions' – Canada, Australia, New Zealand, South Africa – became deeply involved in political and military relationships in their own parts of the world. The transformation was strikingly symbolized in the 1951 ANZUS Pact, by which the United States took over Britain's role in the defence of Australia and New Zealand and from which Britain, on Australian insistence, was excluded. There was no question of Commonwealth unity on foreign policy. Lord Strang, Permanent Under-Secretary in 1949–53, reflecting on his experience could not recall 'any instance' when 'there had been a united Commonwealth view on any difficult issue . . . It was rare to find the Canadians and Australians of the same mind.'[13]

Diminishing power was only part of the problem. The world which Churchill and Eden found on taking office in October 1951 had undergone a metamorphosis even since the Second World War. As well as the obvious changes – the Cold War conflict, the rise of Afro-Asian nationalism, communist control of China – the increase in the number of states, agents and subjects of negotiation since 1945 constituted a sea change in international politics. 'Things have gotten ten or fifteen times more complicated', Churchill confessed to the American President, General Dwight Eisenhower, adding that 'the problems I now face are much greater in number and complexity than they used to be'.[14] A global system had replaced a European-based system in which the main decisions had been made in London, Paris, Berlin and Rome. The rise of multilateralism meant that by 1951 Britain was enmeshed in what Eden called 'the alarming growth of international committees and commissions of every sort and kind' – the United Nations and its specialist agencies, the North Atlantic Treaty Organization (NATO), the Organization for European Economic Co-operation (OEEC), the Council of Europe, and others. The Cold War was a further constraint. Since 1941 the Anglo-American alliance was accepted as Britain's sheet anchor. Only American support, it was argued, enabled Britain to retain a world role. Paradoxically, however, the American alliance accelerated decline. From 1947 the polarization of power blocs around the United States and the Soviet Union reduced the influence which second-rank states like Britain could exercise, and Britain's post-war rearmament, initiated in response to the outbreak of the Korean War in June 1950, overloaded an ailing economy imposing a heavier defence spending per capita than on the American people. By 1953 British defence spending represented 28.5 per cent of total government spending.

The difficulties of policy-making were compounded by the increased interest of the public in foreign affairs. Before the First World War foreign policy had been concerned almost exclusively with relations between governments. In 1914–18 the appeal to peoples as opposed to governments added a new dimension to diplomacy. Policy-makers had perforce to reckon with the impact of policies on domestic and international opinion. Some historians, relying on one or two polls over a period of twenty years, have seriously underestimated public interest in international affairs.[15] However, polls for 1951–5 reveal three principal features: consistently strong support for a superpower summit; large fluctuations of interest in world affairs; and firm views on individual issues. When asked in December 1951 what was 'the most urgent problem the government must solve in the next few months' the majority replied 'foreign affairs', instancing Korea and Egypt.[16] Five months on, in May 1952, 'the cost of living' came first, and international issues was pushed into fourth place. In June 1953 international problems again topped the list. On the hydrogen bomb, Egypt, Korea and German rearmament the public held decided opinions. But strong views did *not* produce demonstrations or letters to MPs. After 1945 opinion impinged on British policy in two ways. First, a growing body of international opinion, especially in the United States, condemned European colonialism; secondly, wartime conferences generated expectations that great power summits would solve world problems and foster international understanding. For the Churchill government opinion was both a spur and a curb. By showing overwhelming support for a summit the polls fuelled Churchill's resolve to arrange such a meeting. Sir William Strang argued 'the need to show the British public that we are not missing opportunities for peace'.[17] But public attitudes also acted as a restraint. To counter ebbing power overseas publicity projected the importance of Britain's moral, democratic and technical leadership. In short the old lion might be past his prime but still had character and brains. This propaganda, however, proved double-edged because Britain was expected to practise what she preached. Egypt exemplified the dilemma. After Britain's withdrawal from Palestine in 1948 Egyptian nationalism posed the most serious threat to Britain's Middle East paramountcy. Egypt, anxious to eliminate the last vestiges of British tutelage, demanded abandonment of the Suez Canal base. Already, in 1946, Bevin's private secretary had acknowledged: 'the days are over when we could treat Egypt *de haut en bas* and act as a great Power . . . This would not only have been out of tune with mid-twentieth century conceptions, but we should have been balled out at the Security Council.'[18] In 1953, while Britain and Egypt haggled over an agreement, Eden made the same point to Cabinet colleagues: to stay in the Canal base 'would almost certainly compel us to reoccupy Egypt . . . We should be likely to have world opinion against us and would find it difficult to make a case if Egypt took us to the United Nations.'[19] Three years later Eden had evidently forgotten his own counsel. Assessing the significance of the 1956 Suez crisis Sir Charles Keightly, commander-in-chief of the Anglo-French forces, wrote:

> The overriding lesson of the Suez operation is that world opinion is now an absolute principle of war and must be treated as such. However successful the pure military operations may be, they will fail . . . unless national, Commonwealth and Western world opinion is sufficiently on our side.[20]

Eden analysed Britain's predicament in a Cabinet paper of 18 June 1952 on 'British Overseas Obligations',[21] and not surprisingly he recommended a gradual reduction of commitments. British governments are sometimes said to have clung to a mirage of power until 1956. Scarce resources, it is contended, were squandered in maintaining vast overseas commitments and a huge defence budget. In fact, as the Second World War ended, planners took stock of Britain's plight. 'The problems in front of us', wrote Sir Alexander Cadogan, Permanent Under-Secretary in 1945, 'are manifold and awful.'[22] Arguably the assessments of the time were not realistic enough, but it is hardly fair to blame the planners for failing to foresee the precipitious decline of the 1960s and 1970s. Initial diagnoses concluded that enfeeblement was temporary and recovery a matter of time. Nevertheless, contraction took place. Between 1945 and 1948 Britain withdrew from India, Palestine, Greece and Turkey. In 1946 Attlee had advocated withdrawal from much of the Middle East and 1949 brought a 'general realisation that there is no solution to our problems over which we ourselves exercise much freedom of choice'.[23] In 1950 Bevin reminded the Commons, 'the day when we, as Great Britain, can declare a policy independently of our allies, has gone'.[24] Thus by 1951–2 few disputed that Britain had to seek a reduced world role anchored in an American alliance.

Eden's 1952 paper identified three fundamental factors governing British policy: 'world responsibilities inherited from several hundred years as a Great Power'; the fact that the United Kingdom was 'not a self-sufficient economic unit'; and the lack of a 'world security system which meant that the United Kingdom ... is faced with an external threat'. 'Rigorous maintenance' of present commitments, warned Eden, placed 'a burden on the country's economy which is beyond the resources of the country ... A position has already been reached where there is no reserve and therefore no margin for unforeseen additional obligations.' The remedy was a gradual shedding of responsibilities while preserving 'the world position of the United Kingdom'. If 'after careful review' this proved too much for national resources the British people faced a difficult choice: 'they must either give up, for a time, some of the advantages which a high standard of living confers ... or, by relaxing their grip in the outside world, see their country sink to the level of a second class Power, with injury to their essential interests and way of life of which they can have little conception'. Drastic and unilateral withdrawal from commitments was rejected: 'the effects of a failure of will and relaxation of grip ... are incalculable. But once the prestige of a country has started to slide there is no knowing where it will stop.' Eden concluded that the only practical course was slowly to shed defence commitments in the Middle East and South-East Asia by constructing international defence organizations and by persuading the United States to take the lead.

Egypt was a practical application of the recommended policy. In February 1953 Eden restated his strategy, urging the Cabinet to accept the loss of the Suez Canal Zone:

> We could undoutedly deal effectively with any immediate attempt by the Egyptians to eject us by force from the Canal Zone. But ... We cannot afford to keep 80,000 men indefinitely in the Canal Zone. Already our current overseas expenditure – mainly military – has risen from £160 million in 1950 to £222 million (provisional estimate) in 1952. This does not include the local cost of our troops in Germany ... With our limited resources, it is essential that we should concentrate on the points where our vital strategic needs or the necessities of our economic life are at stake and that we should utilise our strength in the most economical way.[25]

What went wrong? Why did Eden's recipe fail? Arguably because the prescription was not radical enough. The government wanted to have its cake and eat it. But there was no half-way house between superpower and the second division. Only abdication as a great power would have released sufficient resources to arrest economic decline. Plausible as this argument sounds it is, however, open to several objections. At the time the idea of wholesale withdrawal contradicted long-held, widely supported public policies and assumptions. Britain was the prisoner of her past. The 1945 victory seemed to have vindicated Britain's self-image as a leading world power. The retreats of the 1930s were dismissed as abberrations springing from political ineptitude. Both ministers and public were convinced that the country was and could remain a world power. To criticize this as an illusion is to oversimplify Britain's quandary. Britain still deployed substantial military power in the form of nuclear force, large conventional units and a world-wide network of bases. Just thirteen years before, in 1939, Britain had been an acknowledged world power pursuing an independent foreign policy. Building public support for abdication as a world power would have required several years. Moreover, having power is being seen to have power: Eden and his advisers feared that a rapid run-down might be disastrous for prestige. This was a valid fear. Fast contraction risked destroying Britain's credibility. The power and influence needed for survival as a medium power might be lost. Also, the damage to home morale could have endangered the object of the exercise – economic recovery. In sum, rapid withdrawal from Empire and commitments was not practical politics in the early 1950s. The government with a majority of only 17 would not have carried its own supporters, let alone public opinion. The proof is that withdrawal from the Sudan and the Suez Canal brought a battle with the thirty to forty-strong Suez group of Conservative backbenchers.

Alternatively, and more convincingly, it can be argued that Eden's policy failed for other reasons. First and foremost it was not properly conceived and followed through. It does not seem to have been discussed in Cabinet. No 'careful review' of resources and options took place. Furthermore, the design was flawed. Eden suggested that in order to persuade the United States to shoulder more of the burden Britain had 'to demonstrate that we are making the maximum effort ourselves'. Distrust of Britain and her Empire was strong in the United States. This line of thought seemed to imply that Britain should continue to overstrain her economy so as to satisfy the Americans that we were still a powerful and worthwhile ally. This raised the further and deeper question which Eden and the planners dodged, namely, in what sense, if any, could Britain remain a 'world power' while so demonstrably dependent on American support and goodwill? Key questions such as how much power and influence should Britain seek to retain and in what areas went unanswered. Nor was a timetable mentioned. How 'gradual' was gradual?

Several considerations militated against an orderly and planned retreat. Churchill and Eden lacked the will to see it through. Eden, immersed in immediate problems, could 'see a little ahead' but was 'too keen on popularity to push far-seeing measures through'.[26] Churchill, who only twelve years before had 'not become the King's First Minister in order to preside over the liquidation of the British Empire', opposed further withdrawals and contested Eden's policy on Egypt. Moreover, there was agreement that Britain was overstretched but no consensus on what should be done. The psychological dimension was crucial. The combination of rapid international change and growing awareness of national weakness had a traumatic effect. In the immediate aftermath of war the assumption that ills were temporary shielded opinion from a full perception of decline. By 1951 it was realized that Britain suffered from a continuing haemorrhage. In this mood withdrawals became much harder to stomach. Suspicions that the Americans were 'out to take our place' and 'to run the world' stymied the close partnership with Washington which Eden's strategy required.[27] Rationally the British might acknowledge the need to shed part of the load but instinctively they took for granted that 'our future will be of one piece with our past and that we shall continue as a Great Power'.[28] Churchill recognized in 1952 that 'now that we no longer hold India the Canal means very little to us' and yet fought tooth and nail to stay in Egypt.[29] The discontinuity between present and immediate past was deeply disorientating and produced ambivalent responses. With Churchill back at Downing Street his secretaries hoped that history could be arrested. They attacked Eden and the Foreign Office for their policy on Egypt:

> They thought we should sit on the gippies and have a 'whiff of grapeshot' . . . If we go out of the Sudan and Egypt it will be another stage in the policy of scuttle which began in India and ended at Abadan. It will lead to the abandonment of our African colonies . . . People said at Munich that Britain was

finished and that history was against us, but Winston had proved it wrong.[30]

However, the Foreign Office believed that resistance risked humiliation. 'If we seek to hang on', Kirkpatrick wrote apropos the Sudan, 'we may end up being expelled and that would be humiliating.'[31] Finally, domestic economic crisis combined with international upheaval created an atmosphere of gloom in which problems appeared insoluble. In December 1952 Sir Evelyn Shuckburgh, Eden's private secretary, recorded:

> Slept badly and became very depressed about the world in general. Our economic situation, German and Japanese competition, destruction of British influence in the Mediterranean and Middle East (after Persia and Egypt, the sheikdoms on the Persian Gulf are now being absorbed by Saudi Arabia). The Americans not backing us anywhere. In fact, having destoryed the Dutch empire, the United States are now engaged in undermining the French and British empires as hard as they can.[32]

Tackling Britain's problems required a close and confident partnership between the Prime Minister and the Foreign Secretary. Unfortunately policy-making suffered from 'two men acting as Foreign Secretary at the same time'.[33] Perhaps it was a symptom of the British disease that both transacted business from their beds. Eden's make-up – vain, irascible, overstrung – did not help. The foreign secretaryship was the most demanding job in the Cabinet and after several weeks Eden admitted that he was 'hardly abreast of the daily telegrams'.[34] An arrogant belief in his own perceptions and skills made him unwilling to delegate and the resulting overload generated further stress. The treadmill of constant travelling, very long days and short nights created intense strains for Eden and his staff. The inevitable isolation of the job, with scant leisure time, tended to accentuate overweening self-esteem and confidence in his own judgment. Churchill and Macmillan unwound with Trollope and Austen; Eden lived on his nerves, burned up by work and politics. He was dogged by almost constant ill health (itself ill-treated) until the end of 1953. With the red boxes always went a black tin box of medicines and, according to his private secretary, ill health in the years 1951–3 'undoubtedly coloured his judgement'.[35] His April 1953 operation for gallstones incapacitated him for six months and he was 'far from well' at the Bermuda conference in December 1953.[36] Ambition exacted a much heavier toll than illness. On coming to power Churchill intimated that he would hand over the premiership to Eden within a year. The year became two and then three. The old monarch's procrastination drove the heir apparent demented. Having waited so long for the premiership Eden was prey to every rumour and whisper. He saw the Chancellor of the Exchequer, 'Rab' Butler, as chief rival and even tried to use the Foreign Office to conduct personal propaganda against Butler. Such tensions did not advance Britain's cause. In March 1953 both ministers sailed together for New York. They arrived without apparently understanding what each hoped to get out of the Americans.[37]

Eden's main disability, however, was intellectual. He had great flair but no genius. Unlike Bevin he was a tactician not a strategist, a rifleman setting his sights on 'definite, but limited problems' eschewing 'wide general discussion'.[38] As a negotiator he was first class and scored major triumphs on Indochina, German rearmament and Trieste in 1954, but the vision and ability to think ahead on a broad front were missing. Significantly he allowed the Permanent Under-Secretary's Committee, the Foreign Office planning staff set up by Bevin in 1949, to wither.[39] According to Sir Frank Roberts, Deputy Under-Secretary in 1951–4, Eden 'appeared less conscious' than Bevin of post-war decline and 'less ready to draw the consequences in terms of foreign policy, for example in his relations with Dulles and other American colleagues'.[40] Shuckburgh took a slightly different view: Eden 'recognised the decline in the power and influence of Britain, but ... could never quite reconcile himself to its inevitable consequence – growing American dominance'.[41] Of Eden's *annus mirabilis* in 1954, Robert Rhodes James writes: 'more had been achieved in twelve months to resolve critical issues than in the entire post-war period'.[42] In fact 1954 was not as wonderful as it seemed: the Iranian settlement marked a decline of exclusive British influence since the oil stake had to be shared with American companies; the Egyptian agreement decisively weakened Britain's Middle East position since Cyprus was no substitute for the Suez Canal base; and even Indochina was merely a respite and Eden had 'few illusions' about it.[43]

Triumph and tragedy sums up Churchill's second premiership – personal triumph for a seventy-eight-year-old to stay in office and survive a serious stroke, tragedy for the country because recovery demanded leaders at their peak. The combined assaults of age and economic crisis left Churchill in June 1952 'depressed and bewildered'.[44] Increasingly deaf and with his zest 'diminished', he rebuffed American promptings for swift action on European unity: 'It may be better to bear an agonising period of unsatisfactory time . . . You may kill yourself in getting strong enough.'[45] Nothwithstanding the occasional brilliant speech (except for the 'extraordinary flop' of 5 April 1954 in the hydrogen bomb debate)[46] the Prime Minister's growing incapacity after the 1953 stroke obstructed effective policymaking. 'Terribly drooling . . . fast losing his grip', noted one colleague.[47] Even his secretary Jane Portal admitted he was 'getting senile . . . cannot take in the papers'.[48] Propped up by the Cabinet Secretary, Sir Norman Brook, Churchill coped with day-to-day business but lacked the drive and energy to follow up ideas and to descry the whole field of policy. 'In the worst of the war', he said, 'I could always see how to do it. Today's problems are elusive and intangible.'[49] By the winter of 1954–5 the fag-end ministry 'ceased to be a government'.[50]

More damaging than the individual shortcomings of Prime Minister and Foreign Secretary was the tug-of-war between them. Maxwell Fyfe, the Home Secretary, thought Eden enjoyed more independence than any Foreign Secretary since Lord Rosebery in the 1890s. This was not so. Churchill's consciousness of failing powers made him the more determined to concentrate on his principal interests, defence and foreign policy. On Russia, Egypt and nuclear weapons he felt he had a mission. At least one colleague was sceptical. Lord Salisbury, the Lord President of the Council, explained to Lord Woolton, the Minister of Materials, that Churchill 'thought he was the only person who could bring peace to the world by dealing with Molotov'. Woolton noted, 'This interested me because I remember so well him telling me that he thought he could manage Stalin and that he would bring him to London. Roosevelt suffered under the same delusion.'[51] During the Second World War Churchill dominated foreign policy, controlling all major decisions; in 1951–5 he wanted to be dominant but lacked the energy to do so effectively. Whenever Eden was away – even for his honeymoon in 1952 – Churchill assumed control of the Foreign Office and launched policy initiatives. Not surprisingly their relations were frequently acrimonious.

Churchill's vacillation over his retirement envenomed matters further. His hesitation derived from the hope that he might be able to make a deal with Russia. He was also doubtful whether Eden was really the right man: procrastinating might allow Eden to prove himself; or allow someone who was adequate (Macmillan for example) to emerge as a better candidate. Procrastination forced Eden to swallow policies which he disliked. Thus he at first opposed Churchill's July 1954 approach to Molotov then gave way. 'I am afraid the P.M. has been ruthless and unscrupulous in all this', wrote Colville, 'because he must know that . . . for both internal and international reasons, Eden cannot resign.'[52] Egypt also provoked fierce battles. Churchill interfered, constantly seeking to undermine Eden's policy of withdrawal from the Sudan and Egypt, and Eden himself, seeing party opposition growing, had second thoughts. The only fixed point in policy-making was the Foreign Office which consistently advocated withdrawal and opposed Churchill's initiatives for a summit. Eden, who in 1951 had stressed the East–West divide as 'the cardinal issue in international affairs',[53] also opposed Churchill's 1953–4 initiatives for a summit. His motives were mixed. He obviously did not like Churchill taking centre stage. In May 1954 during the Geneva conference Eden had a very friendly dinner with his co-chairman, Molotov. Shuckburgh noted: 'When it is a question of Winston wanting to throw his arms round Malenkov, it is one thing. But when we ourselves are involved, and playing the beau role, it is a very different matter. These politicians are two-thirds prima donna.'[54]

Although Churchill mistrusted the Foreign Office as 'too prone to appease' and 'riddled with Bevanism',[55] unlike Lloyd George he did not ignore it or attempt to create a separate organization at No. 10. Foreign Office opinions on working with Churchill vary – perhaps reflecting the progress of his decline. In the autumn of 1951 Roderick Barclay, Assistant Under-Secretary of State, found sessions with him 'not difficult . . . there was always a sound reason for any drafting amendments which he made'.[56] But in August 1953 Shuckburgh complained of the difficulties of 'trying to conduct our foreign policy through the P.M. who is at Chartwell and always in the bath or asleep or too busy having dinner when we want urgent decisions'.[57] In 1954 Gladwyn Jebb, before proceeding to the Paris embassy, was briefed by a Prime Minister 'hardly at his best':

What I understood him to say was that I must be very careful not to underestimate the strength of the great French Army. My main function, I gathered, was to go out and, so far as possible, prevent the French from being so tiresome. Detailed instructions on how to do this would be sent to me from time to time.[58]

Churchill's enthusiasm was only roused by cloaks and daggers like the 1953 Operation Boot which, with CIA help, overthrew the Iranian leader Mossadeq.

Britain's retreat was also hobbled by the deficiencies of the government machine. The performance of the Foreign Office, the main engine of overseas policy, fell far short of its potential. The Foreign Secretary and officials were permanently on the defensive, fighting battles on several fronts – with the Cabinet, Whitehall, Westminster, the press. In 1951 the chief preoccupation was with implementing the most far-reaching restructuring in the Office's history, the 1943 Foreign Service Act, known as the 'Eden–Bevin reforms', liberalizing recruitment and creating for the first time a single unified foreign service. Officials knew that Parliament and the press were keeping close watch on the reforms. They felt vulnerable for another reason. The public associated them with pre-war appeasement and Strang and his successor Kirkpatrick had occupied senior posts in the late 1930s. The publication from 1949 of British diplomatic documents for the inter-war years rekindled old controversies about the Office's role and responsibilities. Sorrows also came not 'in single spies'. The defection to the Soviet Union of two senior diplomats, Guy Burgess and Donald Maclean, in May 1951, was 'a shattering blow'.[59] Demands for the cleansing of the Whitehall stables brought an internal purge resulting in the resignation and redeployment of several diplomats. The most important consequence was a new system of 'positive vetting' applicable to everyone, junior and senior. Strang volunteered to be vetted first. The new emphasis on security and security procedures subjected staff and families to greater personal strains. The damage to morale and prestige was the deeper because the Burgess-Maclean affair would not go away. There was no Commons or government statement until 7 November 1955. Year in, year out, Foreign Office spokesmen stonewalled repeated requests for information but the clumsy attempts at damage-limitation only served to keep the hue and cry in full swing.

The Office had long been the favourite whipping boy of politicians, journalists and Treasury watchdogs. It was accused of being overstaffed, extravagent and elitist. Wits claimed that, like the fountains in Trafalgar Square, the young men of the Foreign Office played from ten till four. At Westminster the scourge of the diplomats was Labour backbencher Lt-Col. Sir Marcus Lipton. 'Would it not be in the public interest', he asked in December 1954, 'to have this lush underworld of duty free gin, Scotch and cigarettes independently explored?'[60] Calls for the Foreign Secretary to delegate his work-load by creating four ministers of state with regional responsibilities were supported by Eden's predecessor, Herbert Morrison. The main parliamentary onslaught came in December 1954, when the Commons Select Committee on Estimates proposed an independent enquiry. Kirkpatrick advised acceptance since it would have 'a good effect on the Treasury' and he was confident that a 'carefully selected' committee 'would find ... there was very little wrong with our standards or organisation',[61] but Eden, who detested the Treasury, refused an enquiry.

Parliamentary critics had an ally in Lord Beaverbrook, whose *Express* group of newspapers waged a campaign against the diplomats, alleging that they wasted money and were effete and effeminate. In October 1952 the *Sunday Express* fired a broadside: 'How is it that when the Government changes the blunders go on just the same? Largely because the senior officials ... continue to make policy.'[62] Strang, as Permanent Under-Secretary, was said to personify an Office 'repeatedly overtaken by events'. His reputation, continued the *Express*, was tarnished by Munich 1938 and the failure of the 1939 Anglo-Soviet negotiations. Eden's public defence of Strang only drew another attack: 'If he cannot or will not admit that the Foreign Office requires a thorough shake-up' then the Office needed 'a new political chief'. The principal Whitehall antagonist was the Treasury. Since the 1920s the Office had fought off periodic Treasury bids to assimilate it to the Home Civil Service. 'Officials of the Treasury and other Home Departments', declared one diplomat, 'are (a) jealous of the Foreign Service, and (b) ignorant of the problems of living in foreign countries.'[63] In 1951–2 Treasury economy drives reduced staff from 4,300 (1948) to 3,843 (1952).[64] Early in 1953 the Financial Secretary to the Treasury recommended an enquiry into staffing conditions but Eden, who accused his officials of 'selling out' to the Treasury, opposed any enquiry.[65] As a compromise a Treasury proposal for the inspection of two or three overseas posts was accepted. But the Treasury continued to harry what it considered an elitist enclave. A 1955 report censured the diplomats for leisurely habits of work, over-rigid divisions between departments and a negative attitude to Treasury criticisms.[66]

Within the Office attempts to see the world as a whole were thwarted by a number of obstacles. As British power dwindled, staff and paper multiplied. London staff in 1914 (including door-keepers and cleaners) numbered only 176, in 1952 there were 3,842. Information services, economic recovery, conferences, the British zone of Germany, all spawned new departments. The volume and complexity of post-war diplomacy swamped officials in paperwork and committees. By 1950 incoming papers (630,768) had more than doubled since 1939. Much of the increase was in telegrams requiring urgent action, thus reinforcing a natural bias to react to events. Organization and staffing were in constant flux. The physical separation of staff scattered over several buildings added to the Office's fragmented and amorphous character. The elegant façade of Giles Gilbert Scott's palazzo concealed a Dickensian interior. 'Some staff work in cramped and draughty attics', the Office complained, 'others in gloomy dungeons. Many never see daylight during working hours.'[67] Such conditions impaired efficiency but the main pressure was always the proliferation of paper. In vain Churchill and Eden appealed for brevity. As a result, the urgent drove out the important. 'The increase in staffs and the volume of paper', Kirkpatrick admitted, gave 'little time to think, to look ahead and to make wise long-term plans.'[68]

The downgrading of economics was another substantial handicap. Diplomats could not compete with the expertise of the main Whitehall economic departments. In December 1951 Treasury demands for economies forced the closure of the twenty-three-strong Economic Intelligence Department, where duties had included the co-ordination of secret economic reports, questions of wartime organization, economic warfare planning and the special study of economic reports on the Soviet Union, Romania and Germany. (Reporting on the Soviet Union and Romania was done in London because previous cutbacks had closed the Commercial sections of the Moscow and Bucharest embassies.) The work of the Economic Intelligence Department was transferred to the Research Department but the officer responsible for reporting on the Soviet Union and Romania had 'no specialised economic training'.[69] The Research Department reviewed the treatment of economic issues and found that, whilst the list of departments involved in economic policy was impressive,

> none of these Departments keeps its own files of background material or tries to build up consistently and over a long period of time a 'total' picture of the economy, and the economic trends within any country or area. It is the lack of the constant study of the phases of economic development in foreign countries, and of the interaction between them . . . that seems . . . the most serious feature of the present situation both in the Foreign Office and in Whitehall generally . . . In view of the complexity of the Soviet economic system and the difficulty of interpreting its development accurately the present position does not seem . . . satisfactory.

In 1953 Roger Makins, who had specialized in economic work, left his deputy under-secretaryship for the Washington embassy. His successor was an assistant under-secretary, that is, one grade below. With its strong sense of hierarchy Whitehall understood this to mean that economics had been demoted.

The Foreign Office, although not the effete and extravagant creature which critics alleged, had serious shortcomings. Despite the deluge of paper some officials may not have worked as long hours as their State Department counterparts. Certainly there was scope for much greater co-ordination, particularly between the six departments responsible for east-of-Suez interests. More serious was the lack of machinery for policy review. A formal planning unit was not established until 1957. Nor was there even a daily conference of senior officials until 1964. It was symbolic of the Office's priorities that the library and research department were tucked away in a dingy block south of the Thames. The very qualities prized in diplomats – loyalty, reliability, caution, discretion, avoidance of extremes – discouraged unorthodox ideas. Training and pressure of work focused attention on the execution of day-to-day decisions. It was also a closed society isolated from the world beyond Whitehall. Outsiders tended to be treated as hostile snoopers. Perhaps regretting the publication of inter-war documents the Office clammed up – even withholding the work of its official historian, Sir Llewellyn Woodward.[70]

The Permanent Under-Secretaries in this period, Strang and Kirkpatrick, lacked the daring and imagination to promote new initiatives. Reserved, tactful, cautious to a fault, Strang was 'not a policy-maker such as one might expect from a Permanent Under Secretary'.[71] He ran the Office but no more. Apart from a common training in German affairs he and Kirkpatrick were quite different personalities. Kirkpatrick was brisk, combative and outgoing. But at a time when reflection and reappraisal were desperately needed 'he had little use for research or analysis or for prolonged discussion'.[72] Nor was his management style calculated to restore shaken morale.[73] The driving force in policy formulation came from below – from Deputy and Assistant Under-Secretaries, notably Frank Roberts, Roger Makins, Pierson Dixon and Evelyn Shuckburgh. Yet they were reluctant to push their views. For example, following Stalin's death in March 1953 both Eden and Churchill favoured a meeting with Molotov. Senior officials disliked the idea, but Shuckburgh alone (then Eden's private secretary) took the lead in dissuading Eden 'from whoring after the Russians'.[74]

By far the biggest handicaps in formulating a coherent overseas policy were divided control and the complexity of post-war diplomacy. External relations were carved up between separate departmental fiefdoms. The Foreign Office shared responsibility with the Commonwealth Relations Office and the Colonial Office. Eden had to argue and agree a policy with the Commonwealth Secretary, Lord Swinton, and the Colonial Secretary, Oliver Lyttelton. There was a further complication. The multilateral character of post-1945 diplomacy cut across all departmental boundaries. The urgency of economic, financial and strategic issues meant incessant consultation and bargaining with Whitehall competitors such as the Cabinet Office, Treasury, Board of Trade, Ministry of Defence and the Service departments. The machinery for this process was the system of interdepartmental committees on which the Foreign Office provided only one voice. The harmonizing of different and often conflicting viewpoints swallowed up energies and lengthened the lead times of policies.

Whitehall battles were but the start of a Sisyphean task. Before the Second World War traditional bilateral relations between states were the staple of British diplomacy. Apart from occasional visits to the League of Nations at Geneva a Foreign Secretary stayed at home. By 1951 the Foreign Secretary, junior ministers and aides were a travelling circus. The Council of Ministers of the Council of Europe brought together European foreign ministers, and the Consultative Assembly of the Council provided an open forum for the debate by parliamentarians from both government and opposition parties. Foreign ministers of the three Western occupying powers – Britain, America and France – met regularly for discussion of German and European questions and NATO Assembly meetings gathered fourteen foreign ministers, defence ministers and advisers. In addition permanent delegations were maintained at the United Nations, NATO, OEEC, the Council of Europe and the European Coal and Steel Community. The many overlapping levels of the new diplomacy, plus the fact that everything had to be translated, lengthened negotiating times, making it harder to keep overall objectives in sight. The British papers reflect the exasperation and frustration caused by a complex institutional structure 'in which the same issues were discussed by the same people on different occasions and in different places'.[75]

Such complexities demanded a forum in which ideas, issues and strategies could be reviewed. At the top of the Whitehall pyramid, however, there was no effective machinery for over-view and co-ordination: Downing Street had no 'Think Tank'. In theory the Cabinet provided an arena; in practice, as the Labour minister Kenneth Younger discovered, it was 'a body with no common basis to its thinking . . . quite unequal to big decisions'.[76] Pressure of business left little time for argument and most ministers were too engrossed in their own work to keep up with international affairs. Churchill's professed liking for free-ranging debate usually meant Churchillian monologues, with ministers slipping away as lunchtime approached. More-over Churchill did not hesitate to present the Cabinet with a *fait accompli* as with his 11 May 1953 speech calling for a summit. Another ploy was to forestall Cabinet discussion by sending for Eden and talking him out of circulating papers. Affection and loyalty for the elder statesman also inhibited discussion. Shuckburgh records Lord Salisbury, Lord President of the Council and acting Foreign Secretary during Eden's 1953 illness, saying that 'he disapproves of the P.M.'s policy of trying to get a top-level meeting with the Russians. He says it is one thing to be a member of the Cabinet and to refrain from opposing such policies but quite another to be the responsible Minister.' Shuckburgh noted: 'Now I see why [Eden] gets so little active support in Cabinet when he is fighting the P.M.'s bright ideas.'[77] But affection and loyalty had limits. In July 1954 Salisbury and Harry Crookshank, Leader of the House of Commons, threatened resignation because Churchill approached Molotov without consulting and obtaining Cabinet approval. As for Eden, he regularly briefed colleagues but few offered comment. The only serious challenge came in 1951–2 from the 'pro-Europeans', Macmillan and Maxwell Fyfe, supported by some junior ministers. Having failed to persuade Eden in a personal memorandum about European unity Macmillan sought a Cabinet confrontation in March 1952. Maxwell Fyfe gave only minimal support and Macmillan was defeated. Backed by Churchill, Salisbury and other senior ministers, Eden was impregnable.[78] Nor did Cabinet committees supply the necessary machinery. Churchill did not revive the pre-war Foreign Affairs Committee. The standing Defence Committee did not meet frequently and concerned itself mostly 'with relatively minor problems of current operations and military administration'.[79] Some ministers expressed anxiety about the weaknesses of the Whitehall machine. Lord Woolton urged an overhaul. 'The civil service', he wrote, 'gives us loyal, devoted and competent service; but the chief officers ... like the Ministers, are so encumbered with a host of problems that very few have time or energy left to sit back and think.'[80] As Minister of Defence in 1954 Macmillan believed that Britain was not really winning the Cold War and looked for 'some way of getting everyone to co-operate and pull together – the Cabinet, the Foreign Office, the service chiefs, the information people'.[81] But Eden considered 'it was no use asking the P.M. to undertake any administrative reforms – he simply would not take it in'.[82]

Indeed on external policy the government was more a collection of warring baronies than a single force. The evidence is the handling of overseas information services where successive cuts in expenditure brought parliamentary pressure for an independent enquiry. The Drogheda Committee set to work in July 1952 and reported a year later, recommending a three- to five-year expansion of services. The Foreign Office, Colonial Office and Commonwealth Relations Office jointly urged the Cabinet to accept a five-year programme. But the Chancellor, Butler, blocked any increase in expenditure and the Cabinet appointed a Ministerial Review Committee under the Home Secretary, Maxwell Fyfe. In December 1953 this committee vetoed expansion for 1954–5 while reserving the question of future expansion. In Cabinet, Eden defended 'a valuable report which for the first time provided a definite plan for the effective use of overseas information services'.[83] He continued:

These services formed part of our cold-war strategy . . . the Chiefs of Staff . . . had expressed the view that the expansion of the services was necessary to offset the curtailment in the strength of the armed forces. If the Cabinet were willing to leave cold war propaganda entirely to the United States, that at any rate would be a workable policy. If however we were to continue our efforts we should do so to the best of our ability.

However, Churchill, backed by Butler and Monckton, 'did not see how an expansion . . . could be defended . . . when most damaging sacrifices had to be demanded from the Armed Forces'. In a trenchant memorandum the Prime Minister expressed deep distrust of the information services:

Every effort should be made to reduce or to resist the natural tendency to grow . . . What is wanted is not so much more officials everywhere collecting information to prove how necessary they are but a much smaller number of agents . . . who stay in the same places long enough to learn something about the facts . . . I hope all the reductions will be enforced and no increases granted except out of additional savings suggested by the Service itself . . . As for information that we send abroad, surely that task is accomplished by the newspapers at their own expense. We might help them circulate, but it must be remembered that they say a lot of nasty things about us at the same time.[84]

Nearly another year passed in interdepartmental squabbles. The government withheld the Drogheda Report received in July 1953, releasing only a summary in April 1954. Meanwhile Eden had to run the gauntlet of two Cabinet committees, Lord Swinton's Committee on Civil Expenditure and Maxwell Fyfe's Ministerial Review Committee. By May 1954 an armistice seemed in the making. Eden offered a compromise – expansion over seven years instead of the three to five proposed by Drogheda. The Foreign Secretary knew it was too little and wrote, 'I am more than ever sure that we will have to do more – but this cannot be decided in the present regime.'[85] Then Swinton intervened. As chairman of the Civil Expenditure Committee the Commonwealth Secretary demanded cuts and insisted that no decisions be taken during a lengthy absence overseas. Eden noted: 'Lord Swinton has consistently criticised Drogheda and opposed me. No need for C.R.O. to get a penny.'[86]

On 9 July 1954 Eden returned to the attack, telling the Cabinet that the information services 'were . . . essential to the prosecution of the Cold War and to the maintenance of our international influence'.[87] Before the summer recess Churchill conceded that the services should be exempt from Swinton's proposed cuts. Unfortunately the concession was not minuted and the incident illuminates the central role of the Cabinet Secretary, Sir Norman Brook. On 27 October Eden reminded colleagues that a decision on Drogheda was long overdue and that Churchill had promised exemption. Privately Brook explained to Butler that he had deliberately refrained from recording that Churchill 'had virtually promised that the overseas information services should not suffer the full cut . . . lest it stiffen other Civil Departments in their resistance'.[88] Rab surrendered with good grace. In the Commons Eden on 8 November announced the government's acceptance of Drogheda. But it was a pyrrhic victory. At a time when Britain's case needed vigorous and effective presentation ministers and mandarins had wasted eighteen months arguing about sums of money 'comparable, in the case of the annual additions recommended for the Foreign Office Information Service, to one day's subsidy to the Egg Marketing Board, and as far as the total bill for the Information Services was concerned, to rather less than the cost of two bombers'.[89]

'I feel like an aeroplane at the end of its flight, in the dusk, with the petrol running out, in search of a safe landing', Churchill confided in March 1954.[90] In fact the fuel had run out long before. 'The giant in decay', in Butler's phrase, was a key element in the failure to cope with the problems of rapid decline. Nearly two years of manoeuvrings for the succession made the Churchill administration a broken-backed government incapable of forceful and imaginative management of external policy. Of three possible options in 1951 – keeping the status quo, drastic contraction of commitments or finding a reduced role in world politics – only the third was realistic. Far from blindly pursuing a mirage of power Foreign Office officials recognized that preserving existing interests was out of the question. Pessimism, not optimism, prevailed. Yet abdication as a great power went against the grain of general opinion and might well have proved counter-productive. Carefully planned and executed, a gradual retreat offered at least the possibility of playing a major world role. But the essential components of successful management were missing. Eden and Churchill were at odds: Eden wanted a reduced role but did not will the means; Churchill preferred to do nothing. Much better co-ordination of foreign and defence policies was only part of the answer. Policy-makers were slow to grasp that an era of total war had been succeeded by that of total diplomacy. The Second World War had required and secured the total mobilization of all resources, financial, economic, political, to ensure survival and victory; only a similar mobilization might have restored national fortunes. The will to maximize and concentrate all energies was lacking.

'It's a pity we are governed by crocks', wrote one recently retired Permanent Under-Secretary.[91] New machinery and new approaches were needed but Churchill had no appetite for restructuring Whitehall. Government and civil service had not yet caught up with the scale and complexity of the mid-twentieth-century world.[92] Preoccupied with protecting its patch, the Foreign Office lacked the muscle to push through a controversial policy. To modify attitudes and assumptions on Britain's world role required new initiatives. However, a 'nanny knows best' mentality dominated. When Livingstone Merchant, Assistant Secretary of State in the State Department, described to Shuckburgh how he had 'to appear before Congressional Committees to explain State Department policy, and even to be "quizzed" by Senators on the TV for hours on end', Shuckburgh was horror-struck; Merchant replied that 'Foreign Policy could no longer be a matter handled by experts in secret, but must be the subject of continuous scrutiny by the masses. Even the English would have to give up the "old-fashioned" idea of entrusting vital secrets to experts', but Shuckburgh 'feared that democracy could not survive if *issues*, as opposed to personalities, were to be put before the public. This was the fascist referendum idea. You can fool the public about issues, but not ... about the character and quality of leaders.'[93] The nearest Britain got to more open government was in 1954, when an astonished taxi driver driving down Whitehall heard a cabinet meeting broadcast live over his cab radio.[94]

Notes

1. P. Kennedy, *The Realities behind Diplomacy* (1981), 362.
2. Woolton Papers, Bodleian Library, Diary, 24 Oct. 1955. For two very different judgments on Eden's performance in 1951–5 see G. McDermott, *The Eden Legacy* (1969), chs 9 and 10, and I. McDonald, *A Man of the Times* (1976), ch. 16.
3. For discussion of government policy and the Public Records see Sir Duncan Wilson, 'Public records: the Wilson Report and the White Paper', *Historical Journal*, 1982, 985–94; B. Wasserstein, 'Whose history is it, anyway?', *Times Literary Supplement*, 25 July 1986.
4. Lord Greenhill of Harrow, *The Times*, 7 May 1977.
5. PRO, CAB 129/52, 13 May 1952.
6. G. Mallaby, *From My Level* (1965), 16–17.
7. R. R. James, *Anthony Eden* (1986), 353.
8. CAB 129/48, 31 Oct. 1951.
9. CAB 129/55, 3 Oct. 1952.
10. J. Colville, *The Fringes of Power: Downing Street Diaries, 1939–55* (1985), 650–1.
11. H. Macmillan, *Tides of Fortune, 1945–1955* (1969), 567.
12. Minute of 26 July 1954, quoted in W. R. Louis, 'American anti-colonialism and the dissolution of the British Empire', *International Affairs*, 1985, 413.
13. Evidence to Plowden Committee, 28 Jan. 1963, Strang Papers, Churchill College, Cambridge, file 2/11.
14. Quoted in A. Seldon, *Churchill's Indian Summer* (1981), 34.
15. For example Kennedy, *Realities behind Diplomacy*, 324.
16. G. H. Gallup, ed., *The Gallup International Public Opinion Polls: Great Britain 1937–1975*, I, *1937–1964* (New York, 1977), 258.
17. E. Shuckburgh, *Descent to Suez: Diaries, 1951–6* (1986), 84.
18. P. Dixon, *Double Diploma: The Life of Sir Pierson Dixon, Don and Diplomat* (1968), 232.
19. CAB 129/59, 16 Feb. 1953.
20. Quoted in P. Hennessy and M. Laity, 'Suez – what the papers say', *Contemporary Record*, April 1987, 8.
21. CAB 129/53.
22. D. Dilks, ed., *The Diaries of Sir Alexander Cadogan, 1938–1945* (1971), 782.
23. Diary, 7 July 1949, Younger Papers, by kind permission of Lady Younger and Prof. Geoffrey Warner.
24. Quoted in C. Mayhew, 'British foreign policy since 1945', *International Affairs*, 1950, 478.
25. CAB 129/59, 16 Feb. 1952.
26. Shuckburgh, *Diaries*, 152.
27. Sir Roger Makins, British ambassador in Washington, 25 Jan. 1954, quoted in Louis, 'American anti-colonialism', 396; Shuckburgh, *Diaries*, 187.
28. Sir Oliver Franks, British ambassador in Washington 1948–52,

quoted in P. Darby, *British Defence Policy East of Suez 1947–1968* (1973), 22.
29. Quoted in D. Carlton, *Anthony Eden: A Biography* (1981), 305.
30. Shuckburgh, *Diaries*, 76.
31. Minute, 14 June 1954, quoted in Louis, 'American anti-colonialism', 413.
32. Shuckburgh, *Diaries*, 63.
33. *Ibid.*, 126.
34. *494 HCDeb. 5s*, 19 Nov. 1951.
35. Shuckburgh, *Diaries*, 14.
36. James, *Eden*, 374.
37. Lord Butler, *The Art of the Possible* (1971), 165.
38. *494 HCDeb. 5s*, 19 Nov. 1951.
39. Carlton, *Eden*, 298.
40. 'Bevin and Eden: some personal impressions', unpublished paper in the author's possession.
41. Shuckburgh, *Diaries*, 19.
42. James, *Eden*, 389–90.
43. Carlton, *Eden*, 359.
44. Colville, *Fringes of Power*, 651.
45. *Ibid.*, 660
46. Woolton Papers, Diary, 6 April 1954.
47. Crookshank Papers, Bodleian Library, Diary, 26 Feb. 1953.
48. Shuckburgh, *Diaries*, 141.
49. O. Lyttelton, *The Memoirs of Lord Chandos* (1962), 343.
50. Woolton Papers, Diary, 11 March 1955.
51. *Ibid.*, Diary, 1 Oct. 1953.
52. Colville, *Fringes of Power*, 698.
53. *494 HCDeb. 5s*, 19 Nov. 1951.
54. Shuckburgh, *Diaries*, 193.
55. Pierson Dixon Papers, Diary, 3 May 1953, by permission of Mr Piers Dixon; Shuckburgh, *Diaries*, 251.
56. Sir Roderick Barclay, *Ernest Bevin and the Foreign Office 1932–1969* (1975), 17.
57. Shuckburgh, *Diaries*, 99–100.
58. G. Jebb, *The Memoirs of Lord Gladwyn* (1972), 269.
59. Barclay, *Ernest Bevin*, 100.
60. *535 HCDeb. 5s*, 16 Dec. 1954.
61. PRO, FO 366/3110.
62. Strang Papers, file 2/6.
63. FO 366/3110.
64. FO 366/2981.
65. Shuckburgh, *Diaries*, 152.
66. FO 366.3108.
67. FO 366/3066.
68. I. Kirkpatrick, *The Inner Circle* (1959), 267.
69. FO 366.2983.
70. Dixon Papers, 14 Nov. 1950, minute to Strang. Dixon advised

against publication of Woodward's *History of British Foreign Policy during the Second World War*.

71. Younger Papers, Diary, 29 Oct. 1951.
72. *Dictionary of National Biography, 1961–1970* (Oxford, 1981).
73. Barclay, *Ernest Bevin*, 20.
74. Shuckburgh, *Diaries*, 84.
75. R. Bullin and M. E. Pelly, *Documents on British Policy Overseas*, Series II, vol. I (1986), x.
76. Younger Papers, Diary, 3 Oct. 1951.
77. Shuckburgh, *Diaries*, 100.
78. See J. W. Young, 'Churchill's "No" to Europe: the "rejection" of European union by Churchill's post-war government, 1951–52", *Historical Journal*, 1985, 923–37.
79. C. Seymour-Ure, 'British "War Cabinets" in limited wars: Korea, Suez and the Falklands', *Public Administration*, 1984, 198.
80. Woolton Papers, Box 3, 'The machinery of government', 25 Jan. 1954.
81. C. M. Woodhouse, *Something Ventured* (1982), 132; Macmillan, *Tides of Fortune*, 572–3.
82. Shuckburgh, *Diaries*, 156.
83. Cab 128/53, 29 Dec. 1953.
84. PRO, PREM 11/691.
85. F. Donaldson, *The British Council, the First 50 Years* (1984), 191.
86. *Ibid.*, 192.
87. CAB 128/27.
88. Donaldson, *British Council*, 192.
89. Foreign Office minute, 23 Dec. 1954, quoted in Donaldson, *ibid.*, 193.
90. Butler, *Art of the Possible*, 173.
91. Cadogan Papers, Churchill College, Cambridge, Diary, 16 Sept. 1953.
92. See N. Johnson, 'Change in the civil service: retrospect and prospects', *Public Administration*, 1985, 415–33.
93. Shuckburgh, *Diaries*, 163.
94. I should like to thank the British Academy for a grant which helped me to carry out the research for this essay.

1 The 'Special Relationship' with Washington

Peter Boyle

For Winston Churchill, the maintenance of a close relationship with the United States was the top priority of British foreign policy. This he felt for two reasons. First, he had a romantic affection for the United States and the American people. Second, of much greater substance and importance, Anglo-American partnership appeared to him the *sine qua non* of British security. In 1951 he told his private secretary, John Colville, that one of the main reasons why he sought office again was to restore the Anglo-American relationship which had deteriorated, in his opinion, towards the end of the Attlee government, and which Churchill felt that he was peculiarly suited to repair.[1] How far Churchill succeeded in creating a 'special relationship' with the United States during his peace-time administration, 1951–5, this chapter will explore.

Winston Churchill's association with the United States originated through his mother, Jennie Jerome. A New York socialite, she married Lord Randolph Churchill on 15 April 1874. On 30 November 1874 Winston was born. He was, it was reported, a premature baby, though no record was kept of his weight at birth. Whatever the circumstances of his procreation, it might be suggested that the speed of his production by his young and lively American mother embodied the vitality and exuberance which he would find in the United States throughout his life and in which he delighted. 'Picture to yourself the American people as a great lusty youth', he wrote on his first visit to America in 1895, 'who treads on all your sensibilities, perpetuates every horror of ill manners – whom neither age nor just tradition inspire with reverence – but who moves about his affairs with a good hearted freshness which may well be the envy of older nations of the earth.'[2] There seemed to Churchill, however, to be a volatility in American life, illustrated, for example, by the Wall Street crash, which suggested the desirability of a partnership between the energetic, effervescent but erratic United States, and the more cautious, staid and solid Britain: 'It is in the combination of . . . these complementary virtues and resources, that the brightest promise of the future dwells.'[3]

Between the wars, American isolationism and the absence of Anglo-American partnership seemed to Churchill the causes of the disasters which ensued. As he wrote later to Eisenhower, 'I look back with dark memories to all that followed inch by inch upon the United States withdrawal from the League of Nations.'[4] The combination of close Anglo-American personal association and partnership for security interests achieved its fullest embodiment in the Churchill–Roosevelt relationship in the Second World War. As the Churchill–Roosevelt wartime correspondence makes clear, there were frequent and serious disagreements between the two leaders, as well as ongoing cooperation.[5] Nevertheless, the two patricians, Churchill and Roosevelt, formed an unusually close bond, and wartime disagreements were far outweighed by the remarkable degree of collaboration between the two allies, unique in the history of sovereign nations. In the Far East, it is true, the two nations were never more than, as Christopher Thorne puts it, 'allies of a kind'.[6] Moreover, the overall wartime relationship altered significantly as the war progressed. Even by the time of the Tehran conference in November 1943, Churchill expressed an awareness of Britain's declining position: 'There I sat, with the great Russian bear on one side, with paws outstretched, and on the other side the great American buffalo, and between the two sat the poor little English donkey who was the only one, the only one of the three, who knew the right way home.'[7] As leader of the Opposition in the late 1940s, he witnessed the deterioration of Anglo-American relations in the immediate post-war years. With the common enemy defeated, serious Anglo-American disagreements arose after 1945 over such issues as economics, European unification, atomic information and colonial policy. However, the partnership was brought close together again by the need for collaboration against a new common enemy, the Soviet Union, as Churchill had foreseen and expressed in his Iron Curtain speech at Fulton, Missouri, in March 1946. Churchill, romantic though he was in some respects, was a realist in his appreciation that the heart of the special relationship was Britain's need for American protection against the threat of Soviet aggression, and America's need for

Britain as an essential partner in the containment of Soviet expansion.

Back in office in 1951, Churchill clearly felt a nostalgia for the time when he and Roosevelt had acted like Alexander the Great or Julius Caesar. Eisenhower wrote in 1953, 'Winston is trying to relive the days of World War II . . . In these days he had the enjoyable feeling that he and our President were sitting on some rather Olympian platform with respect to the rest of the world.'[8] By the end of the Second World War, however, Churchill had accepted the decline of British power relative to the United States. The essential objectives of Churchill's government in its relations with the United States, 1951–5, were to achieve as full a degree of consultation as possible, to restrain the more extreme excesses of American foreign policy and to guide American foreign policy in a direction suitable to British interests. The British hoped that Anglo-American personal contacts, on the part of Churchill himself and others involved in Anglo-American relations, would help to achieve these objectives.

Churchill had first met President Harry Truman at Potsdam in July 1945, and felt that they had formed a good relationship. Truman found Churchill's life-style habits a difficulty, as the Missouri farm boy arose at 5 a.m. and was long asleep in the small hours of the morning when Churchill was at his best and his most communicative.[9] But he treated the legendary wartime leader with a degree of deference which flattered the Prime Minister. By the time of Churchill's return to power in October 1951, however, Truman was a seasoned and experienced President. Both he and Secretary of State Dean Acheson were well disposed towards Britain, but neither was overawed by Churchill. Moreover, in spite of Churchill's criticism of deteriorating Anglo-American relations in Attlee's later years, beneath the tempestuous disputes over issues relating to the Korean War in 1950 and 1951 the relationship between the Truman administration and the Labour government was fundamentally very close. Acheson's relationship with Ernest Bevin was remarkably good, in spite of their very different social backgrounds. By contrast, Acheson and Anthony Eden, who seemed mirror images of one another in their Establishment viewpoints and attitudes, had a much more difficult relationship.[10] The closest bond at the personal level was between Acheson and Sir Oliver Franks, British ambassador since 1948, who, as Acheson records in his memoirs, used to meet at least once a week for a *tour d'horizon* of world affairs.[11] The Franks-Acheson liaison, extraordinary as a relationship between a Secretary of State and a foreign ambassador, illustrated that in the Truman-Acheson era, Britain was not really regarded as a 'foreign' country. But neither Franks nor his successor, Sir Roger Makins, had more than a formal relationship with Acheson's successor, John Foster Dulles.

Dulles presented the greatest stumbling block to the development of intimate Anglo-American relations on the personal level during Churchill's administration. After Eisenhower's election in November 1952 Churchill and Eden, dreading the appointment of the ardently anti-communist Dulles, hoped that Eisenhower would instead choose Thomas E. Dewey, the Governor of New York and unsuccessful Republican presidential candidate in 1944 and 1948. After a conversation with Dewey on 12 November 1952, however, Eden cabled Churchill that Dewey wished to continue as Governor, and that the 'man we don't like is still making all the running'. When Eden met Eisenhower a week later, the President-elect told him that Dulles 'would be his Secretary of State at least for a year. General Eisenhower was almost apologetic about it.' Eden concluded that 'we must do the best we can with him'.[12] Churchill found this difficult. As Colville describes Churchill's attitude to Dulles, the latter's '"great slab of a face" was one he disliked and distrusted'.[13] Churchill felt that Dulles severely damaged the image of America in Britain and elsewhere: 'Dulles, in British public opinion, stands nearly as low as McCarthy.'[14] For his part, Dulles felt that Churchill was too steeped in the past. The Secretary of State reported to Eisenhower, after one meeting with Churchill: 'The prime minister followed his usual line. He said only the English-speaking peoples counted, that together they could rule the world.'[15]

Eden was more diplomatic in his dealings with Dulles, and in the course of time they came to have a reasonable working relationship. As Anthony Seldon has argued, 'It is the twenty months of Eden's premiership that have tended to be responsible for the unduly jaundiced view of their relations.'[16] After Eden met Dulles in November 1952, Dulles reported to Eisenhower that they had had a very cordial discussion.[17] Within the Foreign Office, however, the assessment of Eisenhower was low.[18] It was not appreciated by the Foreign Office that, as recent studies of Eisenhower have made clear, the

President was much more fully in command of government than was suggested in the caricatures of leading newspapers.[19] The Foreign Office came to realize, however, that American policy in practice was more moderate than Dulles' rhetorical pronouncements made them fear. With regard to 'liberation' in Eastern Europe, for example, as one Foreign Office official put it in July 1953, 'This administration is decidedly less interventionist in practice than its predecessor, for all the bold talk about "liberation".'[20] At the same time, Eden and Dulles came to know one another well, especially after many daily sessions at the Berlin and Geneva conferences in 1954. Eden found Dulles' moralism rather grating, and he was much more comfortable working with Under-Secretary of State Walter Bedell Smith.[21] But by the summer of 1954, Eisenhower noted to Churchill 'an obvious drawing together of Anthony and Foster in their thinking and relationship'.[22]

The most promising prospect for an intimate Anglo-American relationship by means of personal diplomacy, however, lay in Churchill's relations with Eisenhower. Churchill had first met Eisenhower in Washington in December 1941,[23] and when Eisenhower was in London in 1943 and 1944, he and Churchill developed a strong mutual respect and affection.[24] When Churchill returned to office in October 1951, Eisenhower was NATO's Supreme Commander in Brussels, and the two met on several occasions in 1951–2 and renewed their wartime association. Churchill had his reservations with regard to the replacement of Truman by Eisenhower and the Republicans. When he heard the American election results on 5 November 1952, he said that he was 'greatly disturbed. I think this makes war much more probable.'[25] After meeting Eisenhower in New York in January 1953, Churchill, according to Colville, was 'very disappointed in Eisenhower whom he thinks both weak and stupid'.[26] Certainly, Churchill had gained confidence in the Truman administration, and was distressed over the animosity which developed between Truman and Eisenhower during the 1952 campaign. Dulles suggested, when Churchill visited President-elect Eisenhower in January 1953, that it was not necessary for him to call on the 'lame duck' Truman,[27] but Churchill ignored this and dined with Truman. When Eisenhower made a conciliatory gesture towards Truman later in 1953, Churchill wrote to Eisenhower that he was 'so delighted to read what you said to the press about Harry Truman. He is

.ather a friend of mine.'[28] Eisenhower made a significant recognition of a 'special relationship' by agreeing to meet Churchill for talks on 5 January and 7 January 1953, at a time between the election and inauguration, when he turned down invitations to meet with other leaders. After Eisenhower's inauguration, Churchill hoped to continue the intimacy of the relationship and Eisenhower agreed to his suggestion of a personal correspondence, which continued at regular intervals of a letter approximately every second week until Churchill's retirement.[29] Churchill also sought to meet Eisenhower frequently, but they in fact met only twice while both were in office, at Bermuda in December 1953, and in Washington in June 1954. Churchill suggested meetings in August and October 1953, which Eisenhower declined, as he also declined Churchill's pressing invitation for Eisenhower to visit Britain.[30]

Although Eisenhower was glad to participate in personal correspondence with Churchill, and believed that occasional meetings to clear the air were useful, he favoured orderly governmental processes and was not enamoured by personal diplomacy. As Stephen Ambrose has pointed out, Eisenhower had not been impressed by the personal style of diplomacy conducted by Churchill and Roosevelt, which had caused confusion in the lower ranks.[31] Moreover, Eisenhower felt that Churchill was hanging on to power for too long and should make way for Anthony Eden. Eisenhower noted later: 'I have seen many a man "hang on too long" under the definite impression that he had a great duty to perform and that no one else could adequately fill his particular position.'[32] He put it succinctly to his Cabinet when he said of Churchill in 1953, 'He's just a little Peter Pan.'[33] After Churchill's stroke in June 1953, the President felt even more strongly that he should make way for a younger man. Churchill sent Eisenhower details of his illness, while only a select few in Britain knew more than the official report that the Prime Minister was suffering from exhaustion.[34] Over the next two years, Ambassador Winthrop Aldrich and visiting American statesmen gave differing reports on Churchill's physical and mental condition,[35] and Eisenhower generously wrote that 'your own country, and indeed the world, can hardly spare you even in semi-retirement'.[36] The evidence is clear, however, that the President felt that Churchill ought to have retired. For all that, Eisenhower's fondness for Churchill was undoubted. He wrote of 'our indestructable personal friendship', and they exchanged letters on such matters as their common interest in painting, including a request by Eisenhower for a photographer friend to take photographs of Churchill so that Eisenhower could paint a portrait of him.[37] But Eisenhower's character and style of government were such that personal friendship was unlikely to have undue influence in affairs of state, even with a Churchill in his prime, let alone with the failing Churchill of 1953–5, whose condition caused Eisenhower at times sadness and embarrassment.

Personal acquaintance and previous associations between British and American statesmen during Churchill's peacetime administration did not have sufficient weight to determine the outcome when there was disagreement between the two countries over particular policy issues. Yet the presence in office of such figures as Eisenhower, Truman, Acheson, Eden, Franks and above all Churchill himself gave substantial as well as symbolic embodiment to the special nature of the overall character of the relationship. This was the case, for example, with regard to any tendencies towards isolationism in the United States. Churchill appreciated that despite his apprehensions over a Republican victory in 1952, Eisenhower's election marked the triumph of the internationalist wing of the Republican party and the defeat of Senator Robert Taft and the isolationists. He wrote to Eisenhower in May 1953 that he was 'so glad to read just now your remarks about Taft's speech . . . Thank God you are at the helm.' Eisenhower added further reassurance in his reply: 'If this country should return no matter how reluctantly to a policy of almost complete isolation, or at least to a "Western hemisphere only" philosophy of security and interest, then Heaven help us all.'[38] The Foreign Office was always apprehensive over a reversion to isolationism or unilateralism on the part of the United States. One official, Pierson Dixon, wrote that 'We can never entirely discount that if the Americans should decide that their present European policy was not yielding the expected results, they might consider reverting to their previous ideas about "perimeter defence" or else . . . a direct deal with the Russians.' His colleague, Frank Roberts, did not think that the United States was contemplating such a policy but suggested that 'American moods change very quickly', and warned that such a change might come about 'if we and the other European powers continue to snipe at the Americans on whatever provocation'.[39]

Anglo-American relations at the level of the press and popular opinion were of a somewhat different nature from the relationship at the governmental level. American denunciations of British trade with China, for example, were fully and sensationally reported in the American press. In December 1953 Senator Joseph McCarthy urged 'each and every American who feels as I do about the blood trade with a mortal enemy that they write or wire the President'.[40] The Foreign Office took seriously the response to McCarthy's plea in the form of forty thousand letters and telegrams to the White House. The Consul-General in Los Angeles reported that 'never since he arrived there in 1948 have the public in general been so incensed at "perfidious Albion"'.[41] On the other side, the British press gave wide coverage to such matters as the execution of the Rosenbergs, the casual threats by right-wing and military figures to use the atomic bomb, and above all, McCarthy's outrageous antics. Eisenhower was warned of 'the extraordinary importance which [Europeans] ... attach to Senator McCarthy and his doings';[42] and he pursued a strategy towards McCarthy of allowing the Senator enough rope with which to hang himself, which McCarthy did by the time of his 'condemnation' by the Senate in December 1954. Even Stephen Ambrose, however, in his favourable portrayal of Eisenhower, concedes that the President's above-the-battle approach to McCarthyism gave a damaging impression of weakness.[43] This, together with press reports of sharp disagreements over such issues as Quemoy and Matsu, EDC and East–West trade, poured a considerable amount of acrimony into Anglo–American relations at the popular level. Churchill stated that he hoped that Anglo-American relations should not be expressed in what he called 'McCarthy-Bevanite terms'.[44]

Churchill hoped that good personal relations would produce full Anglo-American consultation. Shortly after Eisenhower's inauguration, Churchill expressed his hope that 'where joint action affecting our common destiny is desired, you will let us know beforehand so that we can give our opinion'.[45] In fact, there were endless complaints by the British at every level over lack of consultation on the part of the Americans. Moreover, Churchill was irritated by American insistence on consultation with other powers, especially France, rather than their relying on the Anglo-American duet. He asked Dulles whether 'the United States sometimes overemphasized the importance of not ganging up, to the extent of falling over backwards to treat us as if we were in the same category as Benelux, Iceland and Portugal'. Dulles replied that 'the United Kingdom was in a totally different category, as far as the United States policy was concerned, to any power in the world'.[46] But Dulles's recognition that this did not happen in practice was illustrated by his suggestion to Eden in 1954 that new machinery for State Department-Foreign Office consultation should be established. Nothing came of this suggestion, especially since it was felt in the Foreign Office that, as one official put it, 'the need is not so much for the creation of new machinery as the conscious effort of mind called for in thinking out potential Anglo-American divergence and then dealing with them *ab ovo*'.[47]

One major reason for the British desire for close consultation was to give Britain the opportunity to restrain the extremes in American foreign policy. The State Department appreciated that Churchill's presence in office helped to feed illusions of the extent of Britain's power. As the State Department's Psychological Strategy Board put it, 'The return of Churchill and the Conservatives has strengthened the nostalgia for the time when Britain was the leading global power, and hypersensitivity to playing the role of junior partner manifests itself in reflections on American inexperience.'[48] This indeed proved to be the case. In January 1952 the British ambassador in Moscow, Sir Alvary Gascoigne, warned that 'the danger of war at the present time seems to be in one of the sore spots becoming too sore and the Americans getting too hot under the collar and taking action "off the cuff"'. William Strang, the Permanent Under-Secretary, shared this view and recommended that 'we should lose no time in discussing specific operations with the Americans, since . . . it is only by co-ordinating our activities with theirs that we can hope . . . to restrain what we consider to be over-zealous activities on their part'.[49]

The influence which resulted from closer Anglo–American personal contacts was not negligible. The essential determinants of policy, however, were economic and military strength, and in these crucial matters Britain was increasingly deficient compared with the United States. Since the Second World War, Britain had developed a condition of dependency on America, which produced a habit whereby the British were disinclined to take any action which would meet with American disapproval, even on minor matters. In 1954, for example, when

Arsenal Football Club were invited to Moscow to play a match against Moscow Dynamo, Sir James Barnes, Permanent Under-Secretary at the Air Ministry, who was associated with Arsenal, originally planned to go to Moscow with the party but decided that 'he had many American friends and he had begun to wonder what they would think! His present inclination was to drop it.'[50] A major theme of Churchill's peacetime administration was the attempt to loosen this dependency on America by building up sufficient independent economic and military strength to meet the Americans, not on terms of equality, but as a strong, fully independent ally. The attempt appeared to meet with growing success in the years from 1951 to 1955, but the success proved ultimately to be illusory.

With the end of Marshall aid to Britain in December 1950, Britain had hoped that there would be no further need of American economic assistance. The Cabinet Mutual Aid sub-committee noted: 'U.K. dependence on U.S. economic aid is not in the longer term compatible with our position as a great power with world wide responsibilities. Nor is it conducive to cordial relations with the United States.'[51] There was lingering British resentment that America had grown rich while Britain impoverished herself in 1939–41, as in 1914–17. The British felt further irritation and humiliation as a result of the overbearing, bureaucratic manner in which American aid programmes were administered. As one historian has put it, during the war, 'Lend-Lease officials sometimes acted rather like a rich uncle putting a nephew through school.'[52] The terms of the 1946 American loan brought dismay in many quarters in Britain. The Marshall Plan was welcomed in 1947 as an imaginative and generous programme, but its operation brought strains and irritations, with Britain's need to placate demanding American officials and irate Congressmen who lectured on the evils of socialism and the waste of American taxpayers' money down a foreign 'rat-hole'.[53] Following devaluation of the pound in 1949 and a turn in the terms of trade in Britain's favour, Britain made such a remarkable recovery in 1950 that Marshall aid was suspended at the end of the year. By the time the Conservative government came to power in October 1951, however, a further turn in the terms of trade against Britain and an overambitious rearmament programme had produced a serious balance of payments crisis. It was clear that further American economic aid would be an essential part of the resolution of the crisis. Such a state of affairs brought much gloom and it significantly affected the Anglo-American relationship in Churchill's peacetime term of office. The State Department Psychological Strategy Board noted in 1953 that 'states which quickly assume commanding positions in the world are viewed with jealousy and suspicion by those who lately exercised great power and who by force of circumstances have lost it'.[54]

Aside from economic aid, Britain had received military aid since 1949 under the Mutual Defense Assistance Program. In 1950 the British government announced a rearmament programme which would cost £3,600 million over three years, but for such a large programme, Britain would need £550 million in aid from the United States. In January 1951 the Attlee government increased the proposed rearmament programme to a new level, which would cost £4,700 million, and counted upon receiving any balance of payments relief necessary for its implementation through arrangements under discussion for equitable sharing of the defence burden among NATO countries. The NATO Burden Sharing Exercise had been set up in September 1950, with a Financial and Economic Board to examine submissions by each country with regard to the impact of rearmament on its economy. When the Board reported in September 1951 a wide gap between existing efforts and stated military requirements, the Temporary Control Committee (TCC) was established to reconcile NATO military requirements with the political and economic capabilities of member countries. The TCC report of December 1951 indicated that Britain was pursuing the maximum effort, which was not the case with respect to many other countries, including the United States.[55] On 14 November 1951 Chancellor R. A. Butler presented the British case to the TCC in Paris, and requested interim American aid. Butler did not ask for aid for the period which was past, but only for the first half of 1952, in which period he estimated a dollar balance of payments deficit of $600 million. Negotiations took place in London with William Batt, head of the Mutual Security Agency in London, who advised that $300 million was the maximum which Congress would allocate for Britain, but at the same time Butler's revised estimates increased the figure of Britain's dollar deficit to $900 million. Thus, American aid was required for a very large amount, and it was required rapidly in order to have an impact on Britain's reserves, a vital matter for the Sterling Area as well as for Britain. The Americans, however, were still willing to give only $300 million, and even this sum would not be delivered immediately. The bills relating to military assistance then made their usual agonizingly slow progress through Congress, and in early 1952 Congress ruled that Britain could receive $300 million, but only in the form of reimbursement for defence-related supplies such as aluminium, copper and steel, and not for Britain's main dollar imports such as wheat and cotton. The result was that only $125 million would be paid by June 1952 and, although the remainder of the $300 million could be received in 1952–3, at the time of Britain's greatest need, American aid was gravely insufficient.[56]

The British felt a deep sense of grievance that they alone had made major sacrifices in their rearmament programme, with a diversion of resources from export industries, whilst the Americans, with considerable economic capacity, had given insufficient assistance for the political reasons that 1952 was an election year, and that after 1952 the Republicans were committed to cutting taxes. By June 1952 the Cabinet Mutual Aid Committee concluded that 'The NATO "burden-sharing" concept has been ineffective in modifying the American assumption that the part which they play in the defence of Europe is entirely a matter for them to determine while at the same time it should give them an important voice in the decisions taken by the other NATO countries about the scale of their defence efforts.'[57] In order to deal with the economic crisis, the British government introduced emergency measures, began an export drive, scaled down the rearmament programme and secured aid from the United States by means of a series of *ad hoc* measures. Britain felt that the damage to her economy and the cuts in defence could have been avoided by an increase in American defence expenditure and aid which the United States could well afford. 'Such is the elasticity of the American economy that their immense effort is demonstrably hurting them scarcely at all', the Mutual Aid Committee concluded.[58] 'The scale of U.S. output', the same committee reported a year later, 'is such that an increased contribution which is quantitatively large could be had by means of a relatively small increase in the proportion of total U.S. resources devoted to defence.'[59] Yet in quantitative as well as qualitative terms, the American military contribution was obviously so much greater than any other country's, that it made it difficult to criticize the United States. 'That puts the Americans in a strong position to criticise others', as the Cabinet Atlantic (Official) Committee noted, 'and they have not hesitated to do so.'[60]

In the absence of substantial amounts of direct economic assistance, the British sought American aid or quasi-aid in whatever form it was available, such as 'off-shore' purchases, an increase in American payments for services for American forces in Britain, compensation for loss of gold to the European Payments Union (EPU) and receipt of agricultural surpluses. All of these means, however, involved a great deal of haggling over details and interpretations of American aid legislation. It was a repetition of the Marshall Plan experience, but whereas Marshall aid amounted to very substantial financial assistance, in the early 1950s the haggling resulted in relatively lean pickings. Britain claimed, for example, that by the terms of the Katz–Gaitskell agreement of December 1950, the United States would compensate Britain for the loss of gold to the EPU as a result of allowing other member countries to meet their current deficits with the EPU out of their existing sterling balances. When Britain claimed $63 million up to January 1952, however, Congress appropriated $50 million and added the condition that (as had been the case with Marshall aid) 5 per cent of the counterpart was to be set aside for the payment of American administrative expenses.[61] American officials, such as Averell Harriman and Harold Stassen, suggested that Britain should win more orders of American off-shore purchases, that is, American defence equipment purchases from foreign suppliers. Britain's position, however, was that her own defence programme, even in scaled-down form, absorbed so much of her potential spare capacity that she was unable to take advantage of off-shore procurement to the same extent as the French, West Germans and Japanese, enabling these countries to take a significant step on the road to overtaking Britain economically. As Eden noted to Franks, 'we are in difficulty because we are the only European country which has responded to the call for action and committed itself to large-scale orders for our own defence and NATO programmes. If we had been as backward as the others, half our programme orders . . . would have been "legitimate" off-shore purchases.'[62] Britain's off-shore procurement increased from $69 million in 1952 to $381 million in 1953, but it was still far behind that of France, which increased from $332 million to $693 million.[63]

The main direct military aid to Britain came in the form of

'commodity aid'. Britain was sent, free of charge, commodities such as wheat and cotton which she would otherwise have purchased for dollars, and the counterpart (that is, the sterling raised by the British government in the sale of these commodities to British suppliers) was used for defence purposes. The programme, however, involved many further details and complications: 5 per cent of counterpart was reserved once again for American administrative expenses; part of the aid was in the form of a loan, rather than a grant ($50 million of the $300 million in the first six months of 1952); and the Moody amendment of 1952 provided that $100 million must be devoted to projects for improving productivity. Congress added a provision that 50 per cent of commodity aid must be carried in American ships, but this Britain refused to accept. Furthermore, again as in Marshall Plan days, American agricultural interests tried to use the programme to foist agricultural surpluses on foreign countries, so that Britain found that, after the passage of the Agricultural Trade and Assistance Act of 1954, aid was offered in commodities which would upset Britain's trade with her colonies. Such difficulties frequently led to a state of affairs in which, as the Mutual Aid Committee described in 1954, there was 'a disposition in Washington to regard us as awkward and to say that if we could not take what was offered we should have nothing'.[64]

When Eisenhower came into office, he made clear that, while he wished cuts in American defence spending, he also wished to maintain or increase foreign aid, which he regarded as good value. Congress, however, was in no mood to spend more and there were steady cuts in aid appropriations. Eisenhower reorganized aid, appointing Harold Stassen director of the Foreign Operations Administration, and with a great fanfare proclaiming a new approach, 'trade not aid'. Eden and Butler came to Washington in March 1953 for talks with Dulles and Stassen, and presented British proposals on 'trade not aid'. In practice, however, modifications on such matters as American tariff policy did not allow a significant expansion of British trade to the United States during Churchill's administration, and the bitter disagreements over the Battle Act and other American restrictions on East–West trade added further salt to the wounds.[65] By 1953, the British economy had recovered from the balance of payments crisis of 1951, but the American response was to cut aid to Britain and to press for increases in the British defence effort! When Butler's 1953 budget included tax reductions, the US House of Representatives responded with a cut in aid to Britain. The Economic Committee was exasperated that 'after all the efforts made by the British Information Service to link the need for defence support with the U.K.'s balance of payments position, Congressmen should still suppose that the need for defence support aid arose only for budgetary reasons'.[66]

The British were always conscious of the awkward element introduced into the Anglo-American relationship by Britain's receipt of American aid. When Eden and Butler went for the meeting with Dulles and Stassen in 1953, they felt that 'it was important not to appear as mendicants'.[67] Above all, it was realized, American aid gave the United States an unspoken lever to use against Britain. In 1954, when Butler expressed disappointment that Special Aircraft Assistance had been reduced by Congress from $75 million to $35 million, Stassen told him that 'there had been adverse reactions as a result of divergencies in policy on South-East Asia'.[68] Churchill told Dulles that he 'particularly deplored threatening speeches such as the recent one of Senator Knowland, which threatened to cut off military and economic assistance unless the British did what we wanted. He said that that was no proper basis for a good relationship.'[69] Yet Churchill found that even Eisenhower could resort to the hint of a cut in aid if he diverged from Eisenhower's wishes on foreign policy. When the Prime Minister suggested, with regard to his favourite theme of a summit meeting with the Soviets, that if Eisenhower was opposed Churchill would go alone to Moscow, Eisenhower wrote that if Churchill did so, 'the effect on Congress which is this week taking up consideration of our Mutual Defense Program and extension of our Reciprocal Trade Act would be unpredictable'.[70] As the Mutual Aid Committee concluded, 'no nation can fully maintain its independence if it is receiving subsidies from another country, at least in peacetime'.[71]

The burden of defence expenditure on the national economy led both countries in a similar direction with respect to defence policy, namely reliance on the nuclear deterrent and a cut in conventional defence. This brought to the forefront the crucial issue of atomic energy, the most important single issue in Anglo–American relations in the decade after the Second World War. During the war, Churchill was one of the very few who knew the secrets of atomic research. He had thought long and deeply about the implications of the development of atomic energy before most others had even an inkling of the matter. In 1941, before American entry into the war, Churchill readily agreed to Roosevelt's request that British scientists share atomic information with the Americans and, in 1942, he agreed to the establishment of the Manhattan Project, with the transfer of work on the atomic bomb to the United States. But he became concerned that Britain was being denied its proper share of atomic information, and attempted to resolve the matter in agreements with Roosevelt, especially the Quebec agreement of 1943, and the Hyde Park *aide-mémoire* of 1944. By the Quebec agreement, each side agreed not to use an atomic bomb without the consent of the other, while, with regard to the peaceful uses of atomic energy, discretion was left to the US President to share information as he saw fit. (Churchill felt that the President would use his discretion in this matter to Britain's benefit.) The Hyde Park agreement stated that full collaboration between the United States and the British government in developing atomic energy for military and commercial purposes should continue after the defeat of Japan, unless terminated by joint agreement. After the war, however, complications arose owing to American desire for international control of atomic energy and the McMahon Act of 1946, which prohibited disclosure of atomic information by the United States to other countries. The British government felt bitterly that the Americans had reneged on the wartime agreements. When the Attlee government decided that Britain should manufacture its own bomb and strive to be a leading nation in the peaceful uses of atomic energy, Britain received virtually no scientific or technical information from the United States. The matter was one of the sorest issues in Anglo-American relations in the late 1940s, though few were aware of the problem since Attlee was as secretive about atomic matters as Churchill had been during the war. The aspect of atomic diplomacy which became much more public was Britain's lack of control over American use of atomic weapons, which became an acute issue with Truman's apparent threat to use the atomic bomb in Korea, and Attlee's flight to Washington to discuss the matter in December 1950.[72]

When Churchill returned to office in 1951, he was favourably impressed by the progress of the Labour government in atomic energy matters, especially in work on an atomic bomb. He grudgingly admired Attlee's deception in concealing the costs by devious accountancy methods, and continued to use similar means. But Churchill was extremely critical of the failure to prevent a breakdown in the Anglo-American atomic partner-ship, which he felt he had developed with Roosevelt. Only in December 1950, with Attlee's trip to Washington, did Churchill learn, to his great dismay, that the Qubec agreement had been rescinded, so that the United States no longer required British consent before using an atomic bomb.[73] Churchill's aims, there-fore, were to gain more information with regard to America's nuclear arsenal and strategic war plan, to win recognition for consultation with Britain before American use of atomic weapons (especially from British bases) and to increase the amount of information exchanged by the United States on atomic energy matters, which Churchill felt Britain should receive as of right, on the basis of Britain's wartime contribution and his agreements with Roosevelt. On his visit to Truman in January 1952, Churchill achieved success with regard to some of these objectives, but he made no progress on others. He received a briefing on America's strategic war plan which was as full as Acheson received.[74] Also, a formula was devised with regard to the degree of consent required from the British government for American use of atomic weapons from British bases, though it was merely a reaffirmation of the agreement made by the Attlee government, and it left the matter vague and imprecise. The 9 January 1952 communiqué reaffirmed 'the understanding that the use of bases in an emergency would be a matter for joint decision by His Majesty's Government and the United States goverment in the light of the circumstances pre-vailing at the time'.[75] Truman was not willing, however, to go further in accepting the need for British consent with regard to the American use of atomic weapons. In the McCarthyist mood of the time, with Acheson under attack as the 'Red Dean', and with Congress only recently apprised that there had ever been an agreement which had restricted America's independent use of atomic weapons, any concession in this regard was out of the question. Nor was any significant progress made on the flow of atomic information. The spy scandals of Fuchs, Pontecorvo, Burgess and MacLean made the United States even less inclined to pass on atomic information to Britain.

Churchill was hopeful of securing more co-operation on atomic energy matters from Eisenhower. When he met Eisen-hower in January 1953, atomic energy was one of the major items in their conversation, and Churchill left Eisenhower with copies of the wartime agreements with Roosevelt.[76] Eisenhower was sympathetic to Britain's case.[77] Moreover, once Britain had successfully tested an atomic bomb in October 1952, it made less sense for the United States to withhold information from her. Throughout his presidency, Eisenhower endeavoured to increase the flow of atomic energy information to Britain, but this did not bear fruit until the late 1950s. The United States was not prepared to yield on the matter of British control over an American decision to use an atomic bomb. The State Department recognized that not only in Britain, but among all of America's NATO allies, there was 'a widespread feeling that the United States is clutching the atom to its bosom, and may at any moment get angry and hurl it in the general direction of the Kremlin'. But the State Department was not willing to go further than to state that 'the balance of feeling of the free world would be much improved if it were generally understood that the United States considers the use of atomic bombs to be a legitimate area of allied discussion'.[78] Dulles found that, after he made a guarded statement on this matter at a North Atlantic Council meeting, Eden wrote a letter which seemed like an attempt to obtain a veto on the use of American atomic weapons, but Dulles was not prepared to go further than to promise consultaton with the allies.[79]

With regard to American bases in Britain, Churchill did not seek with Eisenhower any more precise clarification of the 1952 formula, which remained in force thereafter. Churchill did, however, try to use the existence of American bases with nuclear weapons in Britain as a further lever to secure more atomic energy information from the Americans. He wrote to Eisenhower: 'I am sure you will not overlook the fact that by the Anglo–American base in East Anglia we have made ourselves for the next year or two the nearest, and perhaps the only bull's eye of the target.'[80] Eisenhower instructed Lewis Strauss, chairman of the Atomic Energy Commission, to seek means to increase the flow of atomic energy information to Britain within existing law, and to prepare amendments to American legislation on the subject. A report was drawn up which showed the extent of information disclosed under the existing agreement, the *Modus Vivendi* of 1948. The report indicated that of the nine areas under which there was to be disclosure of information, there had been an exchange of information on six, namely, health and safety, isotopes, extraction chemistry, reactor materials, low power reactors and declassifiable information. Very little information had been exchanged in three other areas, namely, property of the elements, design of power plants and detection of distant explosions.[81] Strauss took an optimistic view of the prospects for increasing information without amendments to legislation.[82] He reported that this could be achieved by adding an item to one of the nine areas of technical cooperation, to permit the exchange of information covering the effects on human beings of heat, blast and radiation from atomic explosions.[83] Any increase in information, however, faced great obstacles. Suspicions remained with regard to the reliability of Britain's security system for safeguarding atomic secrets. Also, any broadening of interpretations of the McMahon Act or *Modus Vivendi* ran into the central difficulty that in many instances a distinction between atomic energy matters of military significance and non-military significance could not be made, and little discretion was left regarding the prohibition of disclosure of information on matters of military significance.[84] Moreover, opposition in Congress to disclosure of information remained strong. Senator Bourke Hickenlooper, for example, chairman of the Senate Commitee on Atomic Energy, 'made clear his reservations in regard to sharing knowledge with other countries and his belief that the United States should base its policies not on friendship, but on self-interest'.[85] The result was that, in spite of Eisenhower's sympathy and Strauss's optimism, the increase in the flow of atomic energy information up to 1955 was not great.

One source of increased British information was through NATO. The United States decided that NATO countries should be supplied with material for training, although atomic weapons would not be delivered prior to use in war. Moreover, NATO countries should be informed of the effects of weapons, the kilotonnage and numbers of weapons committed to NATO, the tactical use of such weapons, Soviet atomic capabilities, defence capabilities against atomic attacks and means of civil defence. Information was withheld from NATO, however, on the manufacture and design of atomic weapons and the numbers, capability and deployment of American nuclear weapons.[86] In early 1955 the United States Atomic Energy Commission prepared a study on atomic military information for the Joint Chiefs of Staff to convey to NATO. When Churchill continued to complain that the degree of information supplied to Britain was insufficient,

Strauss referred to the information which was being prepared for NATO, and wrote that 'quite possibly, Sir Winston has no information that this matter is progressing so favorably'.[87] The information supplied through NATO, however, was a side-track from Churchill's main objective, namely, direct Anglo-American exchange of information. Moreover, Strauss revealed an American motive for improving Anglo-American atomic co-operation: he suggested that the United States should offer Britain use of America's testing site at Bikini (the Australians were raising some difficulties over use of a site in Australia) because, 'If they accepted it, we would no longer be the sole target of Communist propaganda and the sole recipients of irrational protests from Nehru and others.'[88]

Britain was also dissatisfied with the provision of information on atomic energy for peaceful purposes. Churchill endorsed Eisenhower's proposals on 'Atoms for Peace' (to share atomic energy via a UN agency) in December 1953, but was told by Lord Cherwell, his adviser on atomic energy matters, that the prospects of Soviet acceptance of Eisenhower's plan were slim.[89] The Atoms for Peace initiative, in spite of Soviet rejection, helped to spur on the development of the International Atomic Energy Agency, which led to multilateral agreements for ex-change of information, while the Atomic Energy Act of 1954 amended the McMahon Act and allowed a greater flow of in-formation on a bilateral basis. Some progress was therefore made, but the Anglo-American atomic partnership for which Churchill had hoped did not materialize. In spite of his dis-appointments in this matter, he was fairly gentle in chiding Eisenhower. Churchill understood Eisenhower's political diffi-culties over the matter, and was willing to show some patience. 'I am well aware of all your difficulties in view of the McMahon Act, etc.', he wrote, 'and of the efforts you are making to obtain greater freedom to give us the information, and I shall also do my utmost to safeguard our common interests as they are developing.'[90] Churchill was much less patient with the Labour opposition. Winthrop Aldrich reported that 'Churchill has been deeply irritated by left-wing goading that he should take a stronger position vis-à-vis the United States and should demand full information and closer co-operation on atomic matters.'[91] As a result, in an acrimonious debate in the House of Commons Churchill revealed the terms of the Quebec agreement, and made the accusation that the Attlee government had been inept in dealings with America on atomic energy matters. He fore-warned Eisenhower that he felt it necessary to reveal the terms of the Quebec agreement, since 'it will prove decisively that the Opposition, not I, are responsible for our present position'.[92]

Shortly before Churchill's retirement, Eisenhower wrote to him: 'I share your feelings of satisfaction in the progress of your country towards nuclear stockpile; I share your regret that through unfortunate circumstances of the past that develop-ment is not further advanced.'[93] In fact, in industrial as well as in military development of atomic power, Britain by 1955 had made the major breakthrough with relatively little American assistance. Britain had built a stockpile of atomic bombs and was well on the way to testing a hydrogen bomb. In industrial development, Calder Hall and Dounreay had been built, and work begun on twelve other power plants, while Calder Hall had been the first power plant in the world to supply electricity to a national grid. The time of Britain's critical need for American co-operation had been in the late 1940s. In its absence at that time, Britain had developed its own atomic programme at considerable extra cost and delay. By the time of the Conser-vative government much of this was water under the bridge, and the additional American assistance which Churchill sought and only partially gained was of less importance, though it did pry open the flood of information in the later 1950s.

With regard to both economic and military matters, Churchill's peacetime administration marked Britain's last attempt to restore herself to the position of strength and influence which the strains of war had taken from her. Inheriting a serious economic crisis in 1951, the Conservative government felt pride in Britain's recovery by 1953. There were setbacks in 1954–5, which, for example, required the raising of the bank rate to four-and-a-half per cent, the highest rate since 1932. Overall, how-ever, the Conservative government felt that, under Butler's skil-ful Keynesian management, the economy was set on the road to economic growth with full employment, low inflation and a sound balance of payments. This profoundly affected Britain's attitudes in foreign policy. As the State Department Psycho-logical Strategy Board observed, 'In Britain the achievement of a new recovery has tended to produce a renewed assertiveness in foreign policy.'[94] In military matters, Churchill's government made the crucial decision to give top priority to the develop-ment of a British nuclear deterrent, which would give Britain independent security, while allowing reductions in expenditure on conventional forces. This approach, first spelt out in the Global Strategy Paper of 1952 and elaborated upon in defence statements in 1953–5, anticipated the 'New Look' of American defence policy in the Eisenhower years.[95] While the H-bomb brought gloomy pessimism to Churchill in some ways, in other ways he saw in it the balance of terror which would keep the peace. The powerful British nuclear deterrent developed in Churchill's administration, with the successful A-bomb test in 1952 and deployment of the first squadron of Valiants by 1955, profoundly affected the Anglo-American relationship. As Minister of Defence Harold Macmillan argued in 1955, the lack of an independent British nuclear deterrent 'surrenders our power to influence American policy'.[96]

By the end of Churchill's administration, therefore, it appeared that Britain had sufficiently close personal ties with the American leadership, along with economic and military strength and independence, to enable her to reassert herself in world affairs and to exert powerful influence in Anglo-American relations. By the late 1950s, however, this proved to be illusory. Britain's underlying economic weaknesses were laid bare, with the Suez crisis serving as a stark illustration of America's power to force a change in British policy, and the 'Stop-Go' policies of the 1950s revealing Britain's unremitting relative economic decline. Moreover, in military matters Britain's power declined very rapidly in comparison to the two superpowers. Until 1949 it was assumed that Britain would develop an atomic bomb before the Soviet Union. The deep shock of the Soviet atomic test that year was followed by the gradual appreciation in the 1950s that, with the Soviet test of an H-bomb in 1952 and developments in missile technology, Britain was bound to remain massively inferior in nuclear, as in conventional strength, and was dependent on American protection.

On the American side, however, the Truman and Eisenhower administrations gave Britain a vital role in the American world view. With a rejection of isolationism the US government sought to preserve peace, and protect American interests, by involvement in international affairs and rejection of the folly of the policies of the 1930s. In this Britain, though greatly reduced in power and in no way America's equal, played a crucial role as the vital link between the United States and not only Europe, but also the British Empire and Commonwealth.

Fundamentally, therefore, Churchill's peacetime term of office confirmed the essential nature of the Anglo–American relationship as it developed in the late 1940s and beyond. It became clear that, although Britain and America were bound together by ties of language, ideology, cultural heritage, comradeship in arms in two world wars and close personal friendships and associations, at the heart of the special relationship was Britain's need for American protection and America's need for Britain as an essential junior partner in the containment of the Soviet Union. As Eden expressed it shortly after he succeeded Churchill, 'the relationship we have to maintain is not maintained merely because we like each other, though we do, but because unless we can deal with our differences in a friendly spirit, the chances of the peace of the world become slender indeed'.[97]

Notes

1. J. Colville, *The Fringes of Power: Downing Street Diaries, 1939–* (1985), 632–3.
2. R. Churchill, *Winston S. Churchill*, I, Companion, Part I (1967), 600.
3. W. Churchill, *Strand Magazine*, Aug. 1931, 150. Quoted, H. Pelling, *Winston Churchill* (1974), 401.
4. WFIS, Box 16, Churchill to Eisenhower, 28 May 1953.
5. W. Kimball, ed., *Churchill and Roosevelt: The Complete Correspondence* (3 vols, Princeton, NJ, 1984).
6. C. Thorne, *Allies of a Kind* (1978).
7. J. Wheeler-Bennet, ed., *Action This Day* (1968), 96 n.1.
8. R. Ferrell, ed., *The Eisenhower Diaries* (1981), 233.
9. R. Ferrell, ed., *Dear Bess: The Letters of Harry to Bess Truman 1910–59* (1983), 515; R. Ferrell, *Harry Truman and the Modern Presidency* (1983), 52.
10. *Newsweek*, 14 April 1952, 17; D. Carlton, *Anthony Eden: A Biography* (1981), 300–1; R. R. James, *Anthony Eden* (1986), 352.
11. D. Acheson, *Present at the Creation* (1970), 323–4.
12. PRO, PREM 11/52.
13. Colville, *Fringes of Power*, 662.
14. PREM 11/54.
15. J. F. Dulles, White House Memoranda Series, Eisenhower Library, Box 1, 12 April 1954.
16. A. Seldon, *Churchill's Indian Summer: The Conservative Government, 1951–55* (1981), 392.
17. Whitman File, Dulles-Herter Series, Eisenhower Library, Box 1, 14 Nov. 1952.

18. E. Shuckburgh, *Descent to Suez: Diaries, 1951–6* (1986), 50; *FRUS, 1952–4*, I (Washington, DC, 1983), 1947–8.
19. S. E. Ambrose, *Eisenhower: The President* (2 vols, New York, 1983–4); R. Divine, *Eisenhower and the Cold War* (1981); R. A. Lee, *Dwight D. Eisenhower: Soldier and Statesman* (1981); F. Greenstein, *The Hidden-Hand Presidency* (1982).
20. PRO, FO 371/111706/1073.
21. A. Eden, *Full Circle* (1960), 64, 143.
22. WFIS, Box 17, Eisenhower to Churchill, 7 July 1954.
23. *Ibid.*, Eisenhower to Churchill, 22 March 1955.
24. Ambrose, *Eisenhower*, I, 178–9.
25. Colville, *Fringes of Power*, 654.
26. *Ibid.*, 672.
27. WFIS, Box 16, Eisenhower to Churchill, 17 Dec. 1952.
28. WFIS, Box 17, Churchill to Eisenhower, 12 Nov. 1953.
29. WFIS, Boxes 16–18; PREM 11/52–5. Citations are herein made to the Churchill–Eisenhower correspondence in the Eisenhower Library, which is slightly fuller than in the PRO.
30. WFIS, Box 17, Churchill to Eisenhower, 24 May 1954.
31. Ambrose, *Eisenhower*, II, 19.
32. Quoted, *ibid.*, 268.
33. Quoted, *ibid.*, 146.
34. WFIS, Box 16, Eisenhower to Churchill, 20 July 1953; Lord Moran, *Winston Churchill: The Struggle for Survival, 1940–65* (1968), 416.
35. WFIS, Box 16, Aldrich to State Department, 11 Sept. 1953, and Dulles to Eisenhower, 16 Oct. 1953; Dulles Papers, White House Memoranda Series, Box 1, 12 April 1954.
36. WFIS, Box 17, Eisenhower to Churchill, 20 July 1953.
37. *Ibid.*, Eisenhower to Churchill, 29 March 1955, 14 Dec. 1954.
38. WFIS, Box 16, Churchill to Eisenhower, 28 May 1953.
39. FO 371/103514/1024.
40. *Washington Post*, 4 Dec. 1953; FO 371/103508/1016.
41. FO 371/103495/1031.
42. Dulles Papers, White House Memoranda Series, Box 1, Philip D. Reed to Eisenhower, 8 June 1953.
43. Ambrose, *Eisenhower*, II, 160–8.
44. *522 HCDeb. 5s*, 579.
45. WFIS, Box 16, Churchill to Eisenhower, 7 Feb. 1953.
46. FO 371/103519/1053.
47. FO 371/109116/1054.
48. *FRUS, 1952–4*, I, 1486.
49. FO 371/100825/1023.
50. FO 371/111792/1801.
51. PRO, CAB 134/762, 12 Aug. 1952.
52. W. H. McNeill, *America, Britain and Russia: Their Co-operation and Conflict 1941–46* (1953), 233.
53. P. G. Boyle, 'The British Foreign Office and American foreign policy 1947–48', *Journal of American Studies*, 16, no. 3 (1982), 373–89.

54. *FRUS, 1952–4*, I, 1481.
55. CAB 134/492, 20 Dec. 1951; L. Kaplan, *A Community of Interests: NATO and the Military Assistance Program 1948–51* (Washington, DC, 1980).
56. CAB 134/1011, 13 March 1952.
57. CAB 134/1012, 4 June 1952.
58. CAB 134/492, 22 Dec. 1951.
59. CAB 134/1013, 25 Nov. 1952.
60. CAB 134/767, 9 Dec. 1954.
61. CAB 134/1011, 5 March 1952.
62. FO 371/100185/281.
63. CAB 134/1019, 15 Dec. 1953.
64. CAB 134/1025, 16 Dec. 1954.
65. White House Central Files, Subject Series, Eisenhower Library, Box 67, 5 March 1953; B. Kaufman, *Trade and Aid: Eisenhower's Foreign Economic Policy, 1953–61* (1982), 1–55.
66. CAB 134/863, 23 June 1953.
67. CAB 134/1014, 30 Jan. 1953.
68. CAB 134/1024, 23 Sept. 1954.
69. Dulles Papers, White House Memoranda Series, Box 1, 12 April 1954.
70. WFIS, Box 16, 5 May 1953.
71. CAB 134/1012, 4 June 1952.
72. *FRUS, 1952–4*, II (Washington, DC, 1984), 1251–5; M. Gowing, *Independence and Deterrence: Britain and Atomic Energy, 1945–52* (2 vols, 1974), I, 19–321; J. Baylis, *Anglo-American Defence Relations 1939–80* (1981), 1–50; R. Edmonds, *Breaking the Mould: The United States and Britain 1945–50* (1986), 77–93. Less information has been de-classified on atomic energy than on any other subject in both the British and American archives.
73. Gowing, *Independence and Deterrence*, I, 406–7.
74. *Ibid.*, 413.
75. FO 371/114415/11917.
76. WFIS, Box 16, 7 Feb. 1953.
77. *FRUS, 1952–4*, II, 1471.
78. *Ibid.*, 1082.
79. *Ibid.*, 1423.
80. WFIS, Box 17, Churchill to Eisenhower, 21 June 1954.
81. NSC 151/1, Office of the Special Assistant for National Security Affairs, National Security Council Series, Policy Papers Subseries, Eisenhower Library.
82. *FRUS, 1952–4*, II, 1245–6.
83. Whitman File Administration Series, Eisenhower Library, Box 4, Strauss to Eisenhower, 6 Nov. 1953.
84. NSC 151/1.
85. Whitman File, Legislative Leaders Conference, Eisenhower Library, Box 1, 17–19 Dec. 1953.
86. NSC 151/1.

87. Whitman File, Administration Series, Box 4, Strauss to Eisenhower, 3 March 1955.
88. *Ibid*.
89. WFIS, Box 17, Cherwell to Eisenhower, 6 Dec. 1953.
90. *Ibid.*, Churchill to Eisenhower, 29 March 1954.
91. *Ibid.*, Aldrich to State Department, 5 April 1954.
92. Whitman File, Dulles-Herter Series, Box 2, 1 April 1954.
93. WFIS, Box 17, Eisenhower to Churchill, 22 March 1955.
94. *FRUS, 1952–54*, I, 1485.
95. Baylis, *Anglo-American Defence Relations*, 49–55.
96. *537 HCDeb. 5s*, 1897.
97. *530 HCDeb. 5s*, 148.

2 Cold War and Detente with Moscow

John W. Young

On 14 February 1950, during the British general election campaign, Winston Churchill made a speech in Edinburgh which surprised voters by calling for high-level talks with the leaders of Soviet Russia: 'The idea appeals to me', declared Churchill, 'of a supreme effort to bridge the gulf between the two worlds, so that each can live their life, if not in friendship, at least without the hatreds of the cold war ... It is not easy to see how things could be worsened by a parley at the summit.'[1] Although he had favoured diplomatic contacts with Moscow for some time, Churchill was best known in the post-war world for his great anti-Soviet speech at Fulton, Missouri four years before, with its dramatic talk of an 'iron curtain' dividing Europe and its call for an Anglo-American alliance (at a time, soon after the defeat of Hitler, when many still hoped for co-operation with the Soviet Union).[2] By 1950 the divisions of the Cold War were deeply set: the Berlin blockade had raised the spectre of a new world war, the North Atlantic treaty had been signed and a West German state created. The Edinburgh speech came at a time when the American government hoped to launch a major new rearmament effort, and almost simultaneously with Senator Joe McCarthy's first major speech at Wheeling, Virginia against 'communism' in the United States. The Labour party not surprisingly dismissed the Conservative leader's proposals as an election 'stunt'.

In fact, not only did Churchill's desire for high-level talks with Russia prove a lasting one over the next five years, it increasingly became one of his major aims when, following the next general election, in October 1951 he returned to 10 Downing Street. It divided him from his allies in America, Germany and France, from the Foreign Office and many Cabinet colleagues, even from his Foreign Secretary and chosen successor, Anthony Eden. At one time, indeed, the Prime

Minister's obsession with detente came close to destroying
the Conservative government itself. In pursuit of his goal
Churchill demonstrated extraordinary energy, determination
and cunning, but the complexities of the international scene,
divisions and insecurities within the Western alliance and his
own infirmities combined to condemn this, his last crusade, to
failure and disappointment.

Churchill's interest in detente had remained strong during the
1951 election campaign. In a broadcast on 8 October he declared,
'I do not hold that we should rearm in order to fight. I hope that
we should rearm in order to parley', and recalling his 1950
Edinburgh speech he argued, 'It might be that if such a meeting
as I urged had taken place ... the violent dangers of the Korean
War would not have been upon us.'[3] Two weeks later, in a
speech at Plymouth, he underlined the dangers of 'another
world war [which] would not be like the romantic struggles in
former centuries we have read about. It would be nothing less
than a massacre of human beings whether in uniform or out of
uniform by the hideous forces of perverted science'; and he
again hoped that the Soviet leaders would want 'a friendly talk
with the leaders of the free world [to] see if something could not
be arranged which enabled us all to live together quietly'.
Churchill was upset during the election campaign by accusations from some Labour supporters that he was a 'warmonger'
who would drag Britain into a major conflict. Such accusations
only strengthened his desire to be seen as a 'peacemaker' (his
reputation as a great war-leader being already assured). This
was not to say that he wanted negotiations with Moscow at all
costs: in his Plymouth speech he still spoke of the need for
Western strength, and especially for unity with America and
the Commonwealth,[4] and after 1951 he remained as keen as
ever to build a 'special relationship' with Washington. But
Churchill was a statesman raised on the European traditions of
diplomacy, *realpolitik* and balance of power; he may have
condemned Bolshevism in lurid terms after 1917, and shown
little mercy to his 'socialist' opponents at home after 1945, but he
had little sympathy for the rigid, ideological conflict which
characterized the Cold War. The new Prime Minister rejected
both a McCarthy-style anti-communist crusade and a rebirth
of Neville Chamberlain's appeasement, in favour of 'negotiations from strength'. In the late 1940s the West had followed
Churchill's advice given at Fulton, and was now united and well

armed, having seen the communist advance in Europe halted; now was the time to talk to men in the Kremlin, reduce the danger of war and bring about a *modus vivendi* with them.[5] There was therefore a consistency between Churchill the Cold Warrior of Fulton and Churchill the man of detente.

Despite Churchill's hopes for peace during the election campaign, and despite hopes from his Foreign Secretary, Anthony Eden, that there might be a relaxation in East–West tensions,[6] the first year of the Conservative government saw no easing in the Cold War. On the surface it seemed that the Conservative leader's talk of detente had indeed been an 'election stunt'. But there were in fact numerous reasons why he was unable to improve relations with Moscow in his first months in office. Not the least of these was American opposition. Co-operation with the Americans was of course vital to Churchill and it seems that he planned to raise the issue of detente with President Truman when they met in Washington in early 1952. The American press, however, made it plain that the USA had little interest in talks with Russia at this point. By now McCarthyism was a formidable force in American politics, the Truman administration was accused of being 'soft' on communism in the past and the deadlock of the Korean War (where the USA was much more heavily involved than Britain) hardened anti-communist sentiment. Furthermore, in mid-1951, shortly before Churchill returned to office, the Western powers *had* met the Russians – at the Palais Rose, in Paris – only to find it a futile and time-consuming business: officials from America, Britain, France and Russia, charged with preparing for a meeting of foreign ministers, could not even agree upon an agenda. After the Palais Rose experience no one wanted to attempt another four-power conference until there was a greater likelihood of success. In such inauspicious circumstances Churchill did not, in the end, raise the issue of possible Western-Soviet conversations with Truman[7] and in the months following the Washington visit the Russians themselves displayed no willingness to talk on terms that were acceptable to the West. Instead Moscow seemed determined to upset Western co-operation, and in particular to disrupt the formation of a supranational European Defence Community (EDC), through which West Germany was to be rearmed. The Russians were totally opposed to German rearmament and pressed the West from February 1952 to begin negotiations on a German peace treaty, which would create a 'neutralized', united German state, not tied to either alliance block. The Western powers saw this merely as an attempt to prevent German rearmament and were unimpressed by the basis for negotiation which Moscow suggested. It was notable that, once an EDC treaty was signed in May, Soviet pressure for talks on a German peace treaty receded.[8] And by then any chance of East-West talks was out of the question because the United States was locked into a presidential election campaign during which Truman (not himself a candidate for re-election) was unable to take any dramatic initiatives in foreign affairs.

The chances of Churchill being able to take up detente seemed to improve after November when the American election brought Dwight Eisenhower to the presidency. As Supreme Allied Commander during the war he had been a close colleague of the Prime Minister, and Churchill evidently believed he could be manipulated. In January 1953 indeed Churchill made a 'personal' journey to the United States, partly to visit another old friend, Bernard Baruch, but also to meet Eisenhower and among other things to press on him the case for detente. Churchill returned to London, believing that the visit had had some positive effect, but was rather upset that Eisenhower talked of going to meet Stalin alone.[9] In February the new President went further and told a press conference that he was prepared to meet Stalin if this had 'the slightest chance of doing any good', but it still seemed that such a meeting would be on a Soviet-American basis and this was hardly calculated to please the Prime Minister.[10] Any genuine sympathy which the President might have for detente was in any case countered by the professional foreign policy-makers in the State Department. These took a similar approach to detente as that which emerged in the Foreign Office: a policy of firmness was the best way to deal with Moscow; talks must be handled carefully, at foreign ministers' level; and any signs that Russia wanted peace probably disguised a manoeuvre to divide the West (as in 1952). Such views were strengthened by the appointment of the hard-line anti-communist, John Foster Dulles, as Secretary of State. A man of enormous foreign policy experience stretching back to the 1919 Paris peace conference, Dulles believed in an 'irreconcilable conflict' with Russia; he condemned Truman's policy of 'containment' as a defensive posture, unlikely to defeat the Soviets; and he preferred a policy of firmness and 'liberation' to break up the Eastern bloc. In Korea (where 'liberation' had been tried with disastrous results in 1950) he favoured a policy of threats – including talk of using the atom bomb – to bring peace. Although Dulles' appointment was initially an unpopular one with Eden and the Foreign Office, who had clashed with him on earlier occasions, they soon learnt to co-operate with him in controlling any 'unrealistic' hopes of detente.[11]

Churchill's hopes for peace with Russia achieved their first real encouragement not with Eisenhower's election therefore, but with the death of the Soviet leader, Joseph Stalin, on 5 March. Stalin was succeeded by a 'collective leadership' under Georgi Malenkov which soon began to press for an ease in tensions with the West.[12] When a British aircraft was shot down over East Germany the Russians offered to hold talks on the problem;[13] progress suddenly began on an Anglo-Soviet fishing dispute; and, most important, Moscow seemed now to favour a quick resolution of the Korean conflict. Anthony Eden seemed favourable initially to the idea of contacts with the new leaders,[14] and in Washington members of the White House staff were keen to see a major speech by the President, offering talks with the Russians at foreign ministers' level.[15] But the residue of suspicion from the Stalin era was not to be disposed of easily. Eden, after further consideration, decided that talks with Russia might merely damage Western cohesion for little good purpose, and the Foreign Office argued that any apparent changes in Soviet policy were purely 'tactical' – Moscow remained, fundamentally, committed to the cause of world communism.[16] In Washington meanwhile, Dulles urged that the West should await events and avoid 'precipitate' actions. Soviet moves, it was argued, could be designed merely to win the collective leadership a 'breathing space', in order to consolidate themselves in power. The French foreign minister, Georges Bidault, agreed with such doubts and was particularly concerned that talks with Russia would give the French Assembly (which had not yet ratified EDC) an excuse to delay German rearmament: for if peace with the Soviet Union became a real possibility it could easily be argued that German rearmament was unnecessary.[17] Eisenhower did eventually make a speech, on 16 April, calling for a 'fair' peace to be established with Russia and for talks to be held specifically on atomic weapons (an idea which eventually became one of the President's favourite themes). But the speech had been much diluted by Dulles, and Eisenhower demanded evidence of Soviet 'good faith' before any talks could take place. This meant, possibly, a settlement of the Korean War, possibly Soviet agreement to an Austrian peace treaty (which remained unmade after 1945). Even in this form the State Department felt that Eisenhower's speech had gone too far and Dulles insisted on making a speech of his own soon afterwards which was far more negative in tone.[18]

Despite the doubts of the Western foreign ministries Churchill had quickly decided, following the death of Stalin, that the time for an ease in world tensions had come. He hoped to send a personal message expressing this hope to the Soviet foreign minister, Vyacheslav Molotov (another wartime acquaintance), but was dissuaded by both Eden and Eisenhower.[19] Then, in early April, Eden was forced into temporary retirement from the Foreign Office by the need for a gallstones operation, and Churchill made himself acting Foreign Secretary, with greater freedom to pursue his own policies. At about the same time he had received an advance copy of Eisenhower's 16 April speech which, despite its cautious tone and even more cautious covering letter, seemed to show that Eisenhower was open to the idea of detente.[20] By now Churchill was becoming attracted again to a meeting of Western and Soviet leaders (rather than foreign ministers) with a wide agenda, on the lines of the wartime summits at Yalta and Potsdam. He also took up another of his wartime tactics in early May and suggested to Eisenhower that he – Churchill – would visit Moscow alone to establish the opening contact with the new Russian leaders. Eisenhower was unwilling to give any encouragement to such ideas and continued to press the line of his 16 April speech, that talks could be held only after the Soviets proved their good faith.[21] But undeterred, on 11 May, Churchill finally made his own public declaration of the need for peace, in tones very similar to the Edinburgh speech, but this time delivered before an astonished House of Commons. The declaration came at the end of a major foreign policy speech, and though the Prime Minister did say that the Soviets must show their good faith (by agreeing to an Austrian or Korean peace settlement) he went far beyond Eisenhower, stating:

> I believe that a conference on the highest level should take place between the leading powers without long delay. This conference should not be overhung by a ponderous or rigid agenda . . . The conference should be confined to the smallest

number of powers and persons possible . . . It might well be
that no hard-faced agreements would be reached but there
might be a general feeling [that] those gathered . . . might do
something better than tear the human race . . . into bits.[22]

Churchill's speech attracted support from the Labour opposition, some of the Cabinet and at least one junior Foreign Office
minister, Selwyn Lloyd;[23] it was quite well received by the
Russians[24] and had a great impact on public opinion. But it had
been made without consulting the Cabinet, without properly
informing the Foreign Office and without prior notification to
Eisenhower, and almost immediately opposition to it began to
mount. Eden and Lord Salisbury (the government's foreign
affairs spokesman in the House of Lords) were opposed to the
Prime Minister's ideas,[25] and Eisenhower again appealed to
Churchill to show greater caution.[26] The French government
was also appalled, partly because the speech fuelled the case
against German rearmament in the French Assembly and partly
because Churchill seemed to want to exclude France from
the proposed summit. By 20 May the French premier, René
Mayer, became so concerned on these points that he appealed
to Eisenhower to arrange a summit of the three principal
Western leaders (British, American and French) to try to control
Churchill. Despite State Department doubts the President
decided to take up Mayer's idea: if Churchill could not be
silenced by telegrams perhaps he could be silenced by a face-to-
face encounter. The President telephoned Churchill about the
proposal immediately and the latter quickly agreed to a meeting,
confident that *his* arguments, rather than those of his opponents,
would win through on such an occasion. He did, however,
press that the meeting should be held on British territory, at
Bermuda (which also happened to be a US base and close to
America). The scene then seemed set for a grand Western confrontation on the whole question of detente.[27]

Even a Western meeting proved impossible for the moment.
From the first, arrangements for Bermuda were dogged by
problems and the conference was not eventually held until
December. First, on 21 May – the day after the meeting was
arranged – Mayer's own government fell from office in Paris and
another administration, under Joseph Laniel, was not formed
for over a month, by which time the date for Bermuda was put
back to 8 July. Meanwhile, Churchill remained as keen as ever
about talks with Russia, and sent a personal message to Molotov

hoping that Bermuda would lead to this, but elsewhere opposition to this policy only grew. The Americans made clear, publicly, that they did not see the Bermuda meeting as a step to detente.[28] Germany's Chancellor, Konrad Adenauer, was terrified that if Churchill's hopes were realized this would only lead Moscow to press for a reunified but 'neutralized' Germany, which would end the Bonn government's ties to the West. In Britain, the Foreign Office, which regretted the public expectation raised by the decision to call Bermuda, shared Adenauer's fears. In a memorandum to Churchill, on 30 May, the Office pointed out that the 'neutralization' of Germany would ruin NATO's defence strategy (based on the Elbe), upset Adenauer, provide an opening for Soviet expansion and maybe even lead the Americans to abandon Europe. Cabinet ministers were keen to discuss the whole question of detente before Churchill left for Bermuda.[29] But it was then that all the Prime Minister's opponents had their fears eased by his own misfortune. On the evening of 23 June, just before he was to leave by ship for Bermuda, he suffered a stroke. The details were withheld from the public, but the stroke left him unable to appear in public until September. Since Eden was still ill the Chancellor of the Exchequer, 'Rab' Butler, became acting Prime Minister, and Lord Salisbury acting Foreign Secretary, and Bermuda had to be 'temporarily postponed'. In its place it was quickly decided to hold a Western foreign ministers' meeting in Washington in mid-July.

Despite his stroke, the Prime Minister remained mentally alert and on 6 July put a remarkably lucid and forceful memorandum before the Cabinet, arguing in favour of an early meeting of Western and Soviet leaders, with an informal agenda. Though he was now ready to delay such a meeting until *after* the EDC and German rearmament had been approved by the French Assembly, he was as adamant as ever about the need for progress and still ready to meet the Russians alone, on an Anglo-Soviet basis, if necessary. The Cabinet actually agreed that Lord Salisbury should press for an East–West leaders' meeting in the Washington talks but Salisbury himself, a critic of the 11 May speech, doubted that Churchill's proposals would succeed, and these doubts soon proved sound.[30] In Washington both Dulles and Bidault, supported by telegrams from Adenauer, rejected the idea of a leaders' meeting with an open agenda, and pressed instead for a four-power (British, American, French and Soviet) meeting at foreign ministers' level, based on the specific issue of a German peace treaty. Faced with this pressure Salisbury and the British Cabinet had little choice but to agree to the latter proposal: the alternative was to have the Washington talks break down. At least a meeting in some form was to be offered to the Soviets, in answer to the public pressure that had built up since 11 May, but the Labour opposition criticized Salisbury for having betrayed Churchill's vision of detente at Washington and it was clear that neither Dulles, Bidault nor Adenauer expected anything meaningful to emerge from talks with Russia on Germany. They were determined, just as the Foreign Office was, to maintain the Western position in Germany and maintain the informal alliance between Bonn and NATO. The main reason for their acceptance of a meeting in any form was indeed to prove that detente could *not* succeed, so as to deflate public hopes on this point and – more particularly – to induce the French Parliament to approve German rearmament.[31] Over the next months, however, as Churchill recovered from his stroke, the Soviets proved unwilling to respond to the Washington proposal for a foreign ministers' conference. Instead, in a series of interchanges between August and November with the Western powers, the Kremlin insisted on China's inclusion in any talks (a condition the Americans would not agree to after China's 'aggression' in Korea) and again seemed determined to cause mischief in West German politics by offering to discuss reunification with the East.[32]

On 5 November, in the pessimistic atmosphere created by yet another negative Soviet note, Churchill raised the idea of convening the 'postponed' Bermuda conference. The previous month Eisenhower had rejected a proposal from the Prime Minister to meet him alone in the Azores, but it was evident that a face-to-face encounter could not be put off for ever and Churchill remained determined to bring peace with Russia. On 5 November itself he wrote to Eisenhower and pointed out that a major international meeting could end the sense of 'stalemate' in international relations. So an Anglo-Franco-American leaders' meeting was arranged in Bermuda on 4–7 December.[33] Public expectation was again raised, but behind the scenes it was quite evident that Churchill's physical condition would not allow him to press the Americans too strongly. Eden had now returned to the political scene, and was able to challenge the Prime Minister successfully in early November on policy towards Russia, by forcing him to tone down remarks on the subject in a speech to the House of Commons.[34] In mid-November Churchill hit back, by refusing Eden permission to circulate a memorandum to the Cabinet which would have argued that Soviet policies had not fundamentally changed since Stalin's time (this remained the opinion of both the Foreign Office and the Moscow embassy).[35] But then Churchill's desire to break the international deadlock was again upset by Soviet policy. In a note on 26 November Moscow suddenly agreed to four-power talks at foreign ministers' level.[36] At Bermuda, as a result, much time was spent in discussing a reply to the Russians and setting the date for a conference with them. Churchill did not even press for a leaders' meeting, merely for a general opening of contacts with the Kremlin, and the press considered the results of the much-heralded meeting of the Western 'Big Three' to be very disappointing. Bermuda, indeed, was soon overshadowed by two other events.[37] First, on 8 December, Eisenhower developed his own line of detente on atomic issues, by proposing the creation of a UN body to share the benefits of atomic power (an offer which had little effect on Russia, but stole some of Churchill's thunder);[38] and a week later Dulles, exasperated by the continuing delays to the EDC, publicly warned the French that, if German rearmament did not come soon, there would be an 'agonising reappraisal' of America's commitment to Europe. This was a threat which had little effect on France, but it did highlight tensions in the Western alliance, which Moscow could exploit.[39]

In early 1954 Winston Churchill was barely able to keep hopes of real detente alive. The doubts of Eden, Eisenhower and others, combined with his own ill health, had reduced his own pressure for talks with Russia in 1953 to little more than vague encouragement at East–West 'contacts'. And at the meeting of the four foreign ministers, held at Berlin in January–February, there was little more than deadlock. As had always seemed inevitable, the Western powers adopted a concerted position on Germany known as the 'Eden Plan', because it fell to Eden formally to propose it, designed to maintain Adenauer's regime and which would only countenance the reunification of Germany if free elections were held across the country to elect an all-German government. To the Russians this could only seem like an attempt to place all Germany under Adenauer's rule. Their own preferred course was to return to the old system of four-power occupation whilst an all-German government was formed; free elections could then be held but Germany would be 'neutralized', unable to ally with either the Eastern or Western blocs, and the European Defence Community and NATO would be replaced by a 'European Security Pact', excluding America. To the Western powers these proposals seemed designed simply to undermine the cohesion of the Western alliance, destroy Adenauer's position and provide openings for a communist take-over in Europe, and Churchill fully supported Eden in resisting them: negotiation from strength remained, as ever, the Prime Minister's aim. But public concern about a complete East-West breakdown forced Eden, Dulles and Bidault to try to maintain some form of dialogue with Russia when Berlin came to an end, and Churchill was very pleased when it was decided that the four foreign ministers should meet again a few months later, in Geneva. There they would discuss not Germany but the Far East, where there was some hope of fruitful discussion on two subjects: a permanent peace settlement in Korea, following the armistice of July 1953; and a resolution of France's war with the Viet Minh nationalists in Indochina. Dulles was even ready to invite China to this meeting, though as a party to the Korean and Indochinese disputes rather than as a convening power, and without any formal recognition of the Peking government.[40]

It was in the weeks between Berlin and Geneva that Churchill began to consider a major, personal peace initiative towards Moscow. In part this undoutedly reflected a recovery in his health since mid-1953, and a continuing desire to retire as a 'peacemaker' rather than a 'warmonger'. But the Prime Minister also continued to be preoccupied with a new problem that had emerged on to the international scene since 1952, the hydrogen bomb. Both America and Russia had exploded such a bomb, a weapon many times more powerful than those used to defeat Japan in 1945. Churchill was so distressed by scientific reports about its destructive power which reached him during March 1954, that he declared, 'I am more worried about the hydrogen bomb than by all the rest of my troubles put together', and in early April during a debate in the Commons on nuclear issues the government accepted a resolution which called for an Anglo–US–Soviet meeting to discuss nuclear weapons. Churchill feared that, if something fundamental was not done to reduce international tension, the Americans might force a 'show down' with Russia while they could still be certain of nuclear superiority.[41] Eisenhower had actually fed such fears in a letter to the Prime Minister which bitterly attacked the Kremlin and spoke of the need 'to seek renewed faith and strength from . . . God and sharpen up [the] sword for the struggle that cannot possibly be escaped'. Even Eden and the Foreign Office were concerned enough by this to ask Churchill to clarify whether Eisenhower meant a military or spiritual 'struggle'. The Prime Minister agreed to do so, and in his message to the President on 9 March once more raised the idea of an East–West leaders' meeting. Eisenhower in reply was willing to reassure Churchill on the first point – he did not want war with Russia – but he was as unwilling as ever to consider a leaders' meeting.[42] In between the two messages, however, Churchill's son-in-law, Christopher Soames, had been contacted by the Soviet embassy (with whom members of Churchill's entourage had had clandestine contacts for some time) and told that the Soviet leader, Malenkov, would welcome a visit from the Prime Minister! Despite predictable doubts from Eden about this extraordinary approach, and despite Eisenhower's letter, Churchill again became very interested in the idea of a personal visit to Moscow to pave the way for wider detente.[43]

By mid-April Churchill seems to have decided to ignore his opponents and try, once again, to meet the Russians at leaders' level. He planned to do so alone, but he also still realized the necessity of winning Eisenhower's approval for such a visit. So, on 22 April he contacted the President once more and suggested a meeting between them in the near future in Washington. Eisenhower was unenthusiastic but eventually set the date for a meeting with Churchill in late June (at a time when the Geneva conference on the Far East would be in recess). Dulles and Eden too would attend, though Eden was far from enthusiastic about such a meeting.[44] The Foreign Secretary resented the Prime Minister's interference in foreign policy, disliked the work-load which a visit to America would add to his busy schedule and was keen to see Churchill hand over the reins of power to himself. Eden and other ministers felt by now that their leader was mentally and physically unfit to remain in high office.[45] Actually by the time the Anglo-American meetings began on 25 June, they came at a welcome time to discuss differences between Dulles and Eden which had arisen at Geneva. But Churchill's prime concern remained the issue of detente, and in Washington he won surprising presidential approval for his idea of an Anglo-Soviet meeting: Eisenhower even talked of following this up, if it was successful, with a meeting in London with the Russians which he would attend himself. Why the President conceded so much to Churchill can only be guessed: it may have represented a genuine belief in detente on his own behalf which Dulles usually managed to control. Certainly the Secretary of State was surprised by Eisenhower's behaviour and tried to talk Churchill out of a meeting with Malenkov. But the Prime Minister refused to be moved: he had the President's approval – that was the vital thing – and was determined to proceed.[46] Churchill's doctor noted that the idea of a meeting with the Russians 'has completely taken possession of him' and Harold Macmillan felt that the Prime Minister 'was obsessed by his hopes of going down to history ... as the greatest peace-maker in the world'. The hopes had become the main reason (or, perhaps, rationalization) of his desire to remain in office.[47]

On 2 July, whilst sailing back to Britain on the *Queen Elizabeth* in fact, Churchill decided to draw up a message to Molotov to sound out the Russians on whether a meeting (perhaps in Moscow) would, indeed, be possible. At this point Anthony Eden could well have prevented Churchill's message being sent and, indeed, when the Foreign Secretary first saw the Prime Minister's telegram he did raise doubts about it, pointing out that it could upset American opinion, offend Adenauer and other Western leaders, and raise public expectations, without the promise of any result. Eden was also concerned that the Prime Minister wanted to send a telegram to Moscow without obtaining Cabinet approval. Churchill, however, gave further confirmation at this point of his determination and cunning. First, he tempted Eden with talk of handing over the premier-ship to him in September; then he argued that his message to Molotov was not a formal proposal for a meeting, but an in-formal, 'private' sounding which did not require Cabinet approval; and finally he sent off the telegram to the acting premier, Butler, giving Eden the impression that Butler *would* inform the Cabinet. In fact, however, Churchill had no intention of letting the Cabinet see a proposal which he knew they might reject. He sent the telegram to Butler merely asking for comments on it and soon followed this with another message assuring him that the message to Molotov 'does not commit the Cabinet', and telling him to dispatch it to Moscow. Despite Foreign Office doubts Butler did so – and unleashed a storm. Eden's own private secretary Evelyn Shuckburgh was astonished that his chief had not prevented Churchill's action; two junior Foreign Office ministers, Selwyn Lloyd and Anthony Nutting, threatened to resign; and Lord Salisbury expressed horror at the telegram to Molotov on two counts – first because it was likely to harm the Western alliance, and secondly because, despite Churchill's arguments about a 'private' message, it did seem to mark a major foreign policy initiative, without Cabinet discussion.[48] Salisbury was one of those who considered Churchill unfit to head the government and had already considered resigning as a minister on various issues. It was Salisbury who, over the next weeks, led the opposition to a Churchill-Malenkov meeting and brought the Conservative government to the brink of destruction.

The Cabinet first discussed the Molotov telegram on 7 July, and it proved an acrimonious meeting during which Salisbury condemned Churchill's behaviour and threatened to resign. The atmosphere was not helped by the fact that the Soviet Foreign Minister had now written to the Prime Minister saying that a formal proposal for a meeting would be positively received. This message might have pleased the Prime Minister, but for other ministers it merely confirmed that Britain would now find it difficult to refuse this offer without upsetting the Soviet leaders and facing a major international humiliation (since it was expected the Kremlin would then publicize the episode). The Lord Chancellor, Lord Simonds, made moves after the Cabinet to apprise the Queen of the situation, since it was felt that the government might well fall apart, and at the next meeting, the following day, the arguments only became worse. By then Eisenhower had sent a message to Churchill expressing surprise at the speed of his Russian initiative after leaving Washington. A defensive Churchill promised the Cabinet that he would sound out Eisenhower further and – under intense pressure from several ministers, led by Salisbury – actually undertook to abandon the Malenkov meeting, if Eisenhower remained critical of it.[49] The President was thus placed – though he did not know it – in a position where he could have scotched Churchill's enterprise, but incredibly, as at the Washington meetings in June, he proved unwilling to condemn the Prime Minister's efforts. His next message to London stated that 'no-one could be happier than I to find that I have been wrong in my conclusion that the men in the Kremlin are not to be trusted' and in the next Cabinet, on 9 July, Churchill was able to use this to good effect.

He again pressed the case for meeting Malenkov, though he now said that he would only meet him in a neutral capital. He also said that he would demand some evidence of good faith from Malenkov, such as the signature of an Austrian peace treaty. Salisbury was still adamantly opposed to the whole idea, but neither he nor Churchill was yet willing to destroy the government on this issue. Instead ministers decided to put off the hour of decision, using as an excuse the still unfinished Geneva conference. It was evident that success or failure to reach peace in the Far East (and specifically Indochina) at Geneva could greatly affect the chances for a wider peace, and so the Cabinet would revise its discussions on a Churchill–Malenkov meeting when the Geneva conference was completed.[50]

The Geneva conference was in fact brought to a successful conclusion on 20 July and the peace settlement achieved in Indochina boosted Eden's standing in London at a time when his behaviour over the Molotov telegram had threatened to damage it. Cabinet discussion of the two-power meeting was resumed on 23 July. Since the last discussion by ministers the controversy had continued to simmer. Churchill had oscillated between deep concern at the opposition from Salisbury and contempt over his opponents' behaviour. The Prime Minister still had two weapons at his own disposal, to use against ministers: one was an appeal directly to the British people (with a repeat of his May 1953 action); the other was the threat of his own resignation.[51] At the Cabinet meeting all the arguments from earlier in the month were repeated: Churchill insisted on his right to send 'personal' messages to other leaders and on the need for world peace; Eden argued that Butler ought to have consulted the Cabinet in the first place; and Salisbury insisted that a meeting with Malenkov would undermine the Anglo-American alliance and mark a major Soviet diplomatic success. Both Salisbury and Churchill threatened to resign if other ministers did not agree with them, and it was left to the Foreign Secretary, as indecisive as ever, to think of another reason to delay the hour of decision. Seizing on a Soviet declaration, issued that same morning, which criticized US policy at Geneva, Eden argued that time should be taken to study this new Russian step, which might indeed signal an attempt to drive a wedge between London and Washington. With this suggestion, the Cabinet readily agreed.[52] It was a delay which probably saved the government, because the next day, 24 July, the Soviets gave further evidence of a desire to divide the West, when Molotov invited the British, American and French governments to discuss European security and the future of Germany at a foreign ministers' conference. Even the Prime Minister viewed this initiative with contempt and it gave him an ideal opportunity to withdraw with honour from his struggle with Salisbury. Encouraged by Eden, Churchill agreed to send a new message to Molotov pointing out that, since the Soviets were set upon a foreign ministers' conference, a meeting at leaders' level seemed inappropriate. The Cabinet approved this decision on 26 July. The unity of the British government was thus saved, in the end, by clumsy Russian diplomacy. In Moscow it had apparently been decided, in view of the Geneva success, to try to exploit the international situation along the well-established lines of a European security treaty, rather than to wait any longer for Churchill to propose a leaders' meeting.[53]

During August 1954 the Prime Minister in fact continued to hope that a meeting with Malenkov would be possible. Once the Western governments had rejected the Soviet proposal for a European security conference, and once the French finally approved German rearmament in EDC – a vote on this issue was now imminent in Paris – Churchill planned to pursue a two-power meeting with Malenkov again. He told the Cabinet as much in a memorandum circulated on the 3rd of the month, and on the 18th circulated another paper repeating these points. Between these two memoranda the Prime Minister considered that his case had been strengthened by two events. First, it had been announced that a Labour party delegation was to visit Moscow: Churchill saw this as 'proof' that detente could win votes, and that the Cabinet's refusal to back him on the issue would lose the Conservatives support in the next general election. Second, in an extraordinary interview, the Soviet chargé d'affaires in London told a Foreign Office official that Soviet diplomacy must share the blame for the failure to bring about a Churchill–Malenkov meeting, and that the Russians preferred a visit from a Conservative party delegation rather than Labour![54] On 29 August the Prime Minister wrote to his American friend, Bernard Baruch, stating that a meeting with Malenkov was still possible.[55] And meanwhile, despite his promises to Eden, Churchill had dropped all talk of resigning the premiership in September. Rather than bequeath a 'fag-end' Parliament to his successor, he now decided to hold out until 1955 when an election was almost certain to be held. But then, yet again, in the twists and turns of fortune surrounding his hopes for detente events turned against Churchill. On 31 August came a decisive blow, and one that was destined to end all realistic hopes of a meeting with Malenkov, when the French Assembly threw out EDC. All hope of facing the Russians in the near future from a position of strength was thereby lost; instead, the Western alliance was thrown into division and turmoil.

Churchill's pursuit of detente had always been bound up closely with the fate of German rearmament. Although the Prime Minister had always believed in negotiations with Russia from strength, his opponents – in the Foreign Office and the State Department especially – had long feared that talk of detente *before* German rearmament was achieved would provide openings for the Russians to weaken the West, by feeding doubts about EDC. In 1950 it had been the French themselves who had insisted that Germany should only be rearmed, under strict controls and with limited independence, in a 'European army'. But even when the other NATO powers agreed to this, French doubts about German rearmament had continued. Now all the fears of Churchill's opponents seemed to be borne out. The dangers for NATO from the French action were immense: American public opinion was thoroughly tired of the lack of European efforts to defend themselves; Konrad Adenauer, who had fully supported EDC and based much of his foreign policy on rapprochement with France, felt betrayed; and the Soviet Union could be expected to exploit the situation to the full. It was Anthony Eden who called a conference of the most interested NATO states in late September, in London. An alternative route to German rearmament was then found – as Churchill had wanted – within NATO, but the French Assembly did not debate and approve the new agreements until the end of the year, and even then the situation was not safe for the Western alliance: after the Assembly, the accords had to negotiate the French Senate, and a positive vote here was not achieved until March 1955.

Until German rearmament was achieved all further talk of negotiations with the Russians was out of the question; if the French parliament believed that peace with Russia was possible there would be renewed arguments that German rearmament was unnecessary. And the British Prime Minister fully appreciated these arguments. He wrote to Eisenhower at the end of 1954 agreeing that the London accords on German rearmament must be ratified before any talks with Russia could be contemplated – although he still hoped that such talks would eventually take place.[56] During his last six months in office, in fact, the Prime Minister differed little on the surface from Eden and Eisenhower as regards policy towards the Soviet Union. Indeed, if anything, it was Churchill who seemed to offend the Soviet leaders more than anyone else during this period. The publication of the last volume of his memoirs of *The Second World War* (covering the year 1944–5) had given the Prime Minister the chance to demonstrate again his anti-communist credentials, and to reveal his desire to negotiate with Moscow from the strongest possible position. The book was most notable, on this theme, for revealing Churchill's pressures on President Truman in May 1945 to hold on to areas of eastern Germany, as a 'bargaining counter' in talks with Stalin, rather than placing them (as had been agreed) under Soviet occupation.[57] In November 1954 Churchill had followed *Triumph and Tragedy* with a speech at Woodford in which he claimed that he had ordered the stock-piling of German weapons at the end of the war, with a view to arming the Germans for a new war with Russia. This was in fact – as Churchill soon admitted – a baseless claim, but it had a predictably damaging effect on Anglo-Soviet relations (and did little to reassure the public about Churchill's ability to fulfil his responsibilities)![58] Then in January 1955 the French premier, Pierre Mendès-France, as part of his campaign to push German rearmament through the Senate, raised the idea of calling a meeting with the Russians, to satisfy those in France who argued that possibilities for detente had not been fully explored. It was Churchill, exasperated at French delays, who led the Western response to Mendès' suggestion: in a toughly worded note to the French premier, he threatened to isolate France if German rearmament was not approved soon.[59]

In March 1955 Churchill made a speech to Parliament defending his Russian policy, arguing that he had always genuinely sought detente with Moscow, and pinning the blame for the failure of this squarely on the Soviets. The Prime Minister even revealed his hitherto secret exchanges with Molotov in July 1954 and accused the Russians of sabotaging his efforts. This drew an enraged Soviet response, Molotov himself accusing the British of responsibility for the failure of detente and publishing the whole of his correspondence with Churchill in mid-1954 in full.[60] There was still, however, one last danger that the Prime Minister, on the brink of retirement, could revive his bid for peace with Russia. In mid-March President Eisenhower suggested that he might visit Europe in early May – on the tenth anniversary of VE day – in order to exchange the instruments of ratification for the restoration of German sovereignty and German entry into NATO. This would highlight the restoration of Western unity and could also pave the way for talks with Russia from a position of strength. But Anthony Eden, eager to grasp the reins of power at last, scotched this idea with a series of arguments. He did not think a new meeting with Russia was a possibility at present: in February Malenkov had suddenly been overthrown in a Kremlin power struggle and the new leadership, in which the prominent member was Nikita Khrushchev, seemed unlikely to enter major talks at an early date. Neither did the West German entry into NATO in May seem likely to make the Russians willing to talk; rather the opposite. Eden did not think either that the announcement of a visit from Eisenhower would necessarily please the Germans – who would hardly wish to celebrate VE day! – or help the French government – who had still to complete the ratification of German rearmament. In Cabinet on 14 March Churchill pressed ministers to welcome the American initiative. He argued that if it did lead to a Russian meeting it would mark a great achievement, but the Cabinet tended towards Eden's view and the Americans were asked to delay any presidential visit until a later, more opportune moment. Subsequent contact with them revealed that Washington had not, in any case, envisaged an early four-power meeting.[61] By 30 March France had ratified the 1954 agreements on German rearmament and Eden told the Cabinet that he was now ready to work for a new meeting with Russia,[62] but this would take time and, with a general election in the offing, the ageing Churchill had finally decided to retire. He attended his last Cabinet on the morning of 5 April, and in the afternoon, in an address to junior ministers, made one last appeal for Britain to take up contacts with Russia and reduce world tensions.[63]

The irony was that, with Churchill gone, moves towards a meeting with Russia proceeded more quickly than expected, and Eden, Eisenhower and the French went to meet the Russian leaders in Geneva in July. From the Western point of view there was logic in this. The Foreign Office and State Department had always said that they would be willing to hold a meeting with the Russians *after* Germany was rearmed. The German entry into NATO in May gave the opportunity to enter talks with Russia from a position of strength, an argument which Churchill could well appreciate, and the Foreign Office argued that this moment was the optimum one to strike a deal with the Russians, possibly involving a lasting settlement of the German problem. Another reason to talk was that the Russians had finally agreed, in May, to sign an Austrian peace treaty based on the reunification and 'neutralization' of that country. Since America and Britain had always said that such a signature would be treated as proof of Soviet 'good faith', it became difficult to avoid further talks with them. Even so, Eisenhower and Dulles were rather surprised that, once in 10 Downing Street, Anthony Eden should suddenly favour a leaders' meeting, rather than one at foreign ministers' level, and it seems likely that Eden's decision reflected a wish to become the 'peacemaker' that Churchill had failed to be. The Russian motives for agreeing to an Austrian treaty and a leaders' meeting can only be guessed: most likely Khruschev wished to steal the limelight from the Western powers after their success in rearming Germany at last; he and his associate, Marshal Bulganin, may also have wished to strengthen their own domestic position after Malenkov's fall.[64] The Geneva conference did not in fact achieve much by way of concrete results, but it marked the first meeting of Soviet and Western leaders since Potsdam and, as Churchill always hoped, contributed to an ease in East–West tensions. During the meeting Eden kept Churchill informed of events, and on 15 July Eisenhower wrote to his old friend:

> I cannot escape a feeling of sadness that the delay brought about by the persistently hostile Soviet attitude toward NATO has operated to prevent your personal attendance at the [Geneva] meeting . . . Personally I do not expect a miracle. But if we can move a little closer to the dream that has been yours for these many years, if . . . we can create a new spirit of tolerance . . . we shall gain much that will help us.

Three days later Churchill thanked the President by letter and wrote:

> I have never indulged in extravagant hopes of a vast, dramatic transformation of human affairs, but my belief is that, as long

as we do not relax our unity or our vigilance, the Soviets and the Russian people will be increasingly convinced that it is in their interests to live peaceably with us.[65]

There were many reasons why Winston Churchill was unable to attend a summit with Soviet leaders in 1951–5, despite being the leading Western advocate of such a meeting. Some of these reasons were personal. The Prime Minister may not have sought detente purely in order to make a reputation as a great peacemaker, but there was a degree of vanity behind his interest in easing tensions with Russia and this blinded him to some of the problems with his policy – particularly the reaction his ideas would have on Adenauer's policy in Germany and on the French government's efforts to secure EDC. Churchill's age, his ill health, his tendency to doze off in meetings, his refusal to read important memoranda – none of these inspired confidence in him or his ideas in the eyes of many ministers, Foreign Office officials and foreigners; and many believed he should have given power to Anthony Eden at a much earlier date. More directly of course his stroke in 1953 put an end to his hopes of achieving detente during that year. He had recovered enough by spring 1954 to make another bid to meet the Russians, but this would not have got far but for the behaviour of Eisenhower (in encouraging him) and Eden (in failing to prevent the telegram to Molotov), and Churchill's deviousness and arrogance in pursuit of his goal weakened his case in Cabinet, where many considered he had broken constitutional conventions by his actions. After mid-1953 he claimed that it was the hope of reaching a *modus vivendi* with Moscow which kept him in office, but it is difficult to know whether this was a reason or a rationalization for remaining as premier. In such an extraordinary character as Churchill the interplay of personal motives, political realism and visionary idealism was doubtless complex. Certain facts seem to point to a genuine interest in detente as a major goal in itself: after the failure of EDC for example, when hopes for detente were extinguished, Churchill seems to have been dismayed and took less interest, in general, in running the government; then, in March 1955, with the American proposal for a grand conference of the Western alliance, he considered clinging to office a little longer. But too often the Prime Minister seemed to be living in the past, hoping to attend summits and shape the world as he had in wartime. He could still display great energy and imagination at times and his wartime reputation still carried great weight in 1951–5, but he was unable now to face the combined problems of his own physical weakness and the opposition of the professional civil service, the Cabinet and other Western leaders to his policy.

Just as important, however, the Prime Minister was unable to pursue a consistent policy of detente in the face of an unfavourable international situation. In the first seventeen months of the Conservative government the bitter enmities of the Cold War remained undiminished, with both Stalin and the American leaders determined to take a firm stand against the other, and the Korean War as a backcloth. The death of Stalin seemed to present an opportunity for detente, but by then the suspicions between East and West were deeply set. The new Soviet leaders seemed at times to take a more co-operative line towards the West – peace was made in Korea in 1953, the Indochina War was settled in 1954 and in 1955 an Austrian State treaty was signed – but at other times they took a negative attitude (as in their policy towards a foreign ministers' conference in July–November 1953) or seemed to be set on dividing the Western alliance (as in the aftermath of the Geneva conference in 1954). This schizophrenia in Soviet policy may, of course, have reflected the power struggle which was evidently going on in the Kremlin between Malenkov and his opponents. Even more vital than the doubts in Moscow, however, were the doubts and divisions within the Western alliance. Whether or not detente was possible with Stalin's successors is, of course, impossible to say, given the lack of Soviet sources. But the fact is that the West never seriously tried to take up a policy of detente, at least until the 1955 Geneva summit. In part this reflected continuing distrust of Soviet Russia, reinforced by such events as the crushing of the 1953 Berlin rising, in part it reflected the strength of McCarthyism in America, but in part too it reflected doubt and division within the Western camp. The problems which talks with Russia presented for EDC in France and for Adenauer's pro-Western policy in Germany led many to believe that any sign of moderation from Russia was designed to disrupt the Western alliance, and that the policy of Malenkov was fundamentally unchanged from that of Stalin. Actually the appearance of Western divisions once detente was discussed should have caused no surprise: for Western unity was built upon enmity with Russia. But even Churchill of course wanted Western unity and strength as the basis for negotiations with

Russia. Churchill evidently believed in May 1953 that 'negotiations from strength' were possible, but the aftermath of his great speech that month suggested that Western strength itself might be deceptive, and the Prime Minister's desire for contacts with Russia had a damaging effect on his policy of the 'special relationship' with Washington. The fate of EDC was particularly important in all this: French distrust of Germany, and the doubts in Paris about German rearmament in a European army, represented a fundamental flaw for Western unity. Churchill disliked EDC and would all along have preferred to see Germany's direct rearmament within NATO, but it took a grave crisis within the alliance in September 1954 to bring such a solution about, and the experience seemed to prove the Prime Minister's opponents correct on the detente issue. Ironically, it seems that a major reason for Churchill's failure to meet the Russian leaders was his failure to pursue a policy of negotiation from strength. Only when German rearmament was finally achieved in May 1955 were Western leaders really in a strong enough position to meet the Russians, and by then Winston Churchill was Prime Minister no more.

Notes

1. R. R. James, ed., *Winston S. Churchill: His Complete Speeches 1897–1963*, VIII, *1950–63* (1974), 7936–44; and on the 1950 election see H. G. Nicholas, *The British Election of 1950* (1951), 194–203.
2. R. S. Churchill, *The Sinews of Peace* (1948), 93–105.
3. James, *Churchill Speeches*, 8254–8.
4. *Ibid.*, 8281–6; and on the 1951 election see D. E. Butler, *The British General Election of 1951* (1952), 118–28.
5. On this theme see C. Bell, *Negotiations from Strength* (1962).
6. See I. McDonald, *A Man of the Times* (1976), 132.
7. PRO, FO 371/97592/1 (draft agenda, with Russia as first subject); FO 371/90937/3, 21; FO 371/90938/42–4.
8. On the exchanges: FO 371/97877–92; PRO, PREM 11/168; D. Folliot, ed., *Documents on International Affairs, 1952* (1955), 79–80, 85–105, 175–8, 186–97.
9. FO 371/106537/29; PREM 11/422 (8 Jan.); J. Colville, *The Fringes of Power: Downing Street Diaries, 1939–55* (1985), 657–62.
10. D. Eisenhower, *Public Papers of the Presidents of the U.S.: Dwight D. Eisenhower, 1953* (Washington, DC, 1960), 69–70; PREM 11/422.
11. On Dulles' policies see L. Gerson, *John Foster Dulles* (New York, 1967); and on the Korean settlement, R. Foot, *The Wrong War:*

American Policy and the Dimensions of the Korean Conflict (Ithaca, NY, 1985), 204–31.

12. See, for example, Malenkov's speech of 15 March: D. Folliot, ed., *Documents on International Affairs, 1953* (1956), 11–13; and for a general discussion, D. Dallin, *Soviet Foreign Policy after Stalin* (Philadelphia, Pa, 1961).

13. Folliot, *Documents, 1953*, 38–42.

14. E. Shuckburgh, *Descent to Suez: Diaries, 1951–6* (1986), 83–5.

15. FO 371/106524/31; see also A. Eden, *Full Circle* (1960), 49.

16. On discussions in Washington at this time see especially, W. W. Rostow, *Europe after Stalin* (Austin, Tex., 1982), but also: R. J. Donovan, *Eisenhower, the Inside Story* (1956), 72–6; R. Gould-Adams, *The Time of Power* (1962), 109–19; E. Hughes, *The Ordeal of Power* (New York, 1963), 100–15.

17. FO 371/106525/37; FO 371/106537/45 and 57; FO 371/103664/2.

18. See n.16 above.

19. PREM 11/422, 1074.

20. PREM 11/422, 429, 1074.

21. PREM 11/421, 422, 429, 1074.

22. *515 HCDeb. 5s*, 883–98.

23. J. Morgan, ed., *The Backbench Diaries of Richard Crossman* (1981), 241–2; H. Macmillan, *Tides of Fortune, 1945–1955* (1969), 510–11; and, on Lloyd, *515 HCDeb. 5s*, 1071–2.

24. For example, Folliot, *Documents, 1953*, 66–71.

25. PRO, CAB 128/27, CC (54) 49, confidential annex; R. R. James, *Anthony Eden* (1986), 365 and 371.

26. On the US response see FO 371/103527; and in general an Anglo-US relations and the detente issue in 1953 see M. S. Fish, 'After Stalin's death: the Anglo-American debate over a new Cold War', *Diplomatic History*, 1986, 333–55.

27. For a full discussion, J. W. Young, 'Churchill, the Russians the Western alliance: the three-power conference at Bermuda', *English Historical Review*, 1986, 889 and 893–4.

28. PREM 11/420, 428, 1074; FO 371/103527/7; Lord Moran, *Winston Churchill: The Struggle for Survival, 1940–65* (1966), 16 June, 6 July.

29. PREM 11/428, 449, 905; FO 371/103660/32, 34; and on the West German dimension see A. Glees, 'Churchill's last gambit', *Encounter*, April 1985, 27–35.

30. CAB 128/261, CC (53) 39; CAB 129/61, C (53) 186, 187, 194; PREM 11/419, 1074.

31. CAB 128/26, CC (53) 42, 44, 45; PREM 11/419/1074; FO 371/103667/84, 86–7, 90–6; Eden, *Full Circle*, 53–4; Macmillan, *Tides of Fortune*, 517–19; Moran, *Churchill*, 12 and 14 July; *Foreign Relations of the United States (FRUS), 1952–4*, V, 1607–97; Shuckburgh, *Diaries*, 89–92.

32. Folliot, *Documents, 1953*, 77–8, 81–100.

33. *Ibid.*, 100–6; CAB 128/26, CC (53) 64; PREM 11/418, 1074; *FRUS, 1952–4*, V, 1711–15; Colville, *Fringes of Power*, 673, 675, 679–80;

Macmillan, *Tides of Fortune*, 524–5; A. Seldon, *Churchill's Indian Summer* (1981), 402–3; Shuckburgh, *Diaries*, 95–103, 105–10.

34. *520 HCDeb. 5s*, 27–31.
35. PREM 11/418; see also FO 371/106542/14; FO 371/103694/771; FO 371/103695/792; and W. Hayter, *The Kremlin and the Embassy* (1966), 114–15.
36. Folliott, *Documents, 1953*, 107–9.
37. On Bermuda see Young, 'Churchill, the Russians and the Western alliance', 898–907; Shuckburgh, *Diaries*, 110–17.
38. Eisenhower, *Public Papers, 1953*, 813–22.
39. *FRUS, 1952–4*, V, 859–70.
40. CAB 128/27, CC (54) 3, 8, 9, 10; CAB 129/65; C (54) 13; PREM 11/664, 665; FO 371/109269–92; Shuckburgh, *Diaries*, 127–35.
41. CAB 128/27, C (54) 23; *526 HCDeb. 5s*, 36–153; Moran, *Churchill*, 5 and 6 April; and see also A. Howard, *'RAB': The Life of R. A. Butler* (1987), 205.
42. PREM 11/1074; Shuckburgh, *Diaries*, 137, 153.
43. Moran, *Churchill*, 8 April; Shuckburgh, *Diaries*, 149, and see 153–62 on this period.
44. CAB 128/27, CC (54) 39; PREM 11/666, 1074; Macmillan, *Tides of Fortune*, 530–1; Moran, *Churchill*, 28 April, 15 May, 2, 4 and 10 June.
45. Macmillan, *Tides of Fortune*, 553–4; Moran, *Churchill*, 27 May, 2, 4, 10 and 15 June; Shuckburgh, *Diaries*, 173; and for a full discussion of Churchill's health, Seldon, *Indian Summer*, 42–54.
46. CAB 128/27, CC (54) 44; PREM 11/649, 650; Colville, *Fringes of Power*, 691–7; Eden, *Full Circle*, 131–3; R. H. Ferrell, ed., *The Diary of James C. Hagerty* (Bloomington, Ind., 1983), 72–80; Moran, *Churchill*, 25–29 June.
47. Colville, *Fringes of Power*, 691–2; Macmillan, *Tides of Fortune*, 531–3; Moran, *Churchill*, 26 June.
48. Colville, *Fringes of Power*, 697–702; Macmillan, *Tides of Fortune*, 534; Moran, *Churchill*, 2–5 July; Shuckburgh, *Diaries*, 221–2, and for the telegram, see CMD. 9418 (1955), 1. The discussion in James, *Eden*, 380–1 is quite inadequate.
49. CAB 128/27, CC (54) 47th and 48th confidential annexes; PREM 11/1074; Colville, *Fringes of Power*, 701; Macmillan, *Tides of Fortune*, 534; Shuckburgh, *Diaries*, 222–4; and see also Howard, *'RAB'*, 207–8.
50. CAB 128/27, CC (54) 49, confidential annex; PREM 11/1074.
51. CAB 128/27, CC (54) 50; Colville, *Fringes of Power*, 701–2; Macmillan, *Tides of Fortune*, 535–7; and see Shuckburgh, *Diaries*, 224–6.
52. CAB 128/27, CC (54) 52; Colville, *Fringes of Power*, 702; Moran, *Churchill*, 23 July.
53. CAB 128/27, CC (54) 53; PREM 11/670; CMD. 9418, 3–4; Colville, *Fringes of Power*, 702–3; Macmillan, *Tides of Fortune*, 537–8; Shuckburgh, *Diaries*, 235.
54. CAB 129/70, C (54) 263, 271; Colville, *Fringes of Power*, 703, 705; Macmillan, *Tides of Fortune*, 539–41; Moran, *Churchill*, 6, 12 and 18 Aug.
55. Seldon, *Indian Summer*, 621.

56. PREM 11/1074.
57. W. S. Churchill, *The Second World War*, VI, *Triumph and Tragedy* (1954), 496–500.
58. James, *Churchill Speeches*, 8604–5; Moran, *Churchill*, 28 Nov.
59. PREM 11/901; FO 371/118195–7.
60. *538 HCDeb. 5s*, 960–3 and 2268–9; CMD. 9418.
61. CAB 128/28, CC (55) 23, 24, 25; PREM 11/893; Colville, *Fringes of Power*, 705–8.
62. CAB 128/28, CC (55) 27.
63. CAB 128/28, CC (55) 28; J. Boyd–Carpenter, *Way of Life* (1980), 94.
64. CAB 128/29, CC (54) 4–7, 12, 19, 23, 25, 26; PREM 11/893, 894, 895 and see FO 371/118204/29. On USA see especially W. W. Rostow, *Open Skies; Eisenhower's Proposal of 21 July 1955* (Austin, Tex., 1982).
65. PREM 11/981.

3 German Rearmament and the European Defence Community

John W. Young

The greatest problem facing Churchill's peacetime government in Western Europe was that of German rearmament. The issue threatened the future both of the Western alliance and of European unification, it generated enormous criticism of British policy in Europe, but ultimately too it provided Anthony Eden with one of his greatest diplomatic triumphs.

German rearmament had been pressed on NATO states by the Americans in September 1950, at the height of the Korean War crisis, and was seen by US military planners as a vital move to counter the Red Army's strength in Europe. Coming only five years after Hitler's defeat, however, the proposal stunned many Europeans, especially the French, with their bitter memories of three German invasions since 1870. For several months in late 1950 the Atlantic alliance had been thrown into turmoil, before the French themselves produced one possible solution to the disagreements: Germany should be rearmed as part of a federal 'European army' within NATO, without an independent German General Staff; institutions, such as a European minister of defence, would ensure that Germany could never become a menace to the peace again. This marked an extension of the 'supranational' principle, first utilized in the Schuman Plan of May 1950 (which established a European body to control coal and steel production), and was soon accepted by NATO as the only way forward on German rearmament. In February 1951 France, West Germany, Italy, Belgium and Luxembourg, later joined by Holland, began negotiations for a 'European Defence Community' (EDC) in Paris. The Americans, supporters of both German rearmament and European unity, lent the project their full support.

Britain's attitude towards EDC was governed by two sets

of considerations. On one side, because of their world-wide interests, their doubts about the stability of Western Europe and their fear of being drawn into a European federation, the British had refused to join the Schuman Plan. For the same reasons, reinforced by doubts about the practicality of EDC, London refused to enter the Paris talks. But, on the other hand, Britain wanted to see progress in NATO, supported the idea of German rearmament and did not want to appear too negative about European unity ('negative' British attitudes had already been criticized in America and Europe). Thus, in September 1951 Labour's Foreign Secretary, Herbert Morrison, had given Britain's full diplomatic support to EDC and undertook 'to establish the closest possible association with the European continental community'.[1] When Eden returned to the Foreign Office on 27 October, therefore, EDC was the chosen road to German rearmament and Britain was committed to support it from outside; the exact form of 'association' remained to be decided. Many continentals, however, still hoped that Britain might be drawn into EDC and were encouraged by the fact that, whilst in opposition, Winston Churchill had been an advocate of greater European unity: he had even proposed the creation of a 'European army', in August 1950.[2] But Churchill had never said that Britain herself should join such a European federation; rather, he felt, she should act as a 'sponsor' of European integration, whilst maintaining her independence and her links to America and the Commonwealth.[3] He made this plain to the Cabinet, soon after returning to power,[4] and although some ministers – notably Harold Macmillan (the housing minister) and Maxwell Fyfe (the Home Secretary) – took a more genuinely 'pro-European' line, Eden was able to end any illusions about British policy at an early date. In a blunt and widely criticized statement in Rome on 28 November (during a NATO Council meeting) the Foreign Secretary declared that Britain could never join EDC: Labour's policy was to be continued.[5]

Ironically, thereafter, Eden's greatest problems within his own government on EDC lay not so much with the 'pro-European' views of Macmillan and Maxwell Fyfe, as with bitter criticisms of EDC from the previously 'pro-European' Churchill. Like many others the Prime Minister believed that the supranational (or, as he called them, 'metaphysical') elements in EDC made it impractical. He liked to portray the scheme as a motley, confused collection of Italian, Dutch and German privates, being drilled by a French sergeant, and he condemned the whole idea as a 'sludgy amalgam' or 'a bucket of wood pulp'. Churchill had hoped to see a very different kind of European army, more like a coalition of national forces: 'I want a faggot of staves bound by a ring of steel and not a soft, putty affair such as is now contemplated.' From the first, however, Eden resisted these negative arguments. In December he argued forcefully with the Prime Minister in favour of EDC along several lines: EDC was the *only* plan for a European army under discussion, talks on it were progressing and Britain had declared her public support for it; failure of EDC would throw the whole German rearmament question back into the melting pot; furthermore, if the failure was seen to be caused by Britain, she would be condemned by Europe and by Washington as a 'saboteur'. Eden admitted he would prefer 'a more modest scheme without elaborate superstructure' but he was not prepared to disrupt EDC and alienate Britain's allies, in order to bring this about: Britain must only put an alternative policy if EDC failed for other reasons. Impressed by these arguments (and by American views) Churchill avoided public criticsm of EDC, though he continued to castigate it in private. The same arguments also sufficed to silence Macmillan.[6] Eden's policy was thus firmly set: he would not join EDC but neither would he destroy it; instead he would support it from outside, as a sponsor, whilst being prepared to put an alternative scheme forward if it failed.

Eden's efforts on the international scene to secure German rearmament fall naturally into three phases: first, down to May 1952, efforts to secure the signature of an EDC treaty; second, down to August 1954, efforts to secure its ratification; and finally efforts to find an alternative route to German rearmament, after EDC itself collapsed. At the beginning of the first phase there were already grave doubts on the continent about EDC. Indeed, Belgium's foreign minister, Paul van Zeeland, wanted to abandon supranationalism in favour of a looser form of organization, which could include Britain – an approach similar to Macmillan's.[7] In France itself opinion had shifted markedly against EDC especially after the general election of June 1951. The communists (being pro-Soviet) and many socialists and radicals were opposed to German rearmament in principle, partly because of memories of the Occupation, and partly through fears of a German resurgence or the provocation of a Russian invasion; the right-wing *Gaullistes* objected, on national grounds, to merging the French army into a European force. In these new circumstances the French government could only hope to secure the National Assembly's support for EDC by reassuring the Deputies that EDC was indeed the best way forward. This was important for Britain because one vital point, on which Deputies needed reassurance, was that Britain would remain closely tied to Europe's defence, helping to counter both the Soviet menace and any German resurgence. Britain's reputation and military importance still carried great weight on the continent and so pressure was put on London to make Morrison's promise of 'association' as full as possible. It was on the issue of association that most of Eden's problems centred, right down to 1954, as he tried to steer a course which helped the ratification of EDC without making Britain a part of it.

It is unjust to characterize Eden as being 'anti-European' in his attitudes to EDC. In early November British and American representatives readily agreed to a French request for joint guarantees between NATO and EDC so that an attack on a member of either body would be considered an attack on the other (a move which thereby ensured that West Germany would be defended).[8] Later that month, Eden proved that he was willing to go beyond the American position in offering concessions, despite the widespread belief that Britain wished to keep rigidly in line with US policy as a 'co-sponsor' of EDC. The Foreign Secretary suggested both to Dwight Eisenhower (NATO's supreme commander) and Dean Acheson (Amerian Secretary of State) that Britain should offer 'institutional association' with EDC, partly as a way to offset the negative impression of his Rome statement. But, whilst Acheson conceded that British association 'in the end ... might be the catalyst that can pull the whole matter together', both Americans opposed Eden's idea, on the grounds that negotiations for such close British association could cause long delays. Eden took this as confirmation that a policy of supporting EDC without drawing too close to membership was right.[9] Unfortunately, however, it meant that the public heard only of his Rome statement on 28 November and criticism of 'negative' British policy continued: 'From every side, in Europe', wrote Eisenhower, 'I get complaints reference Britain's attitude towards a European army.'[10] And this tended to become the pattern: whatever positive gestures Eden did make failed to offset his refusal to draw too close to the continentals. The Americans too, though sympathetic to his position, were always liable to press him hard on EDC.[11]

At Rome the NATO Council, largely at Washington's behest, pressed the Paris negotiators to complete an EDC treaty before the next council meeting in Lisbon, in February.[12] To help this process, on a visit to Paris in December, Churchill and Eden reiterated British determination to 'associate themselves as closely as possible' with EDC.[13] The following month, on a visit to America, Eden again struck a negative tone about Europe in public when, in a speech at Columbia University, he made it plain that Britain could not join a European federation: 'this is something which we know, in our bones, we cannot do'.[14] But in early February, with the main lines of his policy clear, he was ready to outline Britain's proposals on EDC association to France's foreign minister, Robert Schuman. These included military and air force co-operation (with joint training and exchanges of officers) and a commitment to maintain British forces on the continent as long as they were needed. The proposals did not impress Schuman, however. He wanted to see an Anglo-EDC treaty, embodying an 'automatic' mutual commitment to resist an attack, and lasting fifty years (the intended duration of EDC). He also wanted Britain to guarantee EDC's integrity from within, that is, against disruption by a member state, such as Germany.[15] Schuman's need for British concessions increased at this time because, in February, the National Assembly formally demanded a series of conditions before EDC could be approved; these included solid British and American military guarantees, the predominance of the French army in EDC and a delay to German rearmament until the EDC treaty was ratified by *all* the signatories. (Also in February, the German Parliament made a series of demands including full German equality in EDC and an end to the allied occupation.)[16] Thus, even as the Paris talks produced a draft EDC treaty, new arguments seemed to threaten his future.

It was the funeral of George VI, in mid-February, which provided a fortuitous occasion for resolving many of EDC's short-term problems. Eden, Acheson, Schuman and the German Chancellor, Konrad Adenauer, were able to hold a series of meetings which paved the way for a full agreement at NATO's Lisbon Council. To ensure West Germany's equality in the Western alliance, whilst keeping her from actual membership of NATO (to which the French were rigidly opposed), it was

agreed to hold joint meetings of NATO and EDC when necessary. On the question of guarantees for EDC, it was agreed that
there should be a joint NATO-EDC treaty, a joint Anglo-
American guarantee of EDC's 'integrity' (against external and
internal threats) and a separate British guarantee (reiterating
existing commitments and emphasizing Britain's special links to
Europe). This fell short of Schuman's desire for an Anglo-EDC
treaty but Eden insisted that Britain's long-term military role in
Europe was assured by her NATO membership. Nominally,
members were free to leave NATO after 1969, but Eden was
adamant that Britain would remain in the alliance longer than
that.[17] At Lisbon, Britain's position seemed to be accepted, but
Schuman warned Eden that the continentals might yet demand
more from her[18] and, indeed, a few weeks later, on 14 March,
the EDC states formally asked Britain to enter into a fifty-year
treaty. The pressure for this now came, not from the French so
much as from the Dutch, who viewed themselves as one of
Britain's closest allies and baulked at the idea of entering into a
long-term military commitment which London did not share.
Dirk Stikker, the Dutch foreign minister, suggested that Eden
should extend the terms of the 1948 Brussels Pact, of which
Britain, France and the Benelux were members, to Germany and
Italy. The Brussels Pact, which had paved the way for NATO,
included a fifty-year term and an 'automatic' commitment to go
to war if a member was attacked, and its extension would
draw Britain and the EDC states together. The Americans,
exasperated by these new delays, pressed Eden to give more to
the Europeans, and the Foreign Secretary, though determined
to maintain Britain's Europe, agreed to do so: otherwise, it
seemed, EDC might never be signed.

On 28 March Eden prepared the Cabinet for more concessions
by arguing that 'the more positive form Great Britain's association . . . can take, the more likely the [French] Assembly is to
approve'. Then, on 4 April, the Cabinet was presented with a
new Foreign Office proposal: an Anglo-EDC treaty *could* be
made, *but* it should only last as long as Britain's membership of
NATO; otherwise Britain might be drawn, step by step,
Eden feared, into effective membership of EDC. Eden made it
clear to the Cabinet and to the continentals that this was the
absolute limit of British concessions.[19] Meanwhile agreement
was reached on the technical aspects of Anglo-EDC military
co-operation[20] and, to goad the Europeans into agreement,

Acheson warned that if EDC was not approved, Congress might not agree to further American financial appropriations for NATO.[21] Eden's concessions and Acheson's warning duly had their effect: in early May final agreement was reached on both the EDC treaty and a series of 'contractual agreements' by Britain, America, France and Germany to give West Germany full sovereignty. At French insistence these agreements were linked, so that German sovereignty could not be restored until EDC had been set up. (A last-minute attempt by the Dutch to insert the right to secede from EDC, if NATO was dissolved, was successfully resisted.)[22] As late as 25 May the French Cabinet remained doubtful about signing EDC but diplomatic pressures, includng another American threat to cut off financial support, and some stiffening in the terms of the Anglo-American guarantee, overcame France's reluctance. On 26 May the contractual agreements were signed in Bonn; the next day the EDC treaty was signed in Paris, along with the Anglo-EDC treaty and other guarantees.[23]

Eden has been criticized for the way he retreated on British guarantees to EDC in early 1952.[24] He had been forced to offer far more to Europe than America had done, and he had offered his concessions in what seemed a grudging way, which failed to impress continental opinion. The Foreign Secretary's policy, however, was not without its successes. He had managed to counter the pressures both from those within his own government who were willing to see EDC destroyed, and from those on the continent who hoped to draw Britain into virtual membership of the European army; he had preserved Britain's essential position as a 'sponsor' of the European community; and ultimately he had seen the Paris treaty signed. The compromise of an Anglo-EDC treaty, with a duration equal to NATO, did not seem too great a concession in the light of all that.[25] The problem now was to achieve EDC's ratification.

In June 1952 Eden told the Cabinet that he hoped to see EDC in force by the end of the year,[26] but this proved a forlorn hope. In West Germany doubts arose about whether or not EDC was a 'constitutional' act, and the High Court did not finally judge that it was constitutional until early 1953. This gave other states an excellent excuse to delay their own ratifications, whilst in France opposition to the Paris treaty continued to grow (strengthened in part by France's war in Indochina, which threatened to weaken her contribution to EDC and thus allow Germany to dominate it). Schuman continued to argue that EDC was the only way to rearm Germany under limitations yet as an equal, but even leading officials at the Quai d'Orsay had grave doubts about the new organization.[27] In October the prospects for EDC grew even dimmer, as Franco-German arguments broke out over elections in the Saar (which had been separated from Germany in 1946 under French auspices).[28] René Massigli, the French ambassador, told Macmillan that France might never ratify EDC[29] and Oliver Harvey, Britain's ambassador in Paris, agreed.[30] By the end of 1952, rather than hoping for EDC's ratification, both Britain and America were considering alternative policies to it, though without much success. In Washington the State Department considered a range of alternatives but ruled them out: the abandonment of German rearmanent in favour of a 'non-military' German contribution to defence (through industrial production) seemed inadequate; the withdrawal of American troops from Europe to a position of 'peripheral defence' was an extreme and impractical idea; direct German rearmament outside EDC (but possibly within NATO) was most practical but, of course, would again face strong French opposition. American officials were thus reduced to arguing that EDC *must* remain the way forward, and they hoped to encourage it with a 'carrot and stick' approach: inducements, such as military aid, would be combined with thinly veiled threats to abandon Europe if Germany was not rearmed.[31] Under the new Republican presidency of Dwight Eisenhower, after January 1953, these threats to abandon Europe became more frequent: many Republicans, including the rigidly anti-communist Secretary of State, John Foster Dulles, were quite exasperated by European behaviour.[32]

One important gain for Britain from this American reconsideration of EDC was that US officials from now on saw European pressures for further concessions from London as 'an attempt to squeeze an old lemon even drier'.[33] Acheson told Jean Monnet (the architect of EDC) that it was now quite absurd to blame Britain for Europe's difficulties, and the outgoing Secretary of State seemed fully in agreement with Eden on the responsibility of France for the disappointing state of affairs over EDC.[34] Dulles was keener to see Britain play a fuller role in Europe – the Foreign Office was deeply offended when 'Mr Dulles lumped us together with the French and Germans' in one of his early speeches[35] – but, in general after late 1952, Washington was very sympathetic to Eden's European policy. Foreign Office considerations about the European army at this time were put to the Cabinet on 10 December and had very similar conclusions to those of the State Department: EDC was still the best route to German rearmament and Britain must encourage it through means which 'do not involve any real sacrifice on our part'. Thus Eden was willing to extend military co-operation in its technical aspects and to see British representation in EDC institutions, but he was opposed to, say, a commitment to keep a fixed number of British troops in Europe (an idea which the French were considering) because such a major concession could be 'the first step on a slippery slope' to a European federation. If EDC did collapse Eden was willing to act positively by 'developing the existing organisations, for intergovernmental co-operation in Europe' (importantly, he talked about 'making more of' the Brussels Pact), but he considered that, on German rearmament itself, 'there is no half-way house between the EDC . . . and full German membership of NATO'. Hitherto Eden and his officials had feared that direct German membership of NATO would offend France, antagonize Moscow and open the door to a new German militarism, but now, like the Americans, they saw this course as the only practical alternative to EDC.[36] (Eden actually told the French President, Vincent Auriol, about this NATO alternative during a meeting in December, and argued that France would do well to ratify the EDC: the Foreign Secretary was unimpressed by Auriol's view that a better solution was a European confederation, including Britain.)[37]

In January 1953 EDC faced further complications as a new government under René Mayer came to power in France. Mayer immediately replaced Schuman with the more nationalist Georges Bidault (previously foreign minister in 1944–8) and demanded a comprehensive set of concessions for France before he would try to ratify EDC: he wanted to negotiate certain 'additional protocols' to the Paris treaty, which effectively reinterpreted much of the treaty in France's favour;[38] he wanted a definitive Franco-German agreement on the future of the Saar; and he wanted further political and military links between the EDC and Britain.[39] These demands dominated the efforts to ratify EDC for the next eighteen months (though ratification of the treaty proceeded during this time in Germany and the Benelux states). The 'additional protocols' were largely agreed, on a six-power basis during 1953, a Saar agreement was initialled in May 1954 and a new Anglo-EDC agreement was announced in April 1954. It is the last issue which is of interest to the present discussion.

At first Eden tried to resist Mayer's new demands, telling Massigli that there could be no 'irrevocable guarantees' about British troop levels in Europe and that Britain could not join EDC 'if only for the reasons that behind the plan ... was the conception of a federated Europe'.[40] Instead, on 24 January the Foreign Secretary put forward more proposals on military co-operation with EDC.[41] The French were not to be put off, however. On 12–13 February Mayer and Bidault visited London and presented a memorandum, the main proposals of which were a British guarantee to maintain their current troop levels in Europe (though with an escape clause 'in the event of a serious crisis overseas') and British representation on EDC institutions (so as to achieve 'organic co-operation going further than mere association'). Privately Bidault doubted that Britain would concede much, and was actually considering a transformation of EDC into a 'coalition' of European armies (which of course Churchill might have favoured).[42] But in late February Eden did approach the Cabinet with new proposals. He still opposed a concrete guarantee of troop levels, but was willing to make a promise to consult NATO and EDC before withdrawing troops from the continent; he was also willing to be represented in, but not become a full member of, EDC institutions. As in his concessions of 1952 he was adamant, in winning Cabinet approval, that this was the final limit of his concessions, and only Macmillan showed serious doubts about this policy: Macmillan preferred to end all the concessions, demand EDC's ratification and then, if EDC failed, step forward with a British plan.[43] In March the French continued to press for a solid British commitment on troop levels but the other EDC states (and America) felt Eden was doing enough. Though some more minor concessions were made to France in official talks over the following weeks, a draft agreement was finalized in May which generally followed Eden's line,[44] and on 2 July the Foreign Secretary was able to tell the Cabinet that the British proposals had been formally accepted by all the EDC states.[45]

Yet again, however, an apparent breakthrough proved illusory. By November the 'final' agreement on Anglo-EDC association was ready to be initialled, alongside a memorandum on joint military policy which Eden hoped to publicize at the most opportune moment in order to help EDC's ratification. That same month, however, the French made a new demand for an 'annual review', by Britain and the EDC, of British force levels in Europe. Eden, with strong Cabinet approval, rejected this,[46] but in December Bidault presented Eden with a comprehensive set of new demands, including a British military commitment to Europe as a 'ratio' of EDC forces, fuller Anglo-EDC military links and support for France's position as a 'great power' (to ensure that she was not simply seen in future as 'part' of a European entity). Britain gave long consideration to these ideas in early 1954 and, although the Chiefs of Staff opposed any 'ratio' agreement on troops, Eden asked the Cabinet in March to approve yet another new package of proposals which largely met Bidault's demands: Britain would support France's 'great power' status, place one division in an EDC corps and – most important – would maintain British forces in Europe at their 'present fighting capacity' (a formula which would allow the actual number of units to vary with technological changes in armaments). Even Eden was surprised when the Cabinet agreed to all this,[47] though Macmillan complained that France was being offered 'almost everything but marriage'.[48] On reopening talks with the French, however, Eden actually held the promise on 'fighting capacity' in reserve; it was never revealed to the French, and as it transpired he did not have to offer it to Bidault: the other concessions, particularly the offer of a British division in EDC, proved sufficient to impress the French foreign minister and a final Agreement on Association was signed on 13 April.[49] (In contrast, all the Americans were prepared to offer, in a memorandum of 16 April, was a confirmation of existing guarantees to EDC.)[50] On 15 April 1954, after an intense debate, the French Cabinet agreed to seek EDC's ratification.[51]

The delays to EDC since 1953, it must be said, were not only caused by France. Churchill's search for detente with Russia after Stalin's death in March (discussed elsewhere in this volume) also complicated the situation for EDC.[52] The Prime Minister, at first, saw no need for EDC to hinder detente; he still wanted to goad the French into ratification by threats, and preferred a European 'grand alliance' to the EDC 'amalgam'.[53] However, his views allowed the opponents of ratification in France to cause more delays. They now argued that EDC should be delayed until *after* talks with Russia: for if peace with Moscow was possible, German rearmament was unnecessary. In June 1953 a new government in Paris, led by Joseph Laniel, had come to office and declared that, in addition to all the Mayer government's conditions on EDC, there must also be talks with Russia prior to ratification.[54] This increased the exasperation of those, especially in the United States, who were distressed by all the French delays, but there was little that could be done. At a meeting of American, British and French leaders at Bermuda, in December, the French resisted strong pressure from their allies to ratify EDC.[55] The following week Dulles, to Churchill's satisfaction, publicly warned of an 'agonising reappraisal' of US policy if EDC failed, but this only antagonized French opinion (and in any case, the State Department continued to see no viable alternative to EDC).[56] When a foreign ministers' conference was held between America, Britain, France and Russia, in Berlin, in January-February 1954 it came to nothing, but a further meeting was arranged for May, in Geneva, mainly to discuss the Far East. Britain and America hoped to see EDC ratified in the interim, but Geneva provided France with the excuse for still further delays.[57] It was then that the public reaction to Britain's Memorandum of Association, into which so much time and energy had gone, proved very disappointing. Britain's concessions were again portrayed as grudging and inadequate, and seemed quite unlikely to turn the tide of public opinion in favour of EDC.[58] At the Quai d'Orsay officials were as despondent as ever.[59]

In the spring of 1954 even the most francophile American officials were prepared to be 'cold-blooded' with France;[60] Gladwyn Jebb, the new British ambassador to Paris, believed (like Macmillan) that London should accept EDC's failure and work for a 'less rigid and potentially federalistic' organization, including Britain;[61] Belgium's foreign minister, Paul-Henri Spaak, a great 'pro-European', wanted to see a tangible demonstration of France's isolation.[62] All the renewed talk of threats and alternatives to EDC failed to move the Laniel government towards ratification before Geneva, however – and Geneva proved disastrous for EDC. The conference met just as France's position in Indochina collapsed in defeat at Dienbienphu. Laniel's government fell, to be replaced by another under Pierre Mendès-France, one of France's most remarkable and dynamic politicians. He, inevitably, turned all his attention to the Indochina problem, until it was solved by a comprehensive settlement on 21 July, but behind the scenes it was soon clear that his arrival had not improved EDC's prospects and Jebb reported to Eden that EDC was 'finished'. Mendès' view was that, to avoid further divisions in his country, EDC must be accepted by the whole French nation, not merely a slender majority in the Assembly.[63] On 30 June, in fact, he told Spaak that the European army would not pass in its present form.[64] At the Quai d'Orsay indeed, opinion was no longer divided between 'pro' and 'anti-EDC' factions, but between those who wanted major changes to the treaty and those who wanted to emasculate it completely, until it became no more than a supranational arms control agency. In late July Mendès decided in favour of a series of changes to EDC which diluted its supranational elements in the hope of satisfying those, like the *Gaullistes* and the army, who opposed EDC on 'nationalist' grounds. This approach, which marked the final abandonment of Schuman's 'federalism', included more EDC-NATO links (so that members could leave EDC if NATO ended), a restriction of EDC forces to those present in Germany (leaving French forces independent elsewhere), and a delay in establishing supranational institutions for several years. Mendès planned to discuss this with other EDC states in Brussels, on 19–22 August, then begin the ratification debates.[65] The decisive moment for EDC had come, but in the most inauspicious circumstances.

The British view of Mendès-France was two-sided. On the one hand Eden and Mendès personally got on very well,[66] the Foreign Office hoped the new premier could end the weakness and vacillations of the Fourth Republic's governments, and his ideas on a diluted supranationalism were attractive to people like Gladwyn Jebb. (Jebb, whose links to anti-EDC politicians aroused American suspicions, believed Mendès' advent 'could be the beginning of a real revolution for France'.)[67] On the other hand Britain remained committed to co-operation with Washington and the ratification of EDC. In June Churchill and Eden visited Washington and agreed to pursue EDC to the end, although they also agreed to hold official Anglo-American talks in July (about which Mendès was informed) on a possible separation of the Paris and Bonn treaties of 1952 – so that German sovereignty might be restored, and West German opinion thereby assuaged, even if EDC collapsed.[68] As the Brussels conference approached in August, London and Washington acted together to encourage agreement, despite grave doubts about whether Adenauer, Spaak and the other leaders could accept Mendès' ideas. It was hoped in fact that Mendès' ideas were a tactical move, and that he would be satisfied with more minor concessions.[69] But, to everyone's dismay, these hopes proved unfounded: at Brussels Mendès refused to retreat from any of his demands; three days of talks ended in deadlock.[70]

Mendès flew to London, after leaving Brussels, for a meeting which he had requested with Churchill some days before, hoping to find succour from the foreign government which seemed most friendly to him. But, though Eden flew back from holiday for the meeting (held at Chartwell), and though the British were personally sympathetic to Mendès, London remained loyal to EDC: Mendès was told by Churchill and Eden that ratification *must* be attempted, that France might find the alternatives unpalatable and, indeed, that she might be isolated by her allies if EDC failed. The French premier tried to be positive, declaring himself willing to restore German sovereignty and even hinting that Germany could enter NATO (perhaps via a special European group within the alliance), but he gave little hope for EDC. Gladwyn Jebb hoped that Mendès would now 'finish the job off quickly', so that an alternative to EDC could be sought. He argued that 'there would ... be an overwhelming majority in the Assembly for ... any proposals for a looser European system with only very limited supranational powers, but including ... the United Kingdom' and avoiding German entry into NATO, and he even believed that Mendès himself might call a conference in Paris to pursue such a scheme.[71]

For a time, encouraged by the frank discussions in the Chartwell meeting, Spaak and the Americans hoped that another EDC meeting might be called, with British and American representatives in attendance, but the British feared that this would become a humiliating re-run of Brussels, and preferred to see France's ratification debate take its course.[72] On 30 August, after a debate in which Mendès did little to defend EDC, the whole project was defeated. Four years of negotiation had come to nothing and the Atlantic alliance was thrown into confusion: Adenauer's pro-Western policy was endangered and he felt betrayed; German sovereignty and German rearmament were put in abeyance; Dulles, who had already told Eden that France should be isolated, publicly warned again that America would 'reappraise' its foreign policy;[73] Churchill, denouncing the

French as 'swine', was ready to abandon France for an Anglo-German-American alliance, then bring German rearmament about.[74] The scene was set, however, not for the collapse of the Western Alliance, but for a major diplomatic triumph for Anthony Eden.

In August the Foreign Office had given consideration to the idea of a diluted form of EDC as offering a new way forward, but this seemed likely to recreate all the arguments over EDC and to herald an 'interminable negotiation', and it was not surprising that, on 27 August, before EDC collapsed, Eden had told the Cabinet that the best alternative to EDC was German rearmament through NATO, with some limits on Germany's military independence, but with the restoration of German sovereignty. On 1 September ministers approved more specific moves to bring this solution about, Eden telling them that, if it came to a choice between breaking with France or Germany, he would choose to break with France.[75] Despite ominous rumblings from Washington and Bonn no one, fortunately, was willing to see France isolated just yet, and Eden was determined to avoid this if at all possible: the British Chiefs of Staff had reported that France's loss to NATO would be militarily disastrous. In America, an Anglo-German-American treaty was considered a viable option, and the Pentagon again studied the idea of 'peripheral defence', but Dulles' preferred solution, after careful consideration, was a NATO agreement.[76] Adenauer was deeply angered by the defeat of EDC and was determined to see Germany achieve full equality, via both the restoration of German sovereignty and German rearmament: thus, on 2 September, he rejected the Anglo-American plans to separate the Paris and Bonn treaties and simply carry out the contractual agreements on German sovereignty. He too, however, hoped for a general 'NATO solution' to the problem and even, encouraged by a personal suggestion from Churchill, offered to accept voluntary limits on Germany's military independence. (Churchill himself let Eden pursue a conciliatory policy during September.)[77] But the position still seemed very precarious. The obvious problem was how to win France over to German rearmament – which Washington, London and Bonn were all determined to achieve – whilst providing Adenauer's long-sought full equality in the Western alliance.

According to Eden's memoirs, it was whilst sitting in the bath at his Wiltshire cottage on 5 September that he produced

one possible solution to the difficulties: an extension of the
Brussels Pact from Britain, France and the Benelux to Germany
and Italy, as a way both to preserve a 'European' dimension
to the Atlantic alliance and to draw Britain closer to the continentals, all of which (albeit lacking a supranational element)
would impress opinion in Europe. In fact, of course, the idea of
building on the fifty-year Brussels Pact had been discussed for
some time. A few days after returning to office in 1951 Eden
himself had told the journalist Iverach McDonald that, if EDC
failed, Britain would seek an alternative plan which brought
West Germany into a European grouping within NATO. Dirk
Stikker had raised a similar proposal in 1952, and in December
1953 when Eden and his officials had discussed how to act if
EDC failed, one proposal was to extend the Brussels Pact, form a
single European army (but without federal elements) and agree
not to withdraw British forces from it without consent. It was
an idea which the Office still had under consideration, and
certainly seemed preferable to Dulles' 'agonising reappraisal'.
Furthermore, the idea of extending the Brussels Pact had been
mentioned in the Cabinet, on 27 August, by – predictably –
Macmillan. Neither were the British alone in such ideas. The
Italians too had considered such a course.[78] More important,
so had the French, though their ideas for the Pact were
very different from Eden's. At the Quai d'Orsay an extended
Brussels treaty was seen as the way, not only to draw Britain
closer to the continent, but also as a new means to control
Germany. The French wanted to see a new Brussels military
command separate from NATO and a supranational arms
control agency (an idea discussed earlier, during EDC's decay),
and they wanted Germany to serve a 'probationary' period in the
Brussels Pact before being brought into NATO.[79] As yet, however, though Mendès had hinted at some of these ideas at
Chartwell, and though Jebb had predicted some lines of French
thinking, the British were unaware of French plans in detail.
The Foreign Office and the Cabinet easily approved of Eden's
idea of utilizing the Brussels Pact, but Jebb and others warned
that rather more concessions would be needed to make certain
France's approval of German rearmament, and Eden warned
the Cabinet, on 8 September, that he might, at last, need a
written commitment of British troop levels in order to 'cement'
any agreement. As earlier in 1954, however, he promised to
hold this particular concession 'in reserve' for the time being.[80]

Originally Eden had hoped for a meeting of the EDC powers, with Britain, America and Canada, in mid-September, to resolve the West's difficulties, but Dulles (who, in any case, would have preferred a full NATO meeting) and Adenauer were fearful of moving too quickly, and so the Foreign Secretary decided to pave the way for a nine-power conference via a preliminary tour of EDC capitals.[81] On 11 September he flew to Brussels and found complete support from Benelux ministers for his twin ideas of drawing Germany into NATO and extending the Brussels Pact.[82] Thus encouraged he flew on to Bonn, where an initially sceptical Adenauer also seemed impressed by the British proposals and confirmed his readiness to accept voluntary restraints on German arms.[83] In Rome too Eden found support for his plans,[84] though it was here that he was very upset to receive a message from Dulles, who proposed to visit Bonn and London – but not Paris – within the next few days. Dulles (who had not learnt of Eden's own plans until after the latter's tour of Europe began) had actually warned the Foreign Secretary earlier that such a visit was likely, but Eden felt it was inept thereby to raise the spectre of French isolation, and to show a lack of faith in British diplomacy, just as he was about to make the final, vital visit of his tour – to Paris.[85] Once in Paris, Eden was pressed by Jebb to offer a commitment on troop levels to France, but the Foreign Secretary still held this key concession 'in reserve.' Instead he pressed Mendès, on 15–16 September, to accept Germany into NATO, and offered only an extended Brussels Pact as a concession. At first Mendès refused to move, insisting that the Brussels Pact become a complex military machine in which Germany must serve 'probation' before joining NATO. Ironically the Brussels Pact, far from being a source of unity between Britain and France, was suddenly becoming the principal area of division. Eden, however, warned that France's intransigence would bring her isolation, turn Germany towards Russia and lead America to leave Europe, and eventually his arguments succeeded in mellowing Mendès somewhat. The Frenchman conceded that he might accept Germany's entry to NATO, though still only if effective controls were put on her through the Brussels Pact. Eden agreed to recommend this sympathetically to a nine-power conference.[86]

Eden returned to London on 17 September, and barely had time to report to the Cabinet before meeting Dulles.[87] The Secretary of State still doubted that Eden had sufficient grounds for agreement, and was particularly disappointed at the absence of any supranational element in Britain's plans that might hold out new hope for a European union, but publicly he praised Eden's 'brilliant and statesmanlike ... initiative' and agreed to attend a nine-power conference. Invitations were then sent out for such a conference to begin in London on 28 September.[88] The prospects for a solution still seemed very mixed, however. Neither Dulles nor Adenauer liked Mendès' plans to control Germany via the Brussels Pact,[89] and in a speech in Strasbourg, on 20 September, Mendès still left it unclear what exact controls he wanted on Germany and how she was to be tied to NATO.[90] The key problem therefore remained: how to ensure French acceptance of German sovereignty and rearmament without creating complex safeguards which would alienate Adenauer. Washington was unwilling to put forward new proposals to help the Europeans,[91] so the onus was on Eden to find a solution. Not surprisingly, he now turned to the idea of a promise to maintain the present level of British forces in Europe (four divisions and the RAF). Previously, of course, he had been reluctant to give this concession to EDC because of the dangers of being drawn gradually into a continental federation, because of the difficulties in drafting an 'escape clause' to such a commitment and because the French were likely to 'pocket' such a concession and then ask for more. But he had been willing to offer a troops commitment as a 'final' concession for some time and this was now more palatable since it would be made to the non-supranational Brussels Pact. As to 'escape clauses', Eden wanted to ensure that Britain could alter its commitment in the event of an 'overseas emergency' or a balance of payments crisis (the latter at Treasury insistence). Furthermore, the commitment could be changed at any time with the agreement of a majority of the Brussels powers, not unanimity (thus preventing any French veto). Eden put these proposals in a Cabinet memorandum on 27 September, admitting that he was asking for 'an unprecedented commitment ... but ... it is impossible to organise an effective defence system ... without a major British contribution'. The Chiefs of Staff had already approved of a troops commitment, if it was the only way to save the Western alliance.[92]

The first day of the London conference, 28 September, only further convinced Eden of the need for a troops commitment. Mendès, still as much concerned with feeling in the National

Assembly as with the needs of his allies, pressed for German entry to a complex Brussels Pact machine, but not NATO; Adenauer wanted entry to the Brussels Pact, entry to NATO and the restoration of sovereignty (separate British-American-French-German talks were held on the last question). That evening a small number of Cabinet ministers met and, after some debate, and despite doubts from Churchill, agreed to pursue Eden's plan.[93] The following day, as the deadlock seemed likely to continue, Eden made his dramatic announcement on the future commitment of British forces, which brought an enthusiastic response, even from members of the French delegation. Mendès – as Eden knew – was trapped: having won a long-sought concession from his closest ally he could not reject a settlement without being completely isolated. None the less, Eden's recollection that 'from this point on, the conference moved rapidly forward' was something of an exaggeration. Mendès continued to press hard for a supranational arms production agency and it was agreed that the former EDC states would study this. Adenauer agreed to accept voluntary limits on the manufacture of certain arms, including the so-called 'A.B.C. weapons', atomic, bacteriological and chemical. Dulles (who seems to have overestimated the potential of the Brussels Pact to become a new vehicle of European unity) agreed to extend all America's previous guarantees to EDC to the new Brussels Pact. Eden's was thus the vital, but not the only, concession at London. The Final Act of the conference, including German entry into NATO, an expanded Brussels Pact (known now as the Western European Union), the restoration of German sovereignty, British military guarantees and the arms agency study, was not ready until 3 October.[94] After official talks, to finalize the agreements, they were signed in Paris later that month (where, after some Franco-German argument, a new Saar agreement was added to them).[95]

In December, in an initial vote on the West European Union (WEU), the French Assembly defeated the proposal. There was not, however, to be a repeat of the EDC saga: Mendès put the whole London settlement to a vote of confidence a few days later and, at Jebb's suggestion, Britain issued a stern public warning that German rearmament would be carried out with or without French agreement. Despite some annoyance at Britain's new-found bluntness, the Assembly passed the accords.[96] A similar British warning was issued the following month, when

Mendès revived the old idea of a meeting with Russia, just before the French Senate was due to debate the London agreements. 'Weakness makes no appeal to the Soviets', declared Churchill, 'the sooner we can get our united ratification the sooner the . . . Four-power Conference may come.' The warning, initially in the form of a private letter from the Prime Minister to Mendès-France, included the statement that a long delay in the ratification 'may well lead to the adoption of other solutions which are . . . being studied' (including Anglo-American-German co-operation, to the exclusion of France). This section was quoted to French Senators by the government in March, and the full letter was published (after pressure in both Britain and France) a few days later. Despite Jebb's worries that such continuing pressure might provoke too much French resentment, the Senate then completed France's ratification.[97] In early May 1955, after a last-minute Franco-German argument over the Saar, Germany was formally brought into NATO, exactly ten years since the defeat of Hitler.[98] And so, in retrospect, the September 1954 settlement seemed a resounding success – particularly in contrast to the story of EDC. The West appeared united and, true to their word, both the Americans and British now sought a 'summit' with Russia.[99] Gladwyn Jebb had already warned, however, that the whole experience of German rearmament would leave France an unwilling ally, depressed and resentful of 'Anglo-Saxon' pressure.[100]

Certainly, as a settlement the London agreements were far from original. As early as December 1951 Eden had promised to pursue 'a more modest scheme' if EDC failed, Acheson had predicted that a British commitment to Europe could be the 'catalyst' for a final agreement, and Churchill and Eden had made their first generalized promise to retain British troops in NATO. It has already been seen that the extension of the Brussels Pact was not Eden's idea, and that there was more to the London settlement than the British proposals. Eden's achievement in September 1954 was not to devise a new solution for German rearmament, but to draw together the elements of previous discussions and to carry through a highly successful, pragmatic negotiation, in the midst of enormous pressure, with the dangers of Germany's alienation, France's isolation and America's retreat from Europe. No one else (certainly not Dulles) produced such a comprehensive plan of advance, despite the clear signs that EDC would collapse, and though

Eden's solution was itself hastily conceived, from a motley array of possibilities, it nevertheless allowed him to demonstrate fully his undoubted skills in the art of diplomacy. Churchill's dismissal of Eden's achievement – 'No-one in their senses thought we could bring our troops home from the continent . . . Never was the leadership of Europe so cheaply won'[101] – missed the point: the continentals themselves had erected the proposal for a written British commitment into something meaningful; Eden used their desire for such a proposal with great skill, making it the key element in bringing an agreement. The result, as Paul-Henri Spaak recalled, was that 'Eden saved the Atlantic alliance'.[102]

It is on the issue of British policy vis-à-vis European unity that Eden has been most criticized since 1955. The traditional view of Eden's policy – seen in the accounts of Nutting, Macmillan, Boothby and Kilmuir (among others) – is that it was 'anti-European'. So far as EDC was concerned, it is argued, Eden was grudging in his concessions and unwilling to be constructive in developing European unity; certainly the WEU did not become the force for European co-operation that many hoped for. But Eden's critics were themselves divided on what they expected of him, and his policy was a defensible one. At first, in 1951, there was considerable pressure on him actually to join EDC, but for better or worse British policy on this matter had already been set by the previous government and no Conservative minister, not even the so-called 'pro-Europeans' Macmillan and Maxwell Fyfe, was willing to adopt a federalist European course. Their precise vision of European 'unity' always remained a mystery. In any case the problems of EDC, the divisions among its members and its long, painful demise only seemed to confirm the rectitude of Britain's decision. The fact was that EDC did prove too bold and complex an initiative, which the people of France – the supposed 'leader' of the new Europe – were ultimately too patriotic (and too suspicious) to accept.

Thereafter a more common continental criticism (and one shared by Nutting) was that Eden's help for EDC was too grudging: concessions, usually wrapped in numerous conditions, had to be wrung from him. But Eden was always steering a narrow course, between the need to aid EDC and the fear of being drawn into a European federation 'by the back door'. He was prepared to make concessions when necessary, ultimately to the point of a commitment to maintain troop levels, but he soon became aware of the French tactic of 'pocketing' such concessions, than asking for more. By early 1953 the Americans, and many Europeans, actually accepted that he was doing his utmost for EDC and that France was the trouble-maker.

A third line of criticism, from Macmillan and Churchill, was that Eden should have tried to replace EDC with another institution, under British leadership. Churchill wanted a 'coalition' of forces, Macmillan a non-federal 'European' body; for both courses there might have been support in the French government (from Auriol or Bidault, for example). But this would have been the most dangerous policy of all, and one Eden roundly defeated: it would have seemed like 'sabotage', it would have offended American and continental opinion, and it need not, of course, have resulted in success. The fact was that Eden's policy, though lacking any great 'vision', was coherent, logical and (in September 1954 at least) successful. If Eden can be criticized for anything it is that (like Ernest Bevin before him) his tone too often gave the appearance of being 'anti-European'. His Rome statement of November 1951 and the Columbia speech of January 1952 were understandable as attempts to discourage unrealistic hopes about how closely Britain might co-operate with Europe, but they were not sufficiently offset by more positive declarations about co-operation with the continent. None the less the fact remains that his policy was consistent. From 1951 onwards he planned to support the European army from the outside, and to step forward with an alternative, less ambitious scheme only if EDC failed by itself, and in retrospect he did just that: the London nine-power conference was his vindication. The problem was, of course, that although the Europeans then abandoned all attempts to pursue a Defence Community, Eden's success came less than a year before European supranationalism rose from the ashes, with Messina, Euratom and the Common Market. Within a few years the apparent death-blow to supranationalism in 1954 was forgotten, and Eden's triumph was dismissed as part of a continuing story of British narrow-mindedness in the face of European idealism and imagination.

Notes

1. D. Folliot, ed., *Documents on International Affairs, 1951* (1954), 135–6.
   For background see J. W. Young, *Britain, France and the Unity of
   Europe, 1945–51* (1984).
2. *Council of Europe, Consultative Assembly, 1950* (Strasbourg, 1950),
   222–8.
3. See the 'Zurich Speech': R. Churchill, ed., *Sinews of Peace* (1948),
   198–202.
4. PRO, CAB 129/48, C (51) 32.
5. For a full discussion see J. W. Young, 'Churchill's "No" to Europe,
   1951–2', *Historical Journal*, 1985, 923–37.
6. CAB 128/23, CC (51) 16; *494 HC Deb. 5s*, 2594–6; D. Acheson, *Present
   at the Creation* (1970), 598–9; A. Eden, *Full Circle* (1960), 33–6; R.
   Ferrell, ed., *The Eisenhower Diaries* (1981), 207–8; H. Macmillan,
   Tides of Fortune, 1945–55 (1969), 468–74; R. Massigli, *Une comédie des
   erreurs* (Paris, 1978), 292–3; J. Wheeler-Bennett, ed., *Action This Day*
   (1968), 41, 96–9, 127.
7. *FRUS, 1951*, III (Washington, DC, 1979), 735–8, 907–8; Acheson,
   Creation, 590–1; Massigli, *Comédie*, 294–5.
8. *FRUS, 1951*, III, 917–19.
9. *FRUS, 1951*, III, 746–7, 948–50, 955–7 and 959; Acheson, *Creation*,
   757–8; Eden, *Full Circle*, 32–3; A. Nutting, *Europe Will Not Wait*
   (1960), 41.
10. Ferrell, *Eisenhower Diaries*, 207.
11. In December Eden was annoyed by reports that Acheson was
    critical of British policy: *FRUS, 1951*, III, 973, 977; Eden, *Full Circle*,
    34–5; Massigli, *Comédie*, 303–4.
12. CAB 129/49, C (52) 2; Folliot, *Documents, 1951*, 61–2.
13. Folliot, *ibid.*, 141 2.
14. D. Folliot, *Documents on International Affairs, 1952* (1955), 41–6.
15. CAB 128/25, CC (52) 52; *495 HCDeb. 5s*, 818–20; Eden, *Full Circle*,
    37–8; Massigli, *Comédie*, 307–8.
16. Folliot, *Documents, 1952*, 76–9, 81–3.
17. CAB 128/24, CC (52) 17, 18; CAB 129/49, C (52) 41; CAB 129/50, C
    (52) 92; *FRUS, 1952–4*, V (Washington, DC, 1983) (hereinafter cited
    simply as *FRUS*) 40–86, 247–50; Acheson, *Creation*, 611–21; K.
    Adenauer, *Memoirs, 1945–53* (1966), 408–9; Eden, *Full Circle*, 40–1.
18. Eden, *ibid.*, 41–2; Massigli, *Comédie*, 313.
19. CAB 128/24, CC (52) 37; CAB 129/50, C (52) 90, 92; *FRUS*, 627–34,
    1636–9; V. Auriol, *Journal du Septennat* (7 vols, Paris, 1970–), VI,
    1952; Eden, *Full Circle*, 42–6; Massigli, *Comédie*, 314–18.
20. CAB 128/25, CC (52) 52; CAB 131/12, D (52) 28.
21. *FRUS*, 639–42.
22. The EDC states did agree, however, to consult together if NATO
    was dissolved.
23. CAB 128/25, CC (52) 56; *FRUS*, 646–9, 660–88; Acheson, *Creation*,
    640–50; Adenauer, *Memoirs*, 413–15; Auriol, *Journal*, VI, 314–15,

342–61, 369–70; Eden, *Full Circle*, 46–7; I. Kirkpatrick, *The Inner Circle* (1959), 244–5.

24. D. Carlton, *Anthony Eden: A Biography* (1981), 312–13.
25. On the EDC treaty see Folliot, *Documents, 1952*, 111–70; E. Fursdon, *The European Defence Community* (1980), 150–88.
26. CAB 128/25, CC (52) 60; CAB 129/52, C (52) 185.
27. H. Alphand, *L'étonnement d'être* (1977), 229–31.
28. CAB 128/25, CC (52) 88 and 89.
29. Macmillan, *Tides of Fortune*, 474–5.
30. PRO, FO 371/101738/5, and FO 371/101741/1.
31. *FRUS*, 690–2, 694, 698, 708–17.
32. In February 1953 Dulles made a tour of European capitals partly to encourage EDC. *Ibid.*, 1548–92.
33. *Ibid.*, 690–2.
34. *Ibid.*, 696–700; Acheson, *Creation*, 707–8.
35. FO 371/103510/13.
36. CAB 129/57, C (52) 434; Massigli, *Comédie*, 347–8.
37. Eden did undertake to study Auriol's ideas, however. FO 371/101743/2; Auriol, *Journal*, VI, 804–7.
38. These included the right to withdraw troops from Europe to the French colonies – rather hypocritical (as Massigli pointed out), given France's pressure on Britain to keep troops in Europe.
39. FO 371/101743/3; *FRUS*, 699–700; Auriol, *Journal*, VII, *1953–4*, 14–15, 28–9; Massigli, *Comédie*, 347–8, 352–5.
40. PRO, PREM 11/438; FO 371/101743/3, FO 371/107445/5.
41. CAB 129/59, C (53) 73; Massigli, *Comédie*, 358.
42. CAB 129/57, C (53) 73; FO 371/107445/15, 21, 27; *FRUS*, 730–3; Auriol, *Journal*, VII, 54–5; Nutting *Europe*, 48; Massigli, *Comédie*, 359–61.
43. CAB 128/26, CC (53) 14, 15 and 23; CAB 129/59, C (53) 73, 108 and 111; Massigli, *Comédie*, 364–5.
44. CAB 128/26, CC (53) 32; CAB 129/60, C (53) 158; *FRUS*, 745–55.
45. CAB 129/61, C (53) 186.
46. CAB 128/26, CC (53) 72; CAB 129/64, C (53) 332; PREM 11/618; FO 371/107447/48; *FRUS*, 856–8; Massigli, *Comédie*, 398, 403, 405–6.
47. CAB 128/28, CC (54) 10, 17; CAB 129/65, C (54) 31; CAB 129/66, C (54) 93; PREM 11/618; PRO, DEFE 4/68, COS (54) 7; DEFE 4/69, COS (54) 22, 33; *FRUS*, 802; Nutting, *Europe*, 59–62; and see I. McDonald, *A Man of The Times* (1976), 134–5.
48. Macmillan, *Tides of Fortune*, 478.
49. White Paper, CMD. 9126 (April 1954); *526 HCDeb. 5s*, 1141–4; *FRUS*, 905–6, 921–6, 928; Nutting, *Europe*, 63–4. The main elements of the agreement were: (1) a British minister would attend EDC Councils; (2) a British official would liaise with the EDC Board of Commissioners on everyday matters; (3) Britain would maintain an 'appropriate' share of NATO forces; (4) British forces would remain in Europe so long as there was a threat to security; (5) one British armoured division would be placed in an EDC corps; (6) RAF and

EDC squadrons would co-operate in each NATO air group. A detailed statement on military co-operation was published and Britain declared that NATO was fundamental to its policy and of indefinite duration.

50. *FRUS*, 932–8, 940, 959–65.
51. *Ibid.*, 939–40; Massigli, *Comédie*, 425.
52. See also A. Glees, 'Churchill's last gambit', *Encounter*, no. 374, 1985, 27–35.
53. E.g., CAB 128/26, C (53) 39; CAB 129/61, C (53) 186, 187, 194; PREM 11/419, 618; Lord Moran, *Winston Churchill: The Struggle for Survival, 1940–65* (1968), 6 July 1953.
54. CAB 128/26, CC (53) 40.
55. See J. W. Young, 'Churchill, the Russians and the Western Alliance: the three-power conference at Bermuda, December, 1953', *English Historical Review, 101*, 1986; E. Shuckburgh, *Descent to Suez: Diaries, 1951–6* (1986), 112–16.
56. PREM 11/618; *FRUS*, 868–70; Eden, *Full Circle*, 57–8; Moran, *Churchill, 15, 17 and 18 Dec. 1953*; Shuckburgh, *Diaries*, 120.
57. PREM 11/618; *FRUS*, 879–86, 894–901.
58. E.g., *Le Monde*, 15 April.
59. Auriol, *Journal*, VII, 571; Alphand, *L'étonnement d'être*, 241–4; Massigli, *Comédie*, 415.
60. *FRUS*, 901–4.
61. Lord Gladwyn, *Memoirs* (1972), 271–3.
62. *FRUS*, 951–3, 969–70; P. H. Spaak, *The Continuing Battle* (1971), 159–60.
63. Mendès asked two ministers, General Koenig (Gaullist, anti-EDC) and Bourges-Manoury (Radical, pro-EDC) to find a compromise on EDC but they failed. PREM 11/618; FO 371/112779/40; Massigli, *Comédie*, 430–1.
64. PREM 11/618; Massigli, *Comédie*, 435; Spaak, *Continuing Battle*, 161–3.
65. It was later claimed that, in a secret deal at Geneva, Mendès had promised the Russians he would 'kill' EDC in return for a settlement in Indochina. PREM 11/618; FO 371/112780/75; Alphand, *L'étonnement d'être*, 251–3; A. Berard, *Un ambassadeur se souvient, 1945–55* (Paris, 1978), 560–2; Massigli, *Comédie*, 440; F. Seydoux, *Mémoires d'Outre-Rhin* (Paris, 1975), 185–6.
66. *FRUS*, 979–80; Massigli, *Comédie*, 433–4.
67. FO 371/112780/64, 68; *FRUS*, 970–1, 975–82.
68. CAB 128/27, CC (54) 49, 55; CAB 129/69, C (54) 226, 231; PREM 11/618; *FRUS*, 997–1023 see also FO 371/112781/2, 3.
69. PREM 11/618. Britain and America also acted together to oppose an attempt by Mendès to revive the idea of talks with Russia.
70. PREM 11/618; *FRUS*, 1023–77; K. Adenauer, *Erinnerungen, 1953–5* (Stuttgart, 1966), 274–89; Berard, *Un ambassadeur*, 560–5; Fursdon, *EDC*, 281–91; Massigli, *Comédie*, 440–8; Spaak, *Continuing Battle*, 166–71.

71. PREM 11/618, 672, 891; CAB 129/70, C (54) 271; *FRUS*, 1045–6, 1050–2, 1068–71; Eden, *Full Circle*, 148–9; Kirkpatrick, *Inner Circle*, 260–1; Massigli, *Comédie*, 449–50; Moran, *Churchill*, 16, 18 and 24 Aug.; see also G. Jebb, *The Memoirs of Lord Gladwyn* (1972), 273–4.
72. PREM 11/618.
73. *FRUS*, 1079–81, 1120–2; Eden, *Full Circle*, 149.
74. PREM 11/618; Moran, *Churchill*, 2 Sept.
75. CAB 128/27, CC (54) 57, 58; CAB 129/70, C (54) 276, 280; DEFE 4/72, COS (54) 90; Eden, *Full Circle*, 149–50; Massigli, *Comédie*, 452–3.
76. DEFE 4/72, COS (54) 91; *FRUS*, 1092–4, 1160–77, 1190–1, 1205–9; D. Eisenhower, *Mandate for Change, 1953–6* (1963), 403–4.
77. CAB 128/27, CC (54) 58 (1 Sept.); FO 371/109581/220, 223–4, 231, 234–7; *FRUS*, 1122–32, 1138–42, 1144–5, 1149; Adenauer, *Erinnerungen*, 305–7; Eden, *Full Circle*, 150; Moran, *Churchill*, 2 and 7 Sept.
78. CAB 128/27, CC (54) 57; Eden, *Full Circle*, 151; Fursdon, *EDC*, 311–12; Macmillan, *Tides of Fortune*, 480–2; Nutting, *Europe*, 70–1; R. R. James, *Anthony Eden* (1986), 386–7; McDonald, *Man of the Times*, 132; Shuckburgh, *Diaries*, 121.
79. PREM 11/672; *FRUS*, 1132–5, 1189, 1194–5; Eden, *Full Circle*, 152, 160–1, 169; Massigli, *Comédie*, 459–63; Seydoux, *Memoires*, 189–90.
80. CAB 128/27, CC (54) 59; CAB 129–70, C (54) 286; Eden, *Full Circle*, 151–2.
81. CAB 128/27, CC (54) 59; *FRUS*, 1150–1, 1154–6; James, *Eden*, 387.
82. Eden, *Full Circle*, 153–4, 158; Spaak, *Continuing Battle*, 179.
83. FO 371/109582/247; *FRUS*, 1181–8, 1190–1; Adenauer, *Erinnerungen*, 307–17; Eden, *Full Circle*, 154–7.
84. *FRUS*, 1203–5; Eden, *Full Circle*, 157–8.
85. *FRUS*, 1149, 1159–60, 1192–4, 1197–8; Eden, *Full Circle*, 158–60; Eisenhower, *Mandate*, 404–5.
86. *FRUS*, 1194–5, 1198–1203; Jean Chauvel, *Mémoires*, II (Paris, 1973), 112; Eden, *Full Circle*, 159–62.
87. CAB 128/27, CC (54) 60.
88. *FRUS*, 1209–26, 1230–1, 1234–6; Adenauer, *Erinnerungen*, 308–13; Eden, *Full Circle*, 162–4; Eisenhower, *Mandate*, 405.
89. *FRUS*, 1234–7, 1245–6, 1272–3; Adenauer, *Erinnerungen*, 315–27; Massigli, *Comédie*, 467–8.
90. CAB 128/27, CC (54) 61; *Council of Europe, Consultative Assembly, 1954* (Strasbourg, 1954), 599–606, and see 514–22 on Spaak; see also Nutting, *Europe*, 72 (which is incongruous).
91. *FRUS*, 1253–71.
92. CAB 129/70, C (54) 298; DEFE 4/72, COS (54) 99, 102; FO 371/109434/18; Eden, *Full Circle*, 164–7; Gladwyn, *Memoirs*, 273; Nutting, *Europe*, 72–3.
93. CAB 129/71, C (54) 302; *FRUS*, 1275–7, 1283–93, 1300–4, 1332–8; Adenauer, *Erinnerungen*, 328–31; Eden, *Full Circle*, 167; Macmillan, *Tides of Fortune*, 482–3; Massigli, *Comédie*, 472–3; Spaak, *Continuing Battle*, 181–6; James, *Eden*, 388–9.

94. FO 371/109582/267; FO 371/109773–6; *FRUS*, 1304–30, 135–70, 1378–83; Adenauer, *Erinnerungen*, 331–54; Alphand, *L'étonnement d'être*, 248–9; Eden, *Full Circle*, 168–9; Eisenhower, *Mandate*, 405–6; Massigli, *Comédie*, 473–9; Seydoux, *Mémoires*, 190; Spaak, *Continuing Battle*, 185–6.
95. *FRUS*, 1371–8, 1385–6, 1394–7, 1402–64; Adenauer, *Erinnerungen*, 355–83; Eden, *Full Circle*, 169–70; Massigli, *Comédie*, 482–4.
96. CAB 128/27, CC (54) 79, 86; PREM 11/891; FO 371/109435/57, 62, 65, 68; *FRUS*, 1519–20, 1523–39; Eden, *Full Circle*, 170–1; R.H. Ferrell, ed., *The Diary of James C. Hagerty* (Bloomington, Ind., 1983), 146–52; Gladwyn, *Memoirs*, 274–5; Massigli, *Comédie*, 490–1; and R. Lerner and R. Aron, eds, *France defeats E.D.C.* (1957), 165–96.
97. PREM 11/901; CMD. 9420 (March 1955); Nutting, *Europe*, 80–1; A. Werth, *France, 1945–55* (1956), 708–9; Massigli, *Comédie*, 492–3.
98. CAB 128/29, CC (55) 2, 4, 5, 9.
99. See CAB 128/28, CC (55) 23, 24, 25, 27; Eden, *Full Circle*, 288–9.
100. PREM 11/891.
101. Moran, *Churchill*, 1 Oct. 1954.
102. Spaak, *Continuing Battle*, 188.

4 The Schuman Plan and British Association

John W. Young

In May 1950 the French foreign minister, Robert Schuman, proposed the creation of a supranational authority to control
Europe's coal and steel industries. Five years later, in June 1955,
the six states who had joined in pursuing the 'Schuman Plan' –
France, West Germany, Italy and the Benelux states – met
in Messina and began the negotiations for what became the
European Economic Community. In the intervening years
public attention on European federalism was mainly directed at
the ill-fated attempts to create a European Defence community
(EDC), discussed in the previous chapter. The efforts to create a
'European Coal-Steel Community' (ECSC) slipped somewhat
into the background. In the light of the later importance of
economic integration by the six, however, the purpose of this
essay is to discuss British relations with the ECSC under the
Conservative government of 1951–5, with particular reference to
the establishment of a Council of Association in December 1954.

Britain's decision not to take part in the discussions on the
ECSC in June 1950 has already been fully discussed.[1] Several
considerations affected the British: a belief in intergovernmental
economic co-operation via the Organization for European
Economic Co-operation (OEEC); a dislike of 'premature' and
'idealistic' schemes to build a European federation; the desire to
maintain close links to the United States and the Commonwealth; economic differences with the continentals, who took
only a quarter of British trade (compared to the Sterling Area's
half); and a political fear that economic integration could lead to
the creation of a neutralist 'third force' in Europe, which would
destroy the Atlantic alliance. This did not mean (despite a strong
continental belief to the contrary) that Britain was simply 'anti-
European': the British had led the way in forging economic and
military co-operation via the OEEC, Brussels Pact and NATO.
Neither did it mean that Britain would try to 'sabotage' the

European efforts: London was particularly keen to see a Franco-German rapprochement (which the Schuman Plan seemed to offer) and was only too aware of American support for European economic integration as a way to strengthen the continent in the face of the communist threat. But it did not mean that Britain was determined, herself, to remain outside the attempts by the six to forge a European federation.[1] From July 1950 British policy towards the ECSC centred on the question of 'association', an idea first mooted by Schuman himself as the way to secure British co-operation short of full membership. Ministers quickly agreed to seek some form of association, but the Foreign Secretary, Ernest Bevin, was determined that negotiations on this should not be pursued until after a Schuman Plan institution was created: he believed the Plan might yet face serious difficulties. As it transpired, the negotiations by the Six took considerable time to bring to a successful conclusion. A draft treaty was not ready until November 1950, serious arguments occurred between France and Germany regarding limits on Germany's economic independence, and the supranational elements in the original plan were much diluted. (The problems for the Six were heightened by the debate over German rearmament at this time.) An ECSC treaty was not finally signed until April 1951, establishing a High Authority to control the coal and steel industries of the Six, but the treaty then needed to be ratified. Bevin's successor, Herbert Morrison, reaffirmed Britain's desire to seek association with the ECSC, but when the Conservatives came to office in October the process of ratification by the Six remained incomplete.[2]

On 31 October 1951 the new Foreign Secretary, Anthony Eden, was presented with a brief on British policy towards European integration, which succinctly summed up the established policy:

> We are ready to play an active part in all plans for integration on an intergovernmental basis; defence considerations, our Commonwealth connections and the sterling area inhibit us from subordinating ourselves . . . to any European supranational authority; nevertheless we have encouraged those countries who feel able to go ahead with such plans, and have assured them of our good-will and our wish to be closely associated with their work, short of actual membership.[3]

Eden was determined to maintain Labour's policy, of association short of full membership, with both the EDC and ECSC,
and he successfully maintained this line down to 1955. The story
of the British search for association with the ECSC over these
years falls naturally into three phases. First, down to August
1952, when the High Authority was formally established in
Luxembourg and a British diplomatic representative appointed
to it; then, down to December 1953, a period when both sides
gathered their thoughts about the form which association
should take; and finally the year between the Authority's invitation to Britain to enter formal negotiations and the completion of
an 'Agreement of Association' in December 1954, a period
marked by lengthy delays.

Unfortunately for Eden the first phase began badly, because
of hopes among some continentals (and some Conservatives)
that the new government would take a more positive approach
towards European integration. In opposition Winston Churchill
had been a great advocate of European unity, especially in his
famous Zurich speech of September 1946, and many Conservatives were favourable to closer European integration, including two Cabinet ministers, Harold Macmillan (the housing
minister) and Maxwell Fyfe (the Home Secretary), some junior
ministers like David Eccles and Duncan Sandys, and a group of
backbenchers, including Robert Boothby and Julian Amery.
Many of these had sat in the assembly of the Council of Europe
in Strasbourg, since the creation of that body in 1949. Designed
to foster European co-operation at a popular level, the Council
of Europe was virtually powerless, and worked strictly on intergovernmental lines, but it became a forum for various ideas on
European integration and was used by the Conservatives as a
forum to criticize the Labour government. In fact Churchill had
never proposed that Britain should be more than a 'sponsor' of
European unification, and hardly any Conservatives proposed
British membership of a continental federation, but whereas
Eden maintained Labour's policy towards Europe and was keen
to stress British separation from the continent, the 'Tory Strasbourgers' condemned Labour as 'anti-European' and were keen
to stress a more 'positive' view of European unity (though
Macmillan for one was also fearful that a successful continental
union could prove a long-term economic and political menace to
Britain).

The views of the 'Tory Strasbourgers' never achieved much by way of concrete proposals, but there was an early disagreement between them and the Foreign Secretary in November 1951 over public statements regarding European institutions. On 22 November the Cabinet agreed that, in a forthcoming meeting of the Council of Europe, Maxwell Fyfe should make a favourable statement about the Schuman Plan and Britain's desire for association with it, stating:

> His Majesty's Government . . . welcome the Schuman Plan as a means of strengthening the economy of Western Europe and look forward to its early realisation . . . If the Schuman Plan is ratified [they] will set up a permanent delegation at the seat of the Authority to enter into relations and to transact business with it.

The Parliamentary Under-Secretary at the Foreign Office, Anthony Nutting, was actually responsible for this statement and it can hardly be said to have gone beyond the line Labour might have taken. When Maxwell Fyfe made his speech on 28 November, furthermore, it was received with some disappointment by the continentals. But what upset the 'Tory Strasbourgers' was that the very same evening, in a press conference at the NATO Council in Rome, Eden made a blunt statement that Britain could never join the EDC. The differences between the two ministers might only seem ones of emphasis to outsiders, but Amery, Boothby and others sent a letter to Churchill complaining about Eden's 'negative' attitude and contrasting it to the Home Secretary's 'hopeful' speech. Churchill stood by his Foreign Secretary, but British policy also had its ill effect on the continentals: the Belgian 'father of Europe', Paul-Henri Spaak, resigned as President of the Council of Europe on 11 December, partly as a dramatic protest against British policy.[4]

At first Eden and his officials were unapologetic about his Rome statements. A general paper of 12 December on 'European Integration', by the Permanent Under-Secretary's Committee of the Foreign Office, and a circular telegram to British representatives on the issue three days later, confirmed the general line of British policy as being encouragement of supranational schemes like ECSC from the outside but within the general framework of 'an Atlantic Community based on the three pillars of the United States, United Kingdom (including the Commonwealth) and Continental Europe. In such a Community', it was explained, 'we can reconcile our world-wide commitments with our responsibilities towards Europe and the Commonwealth. This could not be done within the confines of a European federation.'[5] But in late December, in the wake of the Council of Europe meeting, there was some concern in the Foreign Office about the relationship of the Strasbourg body to the new supranational institutions, and about the criticisms of British policy. It was F. G. Gallagher, of the Western Organizations Department, who first suggested on 21 December that 'the Statute of the Council of Europe should be amended ... to allow the existing organs of the Council to become institutions of the Schuman Plan and the European Army'. This would mean that ministerial meetings and sessions of the European assembly would function at three levels: meetings of the six (operating within the EDC and ECSC treaties); meetings of the Six and their 'associates', such as the British; and meetings of the full Council of Europe as an intergovermental body. The first advantage of such a reform was that it would 'put new life into the Council of Europe' by giving it useful tasks to perform, rather than leaving it as a powerless (but frequently embarrassing) 'talking shop'. The second was that it 'would constitute a constructive British initiative which might help convince public option in Western Europe that we are genuinely concerned to encourage ... developments in the European Community'. However, the reform would also smooth the way to British association with the ECSC (and EDC) and thus assumed some significance in the debate over Anglo-ECSC association down to September 1952.[6] Others in the Foreign Office, notably Anthony Nutting, were determined that 'some hard and realistic thinking' needed to be done, following the recent 'Battle of Strasbourg',[7] and a Foreign Office meeting on 21 January 1952 decided to put a plan to Eden, for later submission to the Cabinet, on the lines set out by Gallagher. Following some 'toning down' by Eden of the detailed proposals a memorandum was duly prepared for the Cabinet in mid-February.[8]

Before the 'Eden Plan' – as the scheme to reform the Council of Europe became known – went before the Cabinet it was evident that it would face some opposition from Harold Macmillan. This may seem odd in view of the latter's desire for a more positive British policy towards Europe, but in a memorandum of his own Macmillan argued that the 'Eden Plan' was premature, given that the ECSC and EDC might not even come into being. He expressed the fear that the Six might swallow the

Council of Europe if Eden's proposals were followed and, raising the spectre of a 'German-dominated continental system' if
ECSC and EDC were established, argued that 'our aim should
be to subordinate the Continental Federation to the Council
of Europe' rather than vice versa. (If EDC failed Macmillan
wanted Britain to lead moves towards 'a European Union or
Confederation organised on Commonwealth lines'.) It was clear
that Macmillan's line of thinking was motivated by fear of
the Six as much as a positive view of their efforts, and in
Cabinet discussions on 12 and 13 March the 'Eden Plan' easily
won through against the Minister of Housing's doubts. Even
Maxwell Fyfe seemed well disposed to the Foreign Office ideas,
and Macmillan was left bitterly resentful at the whole experience, even considering resignation from the government!
Thereafter in Churchill's government he kept a lower pro-
file on the issue of European integration.[9] Eden meanwhile
informed the French government of his ideas for reform of
the Council of Europe and on 20 March presented his plan
to the Committee of Ministers of the Council of Europe. He
seemed to win a favourable response,[10] an impression confirmed at the next meeting of the Committee of Ministers on 22–
23 May. There were rumours before this meeting of a new
'Rome-Berlin axis' to exclude Britain from Europe: Italy and
West Germany were keen to prevent any British 'brake' being
put on the ECSC and EDC via the Council of Europe. But Eden
felt that he successfully reassured all his critics, and was particularly gratified by the sympathetic attitude of Schuman. In
the Council of Europe Assembly too the 'Eden Plan' was well
received, and the Foreign Office hoped that it might soon
be possible to put the plan into effect.[11] In early June Eden
told the Cabinet that Britain's standing in Europe was much
improved.[12]

Had the 'Eden Plan' proved successful it would have had a
major effect on the shape of British association with the ECSC,
but it was not to be. An early sign of problems was the decision
by the Six that proposals for a European Political Community
(EPC) should be studied within the ECSC assembly, which was
due to be established, rather than within the Council of Europe.
Following some criticism of the EDC in France, the EPC was
mainly designed to provide for more 'democratic' control of
the latter body and the ECSC (both institutions would be subordinated to control by the EPC), but it would also mark a

further widening of the supranational principle since it was likely to embody such organs as a Six-power European Cabinet and Assembly, with much wider powers than either the ECSC or EDC, and certainly more effective than the Council of Europe. Schuman was prepared to 'harmonize' the EPC study with the Eden Plan, by allowing representatives from other Council of Europe members to sit in (perhaps as observers) on the deliberations of the ECSC assembly, but this situation caught the British in some embarrassment: the Foreign Office viewed the EPC as a premature and unrealistic proposal – Eden told Schuman so, quite bluntly, in a meeting on 27 June; Britain could certainly not join it; but if successful it could fulfil the worst of Harold Macmillan's fears, by developing into a European 'super-state', possibly dominated by Germany. Britain could not do anything to oppose the scheme since this 'would certainly earn us great unpopularity in Europe and in the U.S.A.', and a Foreign Office meeting therefore judged that Britain should adopt a similar line towards EPC as it did towards ECSC and EDC: 'not to discourage the European countries . . . but to try to ensure that the European Political Authority develops in a spirit friendly to us and in a form which permits close association with us'. As a result the British pressed the Six in an *aide-mémoire* in early July to carry out any EPC study 'within the framework of the Council of Europe and in harmony with the British proposals for the future of that organization'. The Six in reply professed to be favourable to the Eden Plan, but in Rome and Bonn in particular the fear persisted that Britain was trying to place a 'brake' on supranationalism, and though Schuman remained well disposed to close co-operation with Britain his compatriot Jean Monnet, head of France's economic reconstruction plan, was less favourable. Monnet had been fearful of British 'sabotage' since he originally conceived the Schuman Plan in 1950, and he was very suspicious of Eden's intentions and keen to study the EPC on a Six-power basis. Monnet saw the EPC as an essential move to 'contain' Germany's reviving power in a wider framework (such containment of German strength was France's main motive for proposing the Schuman Plan in the first place). This was not to say that he was opposed to working with Britain at all: he was in fact very keen to associate Britain (and America) with the work of the Six, not least in order that they could help in controlling Germany. For Monnet the question was how to associate Britain in the European supranational efforts without allowing her to disrupt these. He believed that the Eden Plan threatened just such disruption.[13]

In the second half of 1952 Monnet waged a successful 'war of attrition'[14] against the Eden Plan, not always with the sympathy of the French government. In late July a meeting of the ECSC powers was held to discuss the formal establishment of the organization: the Schuman Plan treaty became formally effective on 25 July with the deposit of all ratifications. Monnet was unanimously chosen as first President of the High Authority and, after an acrimonious debate about possible sites, it was decided the Authority should be 'provisionally' based in Luxembourg. It had been hoped to discuss the Eden Plan and the EPC too but these issues were hardly touched upon owing to lack of time. Monnet's appointment, however, hardly augured well for British hopes.[15] On 10 August the High Authority was formally established in Luxembourg. Eden issued a statement welcoming this and hoping for the 'closest possible' British association,[16] but talks with Monnet in London on 21–23 August failed to remove his doubts about the Eden Plan, which he seemed only partially to understand. He remained determined to minimize any links between the ECSC and the intergovernmental Council of Europe, despite the more favourable views of some French government officials; and he caused no little annoyance to the Foreign Office, especially when he spread (baseless) rumours to the effect that Britain itself planned to withdraw the Eden Plan! Eden even complained to Schuman about Monnet's behaviour in mid-September, and won a reassurance that France still supported links between the ECSC and Council of Europe.[17] The Six did indeed agree that the ECSC Assembly, which first met in September, and which began to study the EPC proposal, should be based in Strasbourg. Whilst the other institutions – the High Authority and ECSC court – met in Luxembourg the Assembly would sit in the Council of Europe's assembly chamber and work closely with the Council's secretariat.

During debates of the Council of Europe Assembly in September in fact the Eden Plan still seemed very much alive. But Monnet was a consistent and determined opponent, who used his position as ECSC President to pursue independent policies. Although he could not completely prevent links to the Council of Europe, Monnet was successful in ensuring that these amounted to little more than a use of common facilities without significant importance, and in retrospect it was clear that, by September 1952, the Eden Plan had been totally undermined.[18] Looking back on these events some years later, Anthony Nutting bitterly recalled that 'our initiative had only aroused the suspicion that we were really trying to sabotage the unity of Europe.'[19] The plan had not been completely useless: for a time it had eased criticisms that Britain was 'anti-European' in its policies. In future, criticism of Britain within the Council of Europe was much lessened, helped by the fact that discussions on a political union of Europe were now taken out of that body for discussion in the ECSC Assembly.[20] But so far as the ECSC was concerned, no means could now be found to smooth the way to British association via the Council of Europe.

While the chances for success of the 'Eden Plan' declined the Foreign Office considered more direct means of association with the ECSC and established formal diplomatic relations with the new body. In March ministers had decided to begin consultations with Britain's coal and steel industries about the full effects of the ECSC on British economic policy, before entering discussions with the High Authority.[21] In late June, somewhat surprised about the speedy progress of the ratification process of the Schuman treaty, the Foreign Office began to consider in earnest how to set up a British delegation to conduct business with the ECSC, as promised in November by Maxwell Fyfe. The Office was keen to keep control of the delegation in its own hands. It was recognized that relations with the Schuman authority would have both a political and an industrial dimension – given the wider, political motivations behind the coal–steel organization – but complications in forming a British delegation were increased by the need to consult other relevant departments.[22] On 17 July the Cabinet agreed that the responsibility for relations with the ECSC should indeed rest with the Foreign Secretary, though he would be advised by an interdepartmental official committee, with representatives from the Foreign Office, Treasury, Board of Trade and the ministries of Fuel and Power, Supply and (when necessary) Labour.[23] This new Schuman Plan Committee (SPC) replaced an earlier official committee set up under Labour,[24] and held its first meeting on 31 July, when the Foreign Office representatives confirmed the pragmatic nature of British policy towards the whole question of association. The Office was determined to put the accent on practical economic co-operation over political links to Europe, and still wanted to see how the ECSC worked before making any formal Treaty of Association with it.[25] In the talks with Monnet in London in late August it was agreed that association should be studied over time rather than defined quickly. It was also agreed that members of a British delegation would arrive in Luxembourg in the near future. The head of the delegation, Sir Cecil Weir, chosen because of his political and industrial experience, had been Senior Economic Adviser in Germany after 1945, and his deputy was a career diplomat, J. A. M. Marjoribanks. Other members, including technical experts, were drawn from the ministries of Supply, and Fuel and Power, and there was provision for management and trade union representatives from Britain's coal and steel industries. Weir arrived in Luxembourg for talks with Monnet in early September.[26]

In the next phase of Anglo-ECSC relations, which lasted down to December 1953, both sides prepared somewhat cautiously for fuller arrangements on a Treaty of Association. Despite the demise of the Eden Plan, the British adopted a benevolent attitude towards the High Authority as it sought to carry into effect the common markets in coal and steel over a 'transitional' period of several months. In particular, the British, though concerned to defend their own iron ore supplies, supported efforts by the Six to have GATT and OEEC arrangements altered to accommodate ECSC arrangements.[27] On 26 September Weir reported that the High Authority was 'beginning to settle down' but that 'we have not yet got a firm basis for routine conversation'. The establishment of the new body was proving a difficult and time-consuming affair and Monnet's earlier hopes to set up a 'Joint Committee', to study British association at an early date, had faded. For the moment the Frenchman indeed seemed to agree fully with Weir's 'informal, natural' approach to the development of links with Britain.[28] Some weeks later, on 15 October, Monnet was able to inform Weir that the ECSC organization was more advanced and that a Joint Committee with Britain could be established in the near future, holding regular meetings which would discuss issues of common interest and allow a 'natural' development of relations. Monnet hoped, amongst other things, that the British might adopt similar rules and procedures to those adopted by the coal and steel industries of the Six.[29] The first meeting of the Joint Committee was finally held on 17 November and, after expressing his general hopes for an 'intimate and enduring association' with Britain, Monnet made some specific proposals for such a relationship including wide-ranging exchanges of information, the application of common rules and the creation of a permanent institutional framework for co-operation. This seemed to mark a return to his earlier, lofty hopes for the rapid creation of quite sophisticated Anglo–ECSC links and was viewed in the Foreign Office with some alarm. In reply to Monnet's ideas, Weir once again pressed the British case for a more cautious approach with the emphasis on practical, commercial cooperation rather than any wider political aims.

In December Weir became concerned at reviving suspicions among the Europeans that Britain was over-cautious towards supranationalism, adopting a 'wait and see' attitude. He was fearful about the possible pace of future developments towards a European 'super-state' via the EPC and was anxious that Britain should decide its policy towards this. In the Foreign Office at the end of 1952, however, it was increasingly felt that problems with the EDC made it unnecessary to fear a 'super-state' just yet. If the EDC collapsed it would certainly destroy all hopes for the EPC, and might even destroy the ECSC, and in such a situation it hardly seemed necessary to answer Monnet's call for far-reaching institutional links with the High Authority.[30] As 1953 began therefore British policy towards the ECSC remained that of taking an empirical approach until the direction of the new organization became clearer.[31] But the year was to see a change in British policy, to the point of willingness to join a European common market on steel – a change which further demonstrated London's willingness to take a positive approach towards co-operation with the continent, albeit one far short of integration on the lines adopted by the Six.

In February a Working Party was established under the SPC, 'to explore the impact on Commonwealth preference of a close association' short of full entry. This Working Party held its first meeting on 12 February with representatives from the Foreign Office, treasury and ministries of Supply, Fuel and Power, and Labour, as well as the Cabinet Office and Paymaster General's Office.[32] A minor trade depression at this time, sparking fears of a reversal of trade liberalization policies, helped to create a more favourable attitude to co-operation with the continent: Peter Thorneycroft, President of the Board of Trade, was even willing to consider a general European 'common market' of free trade as a way to meet the depression![33] The feeling in Whitehall further-more was that the French government themselves might be shifting towards the British emphasis on intergovernmental co-operation, and that the ECSC and EDC marked the limit of France's supranational commitment. Once again, this was felt to be the case because of the problems surrounding the EDC.[34] As a result of EDC's problems Robert Schuman himself fell from favour in Paris and was replaced in January 1953 by a more 'nationalist', and less 'European' foreign minister, Georges Bidault. True, on 10 March a draft EPC treaty was drawn up, embodying a two-chamber European parliament, an executive and Council of Ministers, and dramatic promises of a common foreign policy and a full common market among the Six in trade.[35] But the EPC of course was still tied to the fate of EDC (and eventually collapsed along with the latter proposal in 1954) and the Foreign Office did not think much of the prospects for a full-scale common market. Officials argued that a 'sector-by-sector' approach to European economic unity had achieved little since mid-1950: the ECSC had proved far less dramatic than Monnet and Schuman originally hoped and embodied much that was 'intergovernmental' rather than 'supranational'. In addition negotiations for an agricultural community of 'the Six' had also floundered.[36] If economic union was to proceed it certainly seemed that 'a much more general plunge' (such as a common market) was needed, but the Foreign Office judged that there was simply a lack of political will in France and elsewhere to bring this about at present. A Foreign Office minute noted, with some satisfaction, that 'this suits us since it allows us to participate in whatever forms of co-operation are pursued'.[37]

The ECSC itself was keen to open talks with London on a formal Treaty of Association in this period, and so strengthened the growing feeling in Whitehall that Britain was in a strong position vis-à-vis the Europeans. Monnet and his officials were increasingly eager to end criticisms of the lack of progress in settling Britain's position.[38] Talks were originally proposed by the ECSC in March, but had to be deferred. In April pressures from the High Authority continued; the Foreign Office again tried to delay matters, arguing that it would be better to wait until the common market in steel was operating before taking such a step; but Monnet brushed such arguments aside and pressed for talks on 'real' association to begin in May or

June.[39] The creation of the common market in steel on 1 May [40] strengthened the ECSC President's hand and talks were actually held with Monnet and his deputy, the Dutchman D. P. Spieren-burg, in London on 6–11 May. These however proved to be merely exploratory conversations since the High Authority itself apparently had second thoughts and now planned to draw up a memorandum outlining some technical ideas on co-operation. Once again this suited the British since it allowed them to develop their own views 'without undue haste'.[41] Although it was hoped to have the SPC Working Party's report on associa-tion ready in July, it would then be necessary to consult the relevant embassies about it so that, whilst Britain remained determined to get a formal Treaty of Association at some point, it would inevitably take time to devise.[42] (In July in fact Monnet himself admitted that the technical side of British association was proving more complex to resolve than he had anticipated.[43]) Throughout this period London remained determined to keep its distance from anything that smacked of European 'federa-tion'. This attitude could be seen in Eden's plans for association with EDC, and in April the junior Foreign Office minister, Lord Reading, reminded the House of Lords that Britain was 'only . . . prepared to give general assent, co-operation and encourage-ment to the [European] movement' – a view which drew some criticisms from 'pro-Europeans' in the House.[44]

The SPC Working Party's report was finally produced on 22 July, after consultation with the coal and steel industries. The report included an analysis of the ECSC treaty and policies, and concentrated on economic rather than political issues, though it was recognized that Monnet (whilst respecting British sovereignty and links to the Commonwealth) wanted more than a purely commercial agreement: he would only be satisfied with a treaty of fixed duration and arrangements on such issues as prices, supplies and tariffs. Britain's economic aims as laid down by the report included the preservation of cheap coal and steel supplies (the most vital consideration), good prices for coal and steel exports, price stability and harmonization with the wider trade policy of 'multilateralism' and imperial preferences. With these factors in mind the report looked at three possible approaches to the ECSC. Membership of the organization was judged 'impracticable' because it would require a complete renegotiation of the treaty to suit Britain, and would mean a fifty-year commitment; but importantly it was noted that, since the ECSC 'is going to be well-organized and aggressive we may not be able to afford to stay out of it'. Ignoring the ECSC was equally unthinkable: 'the existence of the Community as an economic *bloc* whose gradual growth might be detrimental . . . to the economic interests of the United Kingdom . . . creates a presumption in favour of coming to terms with it'. Association was thus left as the only viable option, but the exact form of association left Britain with enormous freedom of manoeuvre. Interestingly however the report favoured the boldest possible solution, so far as steel was concerned, namely the establishment of a common market with the ECSC including the end of all trade restrictions and the pursuit of common policies on prices, conditions of sale and actions in the event of shortage or surplus. This would help stabilize the European steel market, and the British steel industry was felt to be efficient and expansive, with everything to gain from healthy competition. On coal the report was less bold, proposing only an import–export agreement, involving quotas, prices and a commitment against 'dumping'. The coal industry was less able than steel to compete in Europe, where increasing power demands were in any case being met by oil and hydro-electricity. The report also proposed certain other arrangements (such as exchanges of information and co-operation on research), a 'transitional' period for the introduction of any changes and a term equal to the life of the ECSC. But the SPC was aware of possible problems: the steel industry had not approved the Working Party recommendations; 'waivers' would be needed from GATT and the OEEC to accommodate Anglo-ECSC trade preferences; and Commonwealth trade would be weakened to some extent.[45]

The Foreign Office was so concerned at the likely reaction to the Working Party report that officials were reluctant to put it before the Economic Steering Committee (the highest official committee concerned with economic issues). The Board of Trade was known to be fearful of being gradually drawn into continental attempts at integration; the Ministry of Fuel and Power doubted the National Coal Board's ability to resist ECSC competition; and Britain's OEEC delegation was concerned at the effect of a coal–steel common market on that organization.[46] But on 7 September the report passed through the Steering Committee with surprising ease. Some concern was expressed at a possible short-term increase in steel prices, and at the reaction of the trade unions and Commonwealth to an Anglo-

ECSC deal, but on balance it was felt that the SPC recommendations were sound. The Treasury's William Strath believed that a common market could be harmonized with Britain's policy of free trade, whilst Sir Edwin Plowden was keen to see the steel industry face the rigours of continental competition. A Foreign Office memorandum, on political considerations, not yet seen by ministers, was also before the committee. It argued cautiously in favour of a close association, as a way to strengthen Western Europe, draw Germany into the West and fulfil Britain's previous promises to the Six, though the Foreign Office was anxious that any decision should primarily be taken for economic reasons and should preserve both Commonwealth trade and multilateral world trade. The Steering Committee decided to consult the coal and steel industries on the SPC proposals whilst awaiting the ECSC proposals on association. A submission would be made to ministers and the Commonwealth consulted once the ECSC views were known.[47] Over the following few months the consultation with the coal and steel industries proceeded, the Foreign Office finalized their paper on the political considerations of association and a draft Cabinet paper was drawn up.[48]

On 23 December 1953, rather later than the British expected, Monnet informed Weir by letter that the High Authority was ready to open negotiations for formal association with Britain. He conceded that it was impossible to expect any British 'delegation of sovereignty' and argued for an association in three parts: an association of markets (with the mutual reduction of protective measures and the creation of common rules on trade); a 'procedure for common action' (by exchanges of information and consultation on policy); and 'the establishment of joint institutions for watching over the operation and the development of the association' (specifically he suggested a 'Council of Association' of three members each from Britain and the High Authority, meeting periodically). Weir and the Foreign Office were pleased by Monnet's ideas which showed flexibility and a desire to treat Britain as an equal.[49] Importantly the Foreign Office now argued that a successful association with ECSC could help the ratification of EDC. The Office was keen to consult the Cabinet quickly on the SPC report and negotiate an agreement with Monnet quickly since 'The whole of our European policy depends upon progress being made in European integration' (by which was mainly meant the creation

of EDC). The scene was thus set for the next phase of Anglo–
ECSC relations, the negotiation of a Treaty of Association, and
conditions seemed very favourable for a far-reaching agreement. Monnet was behaving reasonably and his destruction of
the Eden Plan was largely forgotten; and the British were prepared to be positive, particularly in their proposals on steel,
although the Foreign Office recognized that 'real difficulties will
arise in persuading the interests effected to accept what is
proposed'.[50]

On 18 January 1954, after some further redrafting by the SPC
and Economic Steering Committee,[51] Eden circulated the
Cabinet paper on association, and pressed for swift action to
be taken upon it after the support of British industry and
the Commonwealth was achieved. Importantly the Cabinet
memorandum presented the political arguments for association
first, defining British policy towards the continent as 'support
for the political, economic and military integration of the
Western European countries ... in order to strengthen the
Western alliance ... make it resistant to communism, and ...
provide the means of locking Germany within the Western
Community', without any British surrender of sovereignty. The
Foreign Office now strongly desired institutional links to the
ECSC particularly since, if EDC collapsed, ECSC would be left
as the only form of supranational co-operation. The main thrust
of the economic arguments, as drawn out by the Cabinet
paper, was that the Schuman community 'could create a unit of
great economic power' with which Britain must come to terms;
Britain's steel industry would gain by competition from Europe,
though on coal there was less scope for expanded Anglo-
continental trade (and the coal industry and National Union of
Mineworkers seemed reluctant to enter association even on the
limited terms suggested by the SPC). In the Cabinet discussion
on 21 January Eden received strong support from Duncan
Sandys, Churchill's son-in-law, a former 'Tory Strasbourger'
and now the Minister of Supply, responsible for the steel
industry. But from this moment on the hopes for swift and
dramatic action on association were dimmed. The Cabinet
agreed that Sandys and the Minister of Fuel and Power,
Geoffrey Lloyd (responsible for coal), should continue consultations with the steel and coal industries on the SPC report, whilst
the Commonwealth Relations Office contacted the Commonwealth, so as to prepare for negotiations with the ECSC, but it

was clear that such consultations would be time-consuming. Furthermore, it was decided that initially talks with Monnet should only be 'exploratory'. This was because of fears that, on past experience, the ECSC President might yet demand more than he had included in his letter of 23 December.[52]

Whilst contacts with industry and the Commonweath proceeded, the Foreign Office consulted their European posts on the SPC ideas for association. The Scandinavian countries (even less eager to pursue a supranational course than Britain) were somewhat concerned about closer Anglo–ECSC links, and among the Six there was some suspicion of British motives, but generally it was felt continentals would be favourable to London's policy.[53] Weir had already expressed the view that the SPC proposals on coal were *too* limited,[54] but when Eden met Monnet in Berlin on 10 February, and put some of the British views forward, the Frenchman seemed greatly encouraged.[55] Within Whitehall at this time consideration was also given to the precise make-up of a Council of Association, a brief for the 'exploratory' talks with Monnet was drafted and a reply to his letter of 23 December was drawn up.[56] The delays to effective negotiations caused some exasperation, however, both to members of the SPC Working Party[57] and to the ECSC: on 9–10 April ministers of the Six met, agreed to negotiate a formal association once Britain replied to Monnet's invitation and hoped this would be within the next month.[58]

In fact the British Cabinet had met on 7 April to discuss the results of consultations with the Commonwealth and industry, but the meeting provided a further blow to Foreign Office hopes of rapid progress. The Commonwealth views were not a serious problem: those Commonwealth countries who took the time to express a view on ECSC association showed some fears over future trade with Britain, but Canada and New Zealand supported Anglo-European co-operation on political grounds, whilst Australia and South Africa accepted assurances that Commonwealth interests would be safeguarded.[59] British domestic interests were, however, more troublesome, particularly with regard to steel. A paper circulated by Duncan Sandys revealed rigid opposition to any 'common market' by representatives of the industry on the Iron and Steel Board, and preference for a limited agreement on such issues as pricing and investment. In part this reflected doubts about the ECSC's likely effectiveness: it was felt to be a highly complex agreement, operating over too large an area, and with a fundamental lack of realism in its attempt to separate coal and steel from the rest of the economy. In part, too, the Board's view reflected a feeling that British industry was 'different' from Europe: Britain's steel market in Europe was limited and had not suffered as badly as had the continentals in the minor steel 'slumps' of 1950 and 1953. But most of all the Iron and Steel Board felt that a common market would mean too great an upheaval in policies on pricing, investments, raw materials and imperial preferences. Sandys tried to play down the Board's doubts in Cabinet, arguing that there were political arguments in favour of a common market and that the steel industry could be brought into line if pressed, but the Iron and Steel Federation (of independent producers) and the engineering industry also disliked the idea of a common market. A third Cabinet paper, from the Board of Trade, rein-forced doubts about the idea – especially with regard to changes in British commercial practice – and recommended that a Committee of Ministers should be set up to study the issue. Eden was exasperated at this, bitterly complaining about the four-month delay since Monnet's letter, but the Chancellor of the Exchequer, 'Rab' Butler, suggested a compromise which the Cabinet accepted: a non-committal reply would be sent to Monnet, offering talks on association in London but, since it was known that the Frenchman was unavailable for talks for some weeks, this would allow time for consideration of the form of association by a Committee of Ministers. Such a committee was established under the Commonwealth Secretary, Lord Swinton.[60]

The best that the Foreign Office now hoped for was a toning down of British industry's doubts and association on as close terms as possible, but a common market in steel now seemed out of the question and predictably, in the first meeting of the new Ministerial Committee, it was decided that Britain should instead seek a more limited arrangement covering steel tariffs and quotas.[61] On 29 April Weir handed Britain's non-committal offer of talks to Monnet. After four months' wait the ECSC President was rather disappointed to receive a reply lacking any concrete proposals, but the next day he accepted the invitation to open talks.[62] The SPC Working Party had now finalized a brief for talks with Monnet, and was wound down, to be re-placed by a new Working Party on 'Negotiations with the High Authority'.[63] Fortunately by 24 May the Ministerial Committee completed its considerations, and recommended to the Cabinet that a ministerial delegation (probably led by Eden) should open 'exploratory' talks with Monnet on 18 June, with the object of achieving as close an association as possible, whilst retaining the support of British industry. In the long term this would include mutual reductions in tariffs, but in the short term all that was planned was the establishment of a 'Council of Association' in two tiers: an upper tier of ministers and leading officials to 'steer' work; and a lower one of officials (and representatives from Britain's steel and coal boards) divided into groups working on steel and coal. The purpose of the Council would be to bring about common policies on prices, raw materials, training and safety, to take joint action on scarcity and to make market studies and forecasts, but the Ministerial Committee was determined that other issues (such as working conditions) must be settled by Britain's own system of free collective bargaining. The President of the Board of Trade dissented from the paper, arguing that it would be tactically better to pursue tariff reductions first, and that Monnet would be disappointed with anything less. The Foreign Office supported Thorneycroft's view but Duncan Sandys, supported by Butler, argued strongly in favour of the Ministerial Committee's case. Sandy's logic was that, by establishing a Council of Association as quickly as possible, British industry would become used to working with the Six and might then be won over to greater co-operation. The Cabinet was evidently impressed by the Minister of Supply's performance, because – even though he was not a Cabinet member – Sandys, rather than the disgruntled Eden, was charged with carrying out the negotiations with Monnet. The Committee of Ministers remained in being to advise him.[64]

Having seriously diluted the SPC recommendations of December 1953 the British were at last ready to begin talks on a formal ECSC association. But the next months only saw further delays, though this time due to the continentals. In June Monnet himself became ill, and the practical difficulty in arranging any meetings with the Europeans over the summer meant the date for the 'exploratory' talks was set back until September.[65] By then the EDC had finally and ignominiously collapsed in the face of a vote on 31 August by the French National Assembly. The fading Foreign Office hopes of using an Anglo–ECSC association to encourage EDC ratification disappeared completely, though Weir was able to report that the

ECSC itself was likely to survive EDC's defeat.[66] Interestingly, at the London conference called by Eden in late September to resolve the problems created by the demise of the European army, there was a proposal from Italy that Britain and the Six should make a mutual commitment to economic co-operation 'with the final object of establishing a common market'; but the British not surprisingly decided to oppose the proposal, and the Italians withdrew it.[67] In the meantime there had been some movement on ECSC association. In May Duncan Sandys had suggested that he might hold secret, informal talks with Monnet to pave the way for formal talks in London. The Foreign Office was rather wary of this idea, insisting that Weir must also be involved in any conversations, but Sandys finally had his way and the informal talks were arranged with Monnet (with Weir in attendance) in Paris, on 13–15 September. By early September Monnet was still keen to see an agreement on tariff changes and, with the Foreign Office still keen for as close an association as possible despite the collapse of EDC, Sandys actually considered going back to the industrialists and pressing for a common market in steel![68] But at the talks in mid-September Monnet accepted arguments that the Council of Association would lead to more extensive co-operation later and shifted his pressure to the form the Council would take: in particular he wanted a high-powered delegation from Britain, led by a minister. The broad lines of an agreement were sketched out, a draft arrangement was drawn up and the British Ministerial Committee was impressed enough to approve another session of Sandys–Monnet talks in October, the original idea of 'exploratory' talks in London being pushed aside.[69]

The two sides now proceeded a little more quickly towards an agreement. Sandys' second session of talks with Monnet took place in early October and was largely concerned with efforts to marry together British and ECSC draft agreements.[70] On 5 October the Cabinet approved both the planned agreement and a joint communiqué setting out the aims and role of the Council of Association; by 21 October the redrafting of all the documents was virtually complete.[71] The Cabinet also decided, in late October, that an Act of Parliament could be introduced providing diplomatic immunity to British-based representatives of the ECSC whose supranational status created legal difficulties.[72] On the European side, however, there continued to be delays, principally now because the French premier, Pierre Mendès-

France (who was blamed by many for the collapse of EDC and who was singularly unenthusiastic about European federalism), was engaged in a bitter struggle with Monnet. On 27 October, at a meeting of the ECSC Council of Ministers which should have approved the Council of Association, the French chairman ruled that insufficient time had been given to study the Sandys–Monnet discussions, and that a decision must be deferred until the next meeting in late November.[73] In the intervening period the French government pressed an idea that the Council of Association should be created by bilateral agreements between Britain and each of the Six, and Mendès was reported to favour the transformation of the ECSC into a non-supranational body with British membership. Despite their potential sympathy for such a scheme, the British adhered to their policy of avoiding moves that smacked of 'sabotage' and stood clear of the wrangle between the French premier and the ECSC President. The Council of Ministers on 22 November decided on drafting changes to the association agreement, strengthening the role of member governments over the High Authority. [74] The British Cabinet accepted these on 6 December, and ECSC ministers gave approval to the final documents in a meeting held over the next two days.[75]

The Anglo-ECSC agreement on association was initialled on 11 December 1954 and signed in London ten days later by Sandys and Monnet. It provided for a Council of Association meeting alternatively in London and Luxembourg, made up of four representatives from each side and with a provision for subsidiary committees. The Council was to provide for exchanges of information, and for consultation and joint action on such matters as pricing, raw material supplies, research and safety, relating to both coal and steel. Provision was made for Britain to meet ECSC ministers if necessary, and representatives of the six governments could sit on the Council of Association as observers (or even as participants if a state's special interests were affected). In a separate exchange of letters Sandys agreed that, where possible, the British delegation would be led by a minister and that representatives from the coal and steel boards would be included.[76] French press comment on the agreement was unenthusiastic, however – *Le Monde* and *Figaro* were positively critical[77] – and the creation of a Council of Association could hardly be considered a very inspiring move. Although it led on to closer, practical co-operation between Britain and the

European coal and steel industries, and although Weir's delegation had already succeeded in setting up close day-to-day contacts with the High Authority, the agreement on association was long delayed and limited in content. Britain could not be blamed for all the delays: after May 1954 these had been caused mainly by the continentals. But London had taken a cautious line on the *pace* of negotiations, right from the Labour government's decision to delay talks on association until the ECSC was in operation. And the limited content of the December 1954 arrangement was certainly principally due to doubts in London, and contrasted with Eden's hasty and quite extensive commitments to the continent in the military sphere following the collapse of EDC. On the surface the Sandys–Monnet agreement looked like another example of Britain's reticent attitude towards Europe, a reticence which fell short of a wish to 'sabotage' supranational efforts perhaps, but which also fell far short of encouragement for the Six. It was an attitude which, furthermore, was to prove extremely costly when, in mid-1955, the ECSC states put the failure of EDC behind them and began the negotiations for a full common market. In the long term European integration proved a more successful policy for the Six than did Commonwealth co-operation for Britain.

A closer look at the British efforts to associate with the ECSC under the Churchill administration reveals a rather more complex picture, however, and one more favourable to London. Like the Labour government before it, the Conservative administration of 1951–5 certainly cannot be described as 'anti-European'. Churchill and his colleagues may have appeared less enthusiastic about European integration than they had in opposition and Eden may initially have seemed much too negative about British links to the continent, but there were strong reasons for London to support supranationalism – as a way to tie Germany to the West, strengthen liberal democracy and economic efficiency on the continent, and reassure American opinion – and these were reinforced (at least until August 1954) by a desire to create a European army and so bring about German rearmament. In 1952 the Eden Plan showed Britain's desire to retain close links with the continentals, but it was undermined by the opposition of Monnet and others, who were determined that nothing should interfere with their chosen supranational path and wanted to channel British association along a different course. In 1953 the SPC proposals for a 'common market' in steel revealed both an appreciation of the ECSC's potential strength and a willingness amongst some officials in Whitehall to adopt quite a radical policy towards the Six, but this time the opposition was internal: the steel industry, the coal industry and trade unions, as well as some ministers (like 'Rab' Butler), showed little enthusiasm for continental co-operation and major changes in British commercial practices. To blame Eden and the Foreign Office alone for 'missing the European bus' would certainly be unfair, since even those ministers who did show some sympathy for European co-operation were unwilling to carry this very far: Macmillan's views (easily defeated by Eden in Cabinet) were inspired as much by fears of a European 'menace' as by a positive desire for co-operation, and he had no sympathy for the idea of British participation in a continental 'federation'; Thorneycroft was willing to consider a 'common market' at one point, but was later just as keen to defend existing British practices; Sandys supported the SPC proposals, but later championed the more limited 'Council of Association' (though he evidently hoped it would lead to greater things). Viewed against his original aims, Eden's policy of seeking close association with Europe short of a loss of sovereignty *was* successful. If he and the Foreign Office can be accused in 1952 of a failure to establish a 'middle course' for co-operation with the Six, between supranationalism and intergovernmentalism, this was also due to the refusal of the continentals to accept such a solution. Eden may be accused of a lack of foresight in his European policy overall, but it was a failure shared, often to a far greater degree, by the rest of British government and industry in the crucial years before Messina and the birth of the European Economic Community.

Notes

1. By, for example, A. Bullock, *Ernest Bevin: Foreign Secretary* (1983), A. Milward, *The Reconstruction of Western Europe, 1945–51* (1984) and J. W. Young, *Britain, France and the Unity of Europe, 1945–51* (1984). But also essential is the thorough and impressive collection of documents by R. Bullen, ed., *Documents on British Policy Overseas, Series II vol. II, The Schuman Plan, The Council of Europe and W. European Integration, 1950–2* (1986), ch. 1.
2. On the period from June 1951 to October 1952 see Bullen,

Documents, chs 2 and 3; Young, *Britain, France and Unity of Europe*, 158–66, 177–82.

3. Bullen, *Documents*, 742–4.
4. For a full discussion see J. W. Young, 'Churchill's "No" to Europe: the "rejection" of European Union by Churchill's post-war government, 1951–2', *Historical Journal*, 1985, 923–31. And see Bullen, *Documents*, 755–6, 759–75 (quote from 761–2), 779–81, 794–5, 801–5.
5. Bullen, *Documents*, 781–8, 790–3. And see 812–18 for criticisms of the Foreign Office views by Macmillan.
6. *Ibid.*, 805–9.
7. *Ibid.*, 809–12.
8. *Ibid.*, 819–25, 826–7.
9. Young, 'Churchill's "No" to Europe', 931–4; Bullen, *Documents*, 828–35, 837–41, 844–7.
10. Bullen, *Documents*, 842–4, 846–7, 855–7.
11. *Ibid.*, 862 (Calendar), 867, 870–4, 879–80.
12. PRO, CAB 129/52, C (52) 189.
13. Bullen, *Documents*, 844–90, 893–8, 904–7, 912–13 (quotes from 896, 897–8). Later in the year fears of a European 'super-state' led the Foreign Office to draft a Cabinet paper on the dangers: see Bullen, 979.
14. *Ibid.*, xxvii.
15. *Ibid.*, 915–23. Part of the problem at this meeting was Schuman's desire to turn the Saar into a European 'District of Columbia' in order to resolve its uncertain status (after its separation from Germany, at French insistence, after 1945). See also J. Monnet, *Memoirs* (1978), 369–70; PRO, BT 11/4902.
16. Bullen, *Documents*, 923–5; *The Times*, 12 Aug.
17. Bullen, *Documents*, 928–38, 941–62.
18. *Ibid.*, 862–71, 975–7, 980–3. There was some opposition to Monnet's far-reaching supranational aims among the Six, notably from the Dutch and Belgians; see Bullen, 986–90. In mid-November Eden still believed that Monnet's opposition might yet be overcome and the Eden Plan succeed: Bullen, 1001–3.
19. On the Eden Plan's failure in general see: A. Nutting, *Europe will Not Wait* (1960), 42–6; A. Eden, *Full Circle* (1960), 48; R. Massigli, *Une comédie des erreurs* (Paris, 1978), 330–3; Monnet, *Memoirs*, 380–1; P. H. Spaak, *The Continuing Battle* (1971), 226.
20. See Bullen, *Documents*, xxvii–xxviii.
21. *Ibid.*, 848–55.
22. *Ibid.*, 882–3, 889–93.
23. *Ibid.*, 907–10.
24. The 'Franco-German' committee, set up in May 1950, and chaired by the Treasury, had done very little work since the Convervatives returned to power.
25. CAB 134/1175, SPC (52) 1st–3rd.
26. Until Weir's arrival the British were provisionally represented in

Luxembourg in August by G. C. Allchin. Bullen, *Documents*, 926–8, and see Monnet, *Memoirs*, 377–8; M. Beloff, *New Dimensions in Foreign Policy* (1961), 92–3.

27. See Bullen, *Documents*, 938; and CAB 134/1175, SPC (52) 2nd, 4th, 5th, 7th.
28. Bullen, *Documents*, 971–5.
29. *Ibid.*, 971–5.
30. *Ibid.*, 990–4.
31. PRO, FO 371/105953/1.
32. CAB 134/1177, SPC (E) (53) 1st; FO 371/105953/5.
33. CAB 128/26, CC (53) 15th; CAB 129/50, C (53) 70.
34. On EDC see previous chapter.
35. FO 371/106076/1.
36. Known as the 'Green Pool'.
37. FO 371/106076/1.
38. FO 371/105954/33.
39. FO 371/105954/54 and 60.
40. R. Mayne, *The Recovery of Europe* (1970), 209.
41. FO 371/105954/67.
42. FO 371/105955/82 and 89.
43. FO 371/105955/100; FO 371/105956/114.
44. *181 HLDeb. 5s*, 1215; PRO, PREM 11/430.
45. CAB 134/1177, SPC (E) (53) 29; Beloff, *New Dimensions*, 93.
46. FO 371/105955/107, 108; FO 371/105956/112, 134; Beloff, *New Dimensions*, 93.
47. CAB 134/885, ES (53) 9th and papers 21, 22.
48. FO 371/105957/157, 161, 162. In October the Foreign Office rejected a suggestion from Monnet that a joint meeting of Anglo-ECSC MPs should be held: FO 371/1/105957/152–4.
49. CAB 129/65, C (54) 20, annex A; FO 371/105957/166–8, 171; CMD. 9147 (May 1954), 2–6; Mayne, *Recovery*, 209. The Foreign Office did *not* like Monnet's idea that Britain should deal exclusively with the High Authority, however: officials wanted British access to the Council of Ministers: FO 371/111250/11.
50. FO 371/111250/9, 13, 25.
51. CAB 134/1178, SPC (E) (54) 1st, 2nd and papers 1, 2; CAB 134/888, ES (54) 1st and paper 2.
52. CAB 128/127, CC (54) 4; CAB 129/65, C (54) 20.
53. FO 371/111251/36; FO 371/111252/67, 69, 71, 77.
54. FO 371/111250/10, 30.
55. FO 371/111251/39; FO 371/111252/50.
56. CAB 134/1178, SPC (E) (54) 3rd, 4th; FO 371/111251/44, 45; FO 37/111252/64; FO 371/111253/98.
57. CAB 134/1178, SPC (E) (54) 5th.
58. FO 371/111261/7, 8.
59. CAB 129/67, C (54) 132 (6 April); see also FO 311/111251/40; FO 371/111252/47.

60. CAB 128/27, CC (54) 27; CAB 129/67, C (54) 131, 133; and see also FO 371/111252/51; FO 371/111253/82, 88, 89.
61. The papers of the Ministerial Committee, designated Gen. 462/1, have unfortunately been retained by the Cabinet Office, but see FO 371/111253/100 and 112.
62. FO 371/111253/101, 109, 110, 113, 123; FO 371/111261/9; CMD. 9147 (May 1954), 7–8; Mayne, *Recovery*, 210.
63. CAB 134/1178, SPC (E) (54) 6th; CAB 134/1179, SPC (N) (54) 1st.
64. CAB 128/27, CC (54) 36; CAB 129/68, C (54) 173 and 174; FO 371/111253/128, 131, 138.
65. CAB 134/1179, SPC (N) (54) 6th; FO 371/111254/142, 144; FO 371/111261/12.
66. FO 371/111261/20.
67. The commitment to a common market would have been included in the new Western European Union. FO 371/111275/1.
68. FO 371/111253/127, 128, 135; FO 371/111254/150, 168, 170, 171.
69. At first Monnet also seemed to want supranational elements in the association agreement but he soon dropped this idea. Peter Thorneycroft feared, in the wake of the Paris talks, that both sides expected different things from a Council of Association. FO 371/111254/171/173, 174, 183, 184; FO 371/111255/194; and see CAB 134/1179, SPC (N) (54) 8th and paper 25.
70. There were complaints on the ECSC side that Eden's commitments to Europe in the London talks (following the collapse of EDC) made Britain's proposed commitments to the ECSC seem very thin. FO 371/111255/201–7, 210, 214–16, 219–26, 228–9; FO 371/111256/230, 232–3, 236, 238–9; FO 371/111257/261, 263.
71. CAB 134/1179, SPC (N) (54) 9th, 10th; CAB 128/27, CC (54) 63; CAB 129/71, C (54) 205.
72. CAB 128/27, CC (54) 70; CAB 129/71, C (54) 305; FO 371/111255/227; FO 371/111256/234, 244, 247, 254–5; FO 371/111257/258, 260 266, 275.
73. FO 371/111256/253; FO 371/111257/279; FO 371/111261/22.
74. The SPC Working Party on Negotiations wanted to adopt amendments which heightened the role of the ECSC ministers, but Weir warned that Britain would have to deal primarily with the High Authority. CAB 134/1179, EPC (N) (54) 11th, 12th; FO 371/111257/280, 282–4, 289, 291; FO 371/111258/294, 297, 303, 305, 308, 311–12, 316; FO 371/111261/23–4.
75. CAB 128/27, CC (54) 82.
76. CAB 129/72, C (54) 394; FO 371/111258/315, 322 and 326; FO 371/111261/25; CMD. 9346 (Dec. 1954).
77. 22 December. See FO 371/111258/329.

5 Egypt and the Suez Base Agreement

Ritchie Ovendale

In September 1945 a conference of British officials in the Middle East, chaired by Ernest Bevin, the Foreign Secretary, concluded that the area should remain largely a British sphere of influence. By September 1951 Britain, effectively left with responsibility for the area in allied planning to cope with the cold war situation and a potential hot war, was desperate to involve other countries in its defence. In a future war it was anticipated that Western forces in the Middle East would have to be ready immediately. The Egyptian base was seen as crucial, but in talks on the future of the base, which had begun in 1946, Egypt was determined that Britain should evacuate. Under the terms of the Anglo-Egyptian treaty of 1936 Britain had to go in 1956 anyway if Egypt did not want it to stay. The Middle East was regarded by Britain as a Commonwealth responsibility: the Americans would not be able to participate effectively there for two years after war broke out; Britain had neither the money, the manpower, nor the weaponry to cope on its own; and London therefore hoped for commitments from the old 'white' Dominions. But those countries were hesitant because of the potential costs. Britain outlined its defence policy and global strategy to Dominion defence delegates in the middle of 1951. A firm hold on the Middle East, along with the defence of the United Kingdom and the security of sea communications vital to the allies, were the pillars of this strategy. To retain control of the Middle East within the Western orbit was seen as a vital cold war measure, and military sacrifices had to be made to secure this. In total war the Middle East remained critically important. The retention of some of the oil fields could well be essential economically, and the Middle East was also a potentially important base for offensive air action against southern Russia. The loss of the Middle East would be a catastrophe to the British Commonwealth and to Western Europe. The allied plans, therefore, had to include provision for the minimum forces required to hold a sufficient area of the Middle East to ensure the security of the Egyptian base and the south-west Persian gulf oil fields. Since Britain could not even provide all the forces required to defend the United Kingdom and Western Europe, it seemed inescapable that additional forces for the Middle East would have to be found from other parts of the Commonwealth and from the United States. The idea of a Middle East Command began to take shape at the meeting in London in June 1951 of Commonwealth representatives, and about a month later Britain submitted a paper on the subject to the Standing Group of NATO. Sir Ralph Stevenson, the new British ambassador in Cairo, was then authorized to announce to Egypt details of a Middle East defence scheme in which it was proposed that Egypt would share as an equal partner with Britain and other nations. But on 9 October Egypt, determined to achieve full sovereignty in defence, denounced the Anglo-Egyptian treaty of 1936, in the full knowledge that the Middle East Command proposals were about to be presented. Cairo formally rejected the Command proposals themselves on 16 October.[1]

When it took office the new Conservative government was therefore immediately faced with a potentially explosive and humiliating situation in Egypt. As Prime Minister, Winston Churchill told the Cabinet on 30 October that it was the duty of the British government to keep the Suez Canal open to the shipping of the world, using force if necessary,[2] though he agreed with ambassador Stevenson that an immediate showdown with Egypt to force the existing government out of power should be avoided.[3] Eden wanted to wait a while before putting more pressure on Egypt,[4] but the Chiefs of Staff argued that Britain had lost the initiative and recommended that oil supplies to Egypt be interrupted, a move to put pressure on Egypt which Churchill endorsed.[5] The Prime Minister favoured a full programme of 'immediate suspension', ranging from weapons supplies to control of Egypt's sterling balances.[6] By December there were two British views of the situation. Ambassador Stevenson advised that while it was doubtful that Britain could ever have Egypt's friendship, it might be able to purchase acquiescence in defence matters for a while provided London realized that it could not browbeat Cairo, or stand on its rights under the 1936 treaty: no Egyptian government would be able to go back on the abrogation of the treaty and the consequent administrative measures taken against British forces in the Canal Zone, because the issue of British evacuation had 'already become a truly national sentiment and was fast becoming a national movement'. Churchill however thought that this did not really matter, and the military challenged Stevenson's analysis: Egyptian hostility would not render the Canal base useless; the strategic plans for the defence of the Middle East were dependent on the retention of the Canal Zone base, and here Britain had a responsibility to the Commonwealth and Atlantic Pact powers; Stevenson's policy could result in there being no base at all, a world-wide loss of British prestige and a loss of Arab confidence in British leadership.[7] The scene was already set for the contest between the uncompromising line on policy towards Egypt, identified with Churchill, and a more moderate, diplomatic line, identified with Eden. This contest was not resolved until July 1954, when a settlement was finally negotiated with the Egyptians on the future of the Suez base.

Churchill scorned the Egyptians. He resented their 'cheek', and in private told Eden to let them know if they continued in that vein, 'we shall set the Jews on them and drive them into the gutter, from which they should never have emerged'.[8] When Egyptian crowds ran riot in Cairo on 26 January 1952, burning Shepheards Hotel and British airline offices, symbols of British imperialism,[9] Churchill wrote to Eden that the 'horrible behaviour of the mob puts them lower than the most degraded savages now known'.[10] There was a change of government in Egypt following the disturbances, and the Foreign Office let Cairo know that it wanted to reach agreement with Egypt on the adequate defence of the Canal Zone, which would provide for a gradual assumption of responsibilities by the Egyptian armed forces. Churchill minuted: 'This is the complete "clear-out".'[11] Under pressure from Washington and Paris, however, Eden wanted to resume negotiations, initially on an Anglo-Egyptian basis.[12] Churchill was in no particular hurry. In the prevailing situation Britain could negotiate from strength: Egypt had almost lost its place among civilized states, whereas Britain had remained firm, cool, resolute and immovable. Churchill did not want those assets lost through the feeling that Britain should settle immediately.[13]

In Cabinet on 18 February, Churchill objected to the proposal that the Suez base installations should be handed over to the Egyptian government as a preliminary to their being made available to an allied Middle East Command, and insisted instead that British responsibility should be transferred directly to that Command. Despite Eden's warnings that, if the negotiations were to succeed, the concessions that he had envisaged in his original draft would have to be made, Churchill's amendment was approved by the Cabinet.[14] The Prime Minister did not like 'evacuation': how could control of the Canal and base be entrusted to a strengthened and rearmed Egyptian army which at any time could be taken over by a hostile Egyptian government? He complained to Eden towards the middle of March that Britain's relative strength was growing and he thought that there was no urgency to conclude 'an agreement which sacrifices all we have strived for over so many years'. Churchill was worried about strong forces in the Conservative party which would 'be deeply stirred by our moral surrender and physical flight'.[15] Eden had to explain again that without agreement Britain would have to leave in 1956 anyway; furthermore, if Britain had to maintain its position in the Canal Zone by force there would be no troops available for the defence of the Middle East. Even Churchill viewed that as a difficult situation. The Foreign Secretary insisted that the plain fact was that Britain was no longer in a position to impose its will on Egypt: 'If I cannot impose my will, I must negotiate.'[16] Churchill started to consider what could be saved 'from the wreck'.[17] He could not understand why Britain was 'giving everything into Egypt's power and have nothing in return nor any means of securing the fulfilment of any understanding'.[18]

Preliminary talks with the Egyptians in early 1952 foundered on the same issue that had led to the breakdown of negotiations under the Labour government after 1946: the claim of the Egyptian king to the crown of Sudan, a country which Britain instead insisted had the right to self-determination.[19] On 22 July there was a *coup d'état* in Cairo, however, and a group of military officers seized power. Early in August Stevenson broached the idea of a Middle East Defence Organization with the new Egyptian leader, Neguib: the moment seemed propitious especially since Cairo wanted to buy some British military equipment.[20] Churchill however thought this a dangerous bait: as an old Harrovian he wrote to the Etonian Eden: 'I believe it is an Eton custom to make parents of pupils pay for the birch.'[21] The Prime Minister rejected the idea which had been raised of moving the Suez base to Gaza, and confided to the Minister of State, Selwyn Lloyd, that he had never agreed in principle to Britain's evacuation of the Canal Zone before the treaty expired, and would only evacuate it then if satisfactory arrangements were made for an international defence association with Egypt and the defence of the Suez Canal. Churchill did concede, however, that he was prepared to give Neguib a chance, provided he showed himself to be a friend.[22] While reassuring Churchill that he had no intention of allowing Britain to be kicked out of Egypt, Eden reminded his Prime Minister that the Cabinet had approved an attempt to secure an agreement, providing for both the withdrawal of British combatant forces and the transfer of the base installations to an allied Middle East Command. Failure to settle with Egypt could have serious consequences for the defence of the whole Middle East. The Americans wanted a British agreement with Egypt, and could possibly be persuaded to contribute towards the cost of a redeployment scheme.[23] At the end of October Eden successfully persuaded the Cabinet to authorize the release of a limited number of Meteor aircraft to Egypt.[24]

At the time of the election of the new Republican administration in the United States, British policy in the Middle East was being reassessed. On 4 December Eden told a meeting of the Cabinet, attended by Commonwealth Prime Ministers, that the accession of Turkey to NATO had changed the Middle Eastern problem. It was now proposed to move the British military headquarters from the Canal Zone to Cyprus. In his earlier review to the Cabinet of future defence expenditure, Eden had already anticipated that it might be possible to come to an arrangement with Egypt and other interested parties which would make economies in the Middle East possible. Britain also hoped that a treaty with Libya would make strategic facilities available in that country. Putting these developments together, it might now be possible to devise a successful form of defence for the Middle East based on Turkey, Cyprus and Libya. Furthermore, Eden hoped that Neguib might be forthcoming on defence problems especially since his government had taken the significant step of abandoning the claim to recognition of Egypt's sovereignty over the Sudan.[25]

British officials now had discussions with American diplomatic and military representatives about the basis on which defence negotiations could be resumed with the Egyptian government. During the last year of the Truman administration Washington had conceded that the basis of Anglo-American co-operation in the Middle East should be the agreement of 1948, whereby it was understood that the United States would not compete with or try to displace British responsibilities in the area and indeed would strengthen British interests where it could.[26] The State Department's Policy Planning Staff, however, pointed out that although the defence of the Middle East was primarily a British responsibility, Britain could not defend the area against Russian aggression, or probably even sustain the shortest line of defence east of the Suez Canal.[27] The decline of Britain and France in the area had left a 'growing vacuum' which should, from an American point of view, be filled by elements friendly to the free world.[28] At the beginning of 1953 the American representatives agreed to recommend to their government that Britain open negotiations with Egypt along the lines of 'Case A', which would enable the Western allies to maintain a working base in peacetime, to which they could return immediately after the outbreak of war. (An alternative, 'Case B', would only allow reactivation within sixty days.)[29] American assistance was expected in making representations to the Egyptians, and the Chiefs of Staff were anxious that Washington should not pursue its intention to supply Neguib with military equipment until Egypt behaved satisfactorily in the defence negotiations.[30]

While in the United States in January, Churchill discussed the Middle East with the new President, Dwight Eisenhower, who revealed a limited view of the 'special relationship' in the area by saying that, while Britain and the United States should work together in the area, there should be 'no collusion'. Eisenhower was apparently astonished to hear that Britain had 70,000 men in Egypt. He was told that the situation could not go on indefinitely: there were better uses both for the troops and the money. Churchill thought that British and American policy should have the same focus, even if it operated from different angles. Sometimes joint Anglo-American action had great advantages, though in some cases publicity should be avoided. The Prime Minister told the President of his abhorrence of the view that Britain and the Commonwealth 'was just one among other foreign nations': 'The English-speaking world was the hope. We had 80 million whites, which added to their [the American] population was the foundation of all effective policy.' Eisenhower apparently took this all very well, and Churchill concluded that by 'no collusion' the President meant 'no public collusion'. But the Prime Minister did not like this line of thought.[31]

Churchill returned to London 'passionately interested' in the Egyptian situation. He upset Eden by wanting to stop the delivery of the Meteor jets to Egypt. Furious at Eden's conciliatory policy, he commented that he had 'not known that Munich was situated on the Nile'; John Colville, Churchill's private secretary, was given the impression that Churchill would never give way over Egypt.[32] The Prime Minister even told the Cabinet, on 11 February, that he doubted whether Eden's proposals for the future of the Sudan as an independent state would have sufficient support from Conservative members in Parliament: they would be 'represented as an enormous surrender of our responsibilities in the Sudan and a serious blow to British prestige throughout the Middle East'. But Churchill was told that the Sudanese people expected self-government and nothing would be gained by delay. An agreement on Sudanese self-determination was signed the next day and government supporters in the House of Commons were brought around to accept this.[33] On Egypt, Churchill, as he told the Cabinet on 17 February, felt that Britain needed to ensure that it had the full support and sympathy of Washington in any approach it made. To support the military case he hoped that the British and American ambassadors in Cairo would be assisted by prominent military figures.[34] Churchill explained his envisaged tactics to Eden:

> This military dictator is under the impression that he has only to kick to make us run. I would like him to kick us and show him that we did not run. . . . Unless you can show that we have imposed our will upon Neguib you will find it very difficult to convince the Conservative Party that the evacuation of the Suez Canal Zone conforms with British interest or prestige.[35]

Eisenhower, conscious of the feud between the Foreign Secretary and the Prime Minister, and wanting to strengthen Eden's hand, wrote directly to the Foreign Secretary on 16 March, saying that he hoped that the proposed plan would operate to the advantage of Egypt and would also assure the free world that the Suez Canal would remain available for use. At the same time the President in effect again devalued the 'special relationship': he argued that Britain and the United States should avoid giving the appearance of attempting to dominate the councils of the free world; Britain and the United States should consciously preserve 'an attitude of absolute equality with all other nations'.[36]

It was against this unpromising background that London fought to secure American acquiescence, if not active support, for its stand against Neguib in negotiating a new Anglo-Egyptian treaty. Early in March Eden went to Washington still hoping to secure control of the Suez base after British evacuation via an international agreement. Together with most British officials involved in the affair, Eden distrusted the American ambassador in Cairo, Jefferson Caffery: too often Caffery had given the impression of being a neutral arbiter between the British and the Egyptians. What Britain in effect wanted was a joint Anglo American démarche, and by placing a military emphasis on the talks the British hoped that Caffery's influence would be weakened. The British and American ambassadors in Cairo would be assisted by Field Marshall Sir William Slim, due to become Governor-General of Australia, and General John E. Hull, the American Army Vice Chief of Staff. Eisenhower went along with this idea, but otherwise was not so helpful: he said that the Americans needed time to consider more fully the envisaged Middle East Defence Organization and insisted that American participation in the talks be made contingent on an Egyptian invitation.[37]

Churchill, faced by the American views, wanted Britain to 'go on alone'. 'If we cannot be united in a definite demand on the Egyptian dictator, there can obviously be no joint action, but only resolute British action within the limits already agreed.' Slim backed him.[38] Eden continued to argue that a joint Anglo-American approach with the Americans in at the beginning offered the best chance of success,[39] but Churchill was unmoved and told Eden to pass a message to his 'dear Friend', Eisenhower. Mentioning the United Nations 'crusade' in Korea, Churchill hoped that Britain and the United States could work together to avoid a costly indefinite stalemate both in the Middle East and the Far East. The Prime Minister concluded: 'If on consideration you do not feel you can go in with us now in Egypt we had much better do the best we can ourselves hoping for and counting on your goodwill.'[40] Eden was even more distressed: he feared the consequences of failing to act together with the Americans over Egypt on Anglo-American relations not only the Middle East but in the wider sphere.[41] Churchill, however, believed that the negotiations if pursued would break down, with Neguib and the Americans arrayed together on one side, and Britain left alone shouldering the burden on the other. He allowed Eden a little latitude,[42] and the Foreign Secretary managed to secure a compromise where there would be no modification of 'Case A' without the concurrence of both the British and American military representative.[43] But the Egyptians then declined to invite the Americans and there thus seemed no early prospect of resuming the negotiations.[44] Even Eden found it difficult to believe that the Americans could not find some way to persuade the Egyptians to invite them.[45] Churchill informed Eisenhower: 'I have reached my limit. We are neither unable nor afraid to deal with Neguib ourselves.'[46] Eisenhower merely replied that Britain and the United States should not be inflexible about procedure.[47]

Early in April 1953 Eden was stricken by illness and Churchill assumed control of policy towards Egypt. Just before doing so the Prime Minister reminded Eden that he did not like Britain being treated by the United States as if it were one of a crowd. Churchill developed this theme in a letter to Eisenhower on 5 April: 'My hope for the future is founded on the increasing unity of the English-speaking world. If that holds all holds. If that fails no one can be sure of what will happen.' Churchill felt that there were instances where a joint initiative by Britain and the United States could settle a dispute peaceably to the general advantage of the free world, and that Egypt was a case in point. Churchill mentioned the Opposition's argument that Britain should abandon Egypt and wanted to know whether Eisenhower also felt that Britain should wash its hands of the whole business. In any case Britain could not indefinitely keep 80,000 men there at a cost of £50 million to discharge an international duty.[48] Eisenhower replied, perhaps disingenuously, that he would find it difficult to disagree with a single line of Churchill's letter: could the Americans be brought into the conversations through the issue of additional arms for Egypt?[49]

At this time too, Churchill was excited by a Foreign Office document on the validity of the Anglo-Egyptian treaty of 1936, which argued that as Egypt had denounced the treaty it was no longer entitled to require negotiation for a revision. Pending revision, or unless both parties agreed to terminate the treaty, it remained in full force. Furthermore, the treaty did not provide for the automatic withdrawal of British forces at any given date: in 1956 the continued presence of the British troops could be dependent on whether Egypt was able to defend the canal, and that issue could be submitted by either of the parties to arbitration, in effect by the United Nations. But, in any case, it could be argued that Egypt's denunciation deprived it of the legal right to insist on negotiations or other steps for withdrawal.[50] British intelligence also reported that ex-Nazi German officers and technicians were training and advising the Egyptians at all levels.[51] The Minister of State, Selwyn Lloyd, advised on 21 April that Britain had information that the Neguib regime wanted to play Britain along for another six months to prepare guerilla formations to be used against British forces in the Canal Zone, and that the German advisers were encouraging this. It was just 'no good the Americans expecting us to lower the price in view of what we suspect to be the real intentions of the Egyptians'.[52] The Chiefs of Staff argued that if there were further trouble in Egypt there would be a need for a rapid decision to take immediate and resolute action.[53] On 26 April Churchill met military chiefs at Chequers to prepare for contingencies, and in view of possible developments in Egypt it was decided that Britain could not dissipate its resources by giving aid to the French in Indochina.[54]

It was against this background that talks between Britain and Egypt were finally reopened in Cairo. General Sir Brian Robertson relinquished his command in the Middle East to assist Stevenson, Slim having left to take up his post in Australia. The negotiations were marred by distrust and ill will on both sides. Churchill told the British team to stand firmly by 'Case A',[55] and approved the line that an agreement of less than twenty years would not be regarded as being of much value.[56] At first the American attitude seemed unhelpful: there were fears that Washington was due to offer Cairo economic and military aid, and Churchill drafted an angry note to Eisenhower arguing that, in view of the Anglo-American agreement on the 'package', Britain had hoped for at least 'moral aid' from the United States. He also warned that Britain would defend itself if attacked.[57] In reply, Eisenhower pleaded that he might not have understood the background to the situation and agreed to delay action on the whole matter until his Secretary of State, John Foster Dulles, had seen Neguib.[58] Churchill's initial response was blunt: 'I should find it very difficult if our soldiers were killed and the massacre of our people as well perhaps as Americans were taking place in Cairo, to justify your support of the creation of an Egyptian army under the tutelage of Nazi criminals and furnished with American weapons.'[59] In the event, however, Dulles made what Churchill regarded as an 'excellent' statement on visiting Cairo.[60] Indeed for a time Dulles apparently supported the idea of an Anglo-American 'special relationship': the Secretary of State told the Egyptians that the United States was not ashamed of close Anglo-American ties. He conceded that the United States did not automatically accept British policies as its own, but the two countries were 'fundamentally agreed on broad principles'.[61]

By the middle of May the Anglo-Egyptian negotiations had effectively been suspended: there was deadlock over the arrangements for technical supervision of the base installations in the Canal Zone. Egyptian ministers made provocative speeches and the sporadic attacks on British troops and property in the Canal Zone increased,[62] but Churchill ramained convinced that there was no hurry to settle affairs in Egypt.[63] Dulles returned from his tour of the Middle East convinced that the United States suffered from being linked with British and French imperialism. Rather than a Middle East Defence Organization with Egypt as the centre (which now seemed impossible to achieve) he favoured a defensive arrangement of the Northern Tier of states: Turkey, Iraq, Syria and Pakistan.[64] Eisenhower now suggested to Churchill that it might not be possible to settle on 'Case A' and offered American technicians to help maintain the base,[65] but this did not modify Churchill's views.[66] He resisted Eisenhower's pleas for concessions and instructed the Foreign Office to 'remain firm and calm'.[67] Churchill sent Lord Salisbury to Washington in July, and discussions were held on the matter, but the Americans took pre-emptive action and approached Neguib themselves – an act which the Foreign Office thought 'most unhelpful'.[68] In Washington Dulles lectured Salisbury about changing times: there was a feeling in the United States that the British approach with people like the Egyptians was to be completely stern and firm, and to deliver a well-placed kick when they made difficulties – such action was no longer appropriate. Salisbury found all this rather hard to bear, but it was felt that Britain should avoid giving the impression that it was being merely 'obdurate'.[69] Lloyd, however, warned the Cabinet that Britain should not be manoeuvred into a position where the United States could act as an intermediary between it and Egypt.[70]

In the wake of the Washington talks and while Britain was negotiating a treaty with Libya (which it was hoped would largely satisfy requirements for air facilities and training areas)[71] negotiations were resumed with Egypt. It was felt that Neguib's influence was lessening at this time, and there were hopes that the Americans could be persuaded to take part in a multilateral approach to Egypt over freedom of navigation in the Suez Canal.[72] By 8 September there seemed some possibility of agreement, but it was felt that American help would be needed to overcome the remaining points of disagreement over technicians, the availability of the base and the duration of the treaty.[73] American enthusiasm for Egypt cooled when Egyptian leaders attacked that country for not giving aid they said had been promised, but when Cairo threatened a policy of neutrality Washington warned London that the aid might be sent. Stevenson summed up American policy as reflecting the view that Egypt was the victim of British 'colonialism' and as such deserved American sympathy. The United States seemed disinclined to take second place in an area where the responsibility was not theirs.[74]

By the time Eden returned to the Foreign Office in October, Churchill had finally come around to the view that American help might be necessary. The Prime Minister was increasingly disturbed by the prospect of a back-bench revolt on the issue: some government supporters – the 'Suez group' – were convinced that British troops should remain in Egypt to ensure the right of free transit through the Suez Canal. Churchill now conceded that the strategic importance of the base in peace and war was much less than it had been. An *international* base in Egypt could meet British requirements provided there were a few thousand British troops on it, and American support could lead to Egyptian concessions. Eden still doubted whether Cairo would agree to any international organization for the defence of the Middle East but of course he liked the idea of winning American support, and thought the issue could be raised at the forthcoming conference with the Americans and French at Bermuda.[75] Churchill hoped for American agreement there to a plan for the disposition of forces in the Middle East in support of NATO.[76] At Bermuda in early December, however, the Americans did not give way to British demands. The Assistant Secretary of State, Henry A. Byroade, instead presented Eden with a new formula which the Foreign Secretary thought inadequate as it gave no automatic right to return to the Suez base, even in the event of a United Nations decision. Eden told him that the British government could make no further concessions; if only the Americans would back Britain, instead of allowing their ambassador in Cairo to undermine the British position, the Egyptians could be brought around.[77]

Eden wrote to Churchill, on 21 December, that the Americans were trying to treat Britain over Egypt in the same threatening manner with which they handled France over the question of the European Defence Community: they would have no friends left if they went on that way.[78] The Prime Minister then warned the President that although the Egyptian issue might seem petty to the Americans, it was one that could cause 'a deep and serious setback' to relations between their two countries, and that would be a disaster for all.[79] On 28 December Churchill outlined a new policy to Eden: Britain should present Egypt with an ultimatum, all negotiations would then lapse and Britain could act in Egypt 'in accordance with what we think are our long-term interests'.[80] He was, however, confronted with the arguments of the Chiefs of Staff that it was important from the general strategic point of view to reach an agreement with Egypt even if it had 'serious military disadvantages'.[81] In late January, Britain also learnt through its Oriental Counsellor in Cairo, Trevor E. Evans, who regularly entertained the revolutionary officers, that Nasser, at that time the Deputy Prime Minister, had told him that time was on the side of the Egyptians, and that no concessions should be made to Britain; the Egyptian objective would be achieved and that day would not be put off by Britain resorting to violence.[82] Churchill (who had taken over Egyptian policy again from Eden while the Foreign Secretary was away at the Berlin conference) said that he was not going to be blackmailed,[83] but he faced increasing opposition to his Egyptian policy early in 1954. In Egypt itself, at a time of disturbances in the Sudan early in March, during which Churchill briefly contemplated a British occupation of Khartoum, the power base shifted from Neguib to Nasser. Britain's financial straits were also becoming more pressing, and only evacuation of the Canal Zone seemed to offer the prospect of substantial savings. This helped to convince Churchill of the need for a settlement with Egypt.[84]

On 11 March, at a Foreign Office meeting, Evelyn Shuckburgh suggested that a new, positive approach should be made to Egypt: the Egyptians had said that they *would* allow Britain to re-enter the base if there were a threat of aggression against Turkey (an important concession for British military planners) and that really only left the issue of whether British technicians left on the base could wear uniforms and carry personal arms (a question which touched the delicate nerve of Egyptian sovereignty). A paper for the Cabinet was drafted along these lines and discussed on 15 March. In it Eden argued that the concession on Turkey was important not only because of its geographic position but because that country was a member of NATO. If the Egyptian government made their concessions public and it became known that the only outstanding issue was the wearing of uniforms, Britain could be seriously embarrassed at home and abroad. In any case Eden felt that if around 4000 British soldiers were left on the base they would just become 'hostages to fortune'. He asked the Cabinet to consider whether essential installations on the base could not instead be maintained by civilian contract labour. As part of any agreement, Egypt would also have to undertake to behave properly in the Sudan and not attack British public servants there. British concessions might justify a request that the agreement last for twenty years rather than seven, and that around two years be allowed for the withdrawal of British troops. The Foreign Secretary was supported by the Minister of Defence, Field Marshal Lord Alexander: the new proposal would enable Britain to remove all its troops from Egypt, reduce its overseas military expenditure and redeploy forces in the Middle East to better advantage. Some ministers feared that the suggested agreement could be represented as a complete surrender to the more extreme demands of the Egyptian government, and argued that public opinion in Britain would want safeguards to provide for the right of international passage through the Suez Canal. But Eden explained that the matter was of concern to a number of maritime nations: a bilateral agreement with Egypt would not be possible. In any case Britain had to redeploy its forces in the Middle East to enable it to maintain its prestige in the area and exert effective power if Egypt failed to keep the agreement: plans being contemplated envisaged the stationing of an armoured brigade in Libya, a brigade in Cyprus and possibly a brigade in Jordan. Churchill was worried about the Foreign Office plan and the political criticism that it might arouse. The Prime Minister favoured an alternative policy: Britain should break off the defence negotiations with Egypt and start its programme of redeployment immediately; and the maritime powers should take multilateral action to ensure the rights of passage through the Canal. Eden successfully opposed this extreme solution,though he did like a suggestion that American civilian contractors could be involved in maintaining the installations on the base.[85] Dulles approved of the new proposals and said that the United States was in principle prepared to co-operate provided there was no new American commitment and that Washington would only take part in the negotiations if asked to do so by the Egyptians. But Churchill continued to insist that he would have preferred a definite rupture in the negotiations with the Egyptian government and a stand on the 1936 treaty.[86]

Opposed by Eden, the Foreign Office and now the military, Churchill still would not give up Egypt. Early in April the Prime Minister reminded Eden of his 'constant interest' in the problem.[87] More and more Churchill, in contrast to his earlier views, wanted American involvement. Approaches over the possibility of a collective defence organization for South-East Asia led the Prime Minister to hope that the Americans might be persuaded to join the British in a similar assurance about the security of the Middle East and the Suez Canal. Eden doubted whether the Americans could be persuaded.[88] The Chiefs of Staff did, however, urge on Admiral Radford, the Chairman of the Joint Chiefs of Staff, the view that Britain needed to reduce its commitments in the Canal Zone in order to build up a strategic reserve which would be able to fight communism anywhere in the world. With American support it might be possible to get a sound agreement with Egypt that would ensure the maintenance of the allied position in the Middle East.[89] At the Geneva conference in May, however, Eden did not get on well with the Americans: Shuckburgh recorded that the Foreign Secretary privately thought that all the Americans wanted to do was to replace the French in Indochina, take over from Britain in Egypt and run the world.[90] Churchill continued to believe that a joint Anglo-American settlement with Egypt was the solution,[91] but Eden warned that there would be serious difficulties in asking the Americans to join Britain in negotiating a settlement with Egypt. It would make agreement more difficult for the Egyptians: Nasser would face the charge of having allowed two great powers into the Canal Zone instead of one. In any case Eden doubted whether any arrangement like that would make the settlement more popular in Britain. There was also the danger of the effect on Iraq and the Persian Gulf states if it seemed that Britain had to ask for help from the Americans. In any case Dulles was being disagreeable, and it was important that any British approach to the Egyptians should not appear to have been dictated by the Americans. American diplomatic support would be preferable to bringing them directly into the negotiations.[92]

The Cabinet debated the whole Egyptian situation again on 22 June. It was emphasized that Britain's strategic needs had been radically changed by the development of thermo-nuclear weapons. On 12 May the Chiefs of Staff had concluded that 'by far the most important factor to be taken into account in any consideration of United Kingdom strategy was the introduction of the H-bomb',[93] and on 2 June Sir William Dickson, the Chief of the Air Staff, had outlined how the defence problems of the Middle East had been changed by the development of the hydrogen bomb: in view of the weight of an atomic attack to which the Russians would be subjected in the opening stages of a major war, they were now less likely to be able to develop a substantial offensive through the Caucasus; and so Britain now had a better chance of holding the north-east of Iraq, a development which increased the strategic importance of air bases in Iraq.[94] It also followed that it was no longer expedient to maintain so large a concentration of stores, equipment and men within the narrow confines of the Canal Zone. Faced by these considerations Churchill now accepted the military argument for redeploying the British forces in the Middle East, but he remained impressed by the political disadvantages of abandoning the position Britain had held in Egypt since 1882 and still believed that, if the settlement could be presented as part of a comprehensive Anglo-American plan for building up a defensive front against communist aggression throughout the world, it might become more acceptable to sections of the Conservative party.[95]

Churchill finally gave in to Eden in July. On 26 and 27 June, in Washington, the Prime Minister and the Foreign Secretary discussed the whole problem with Eisenhower and Dulles. Churchill declared in the talks that, although initially he had originally thought it best that any agreement should be between Britain and the United States on one side, and Egypt on the other, he now acknowledged that the Americans would not participate unless invited to do so by the Egyptians and that such a solution was unlikely.[96] Eden was able to tell the Cabinet on 7

July that Washington had come as far to meet the British requirements as could reasonably be expected: the provision of American economic aid to Egypt would be conditional on the Egyptian fulfilment of any agreement relating to the Canal Zone base, and the United States would also support publicly the principle of free transit through the Suez Canal. Churchill confessed that, despite his earlier doubts, he was now satisfied that the withdrawal of British troops from Egypt, together with an arrangement to 'reactivate' the Suez base in time of war, could be fully justified on military grounds. British requirements in the Canal Zone had been radically altered by Turkey's admission to NATO and the extension of a defensive Middle East front as far east as Pakistan (which was now taking American arms) whilst thermo-nuclear weapons had increased the vulnerability of a concentreated base area and it would not be right to continue to keep in Egypt 80,000 troops who would be better placed elsewhere. Churchill was supported by Alexander,[97] and the Prime Minister himself repeated these arguments against the Conservative 'Suez group' rebels in the House of Commons, in a stormy debate at the end of the month when twenty-seven Conservatives voted against the government.[98]

The Secretary of State for War, Antony Head, led the British delegation to Cairo to work out an agreement with the Egyptians along the lines agreed by the Cabinet. The terms of the agreement which was negotiated included: the maintenance of the base in peacetime by British and Egyptian civilian technicians (without military uniforms therefore); provision for placing the Suez base on a war footing if an attack took place on certain Arab states or Turkey; the withdrawal of British armed forces from Egypt within twenty months of the signature; confirmation of the 1888 convention on freedom of navigation in the Suez Canal (which of course still remained largely British-owned); and a seven-year term. The Egyptians had thus succeeded in defending their sovereignty, restricting the duration of the treaty and avoiding a commitment to any general Western defence organization. The new Minister of State, Anthony Nutting, finalized the arrangements early in October and the agreement was signed on the 19th of that month.[99] An improvement in Anglo-Egyptian relations then seemed apparent. Just before becoming Prime Minister Eden, in February 1955, met Nasser in Cairo. Six months later, in a note drafted but not sent to the new

British ambassador in Cairo, Sir Humphrey Trevelyan, Eden recalled this encounter: Nasser had taken his hands in his and assured him that a new chapter had opened in Anglo-Egyptian relations. Eden could rely on Egypt's friendship.

But relations with Egypt, following the conclusion of the Anglo-Egyptian treaty, proved to be a deep disappointment to Eden. In Eden's view Egypt, from the day of the signature of the agreement, never ceased to attack Britain and to oppose it on every conceivable issue. By October 1955 Eden suspected Nasser of anti-Western sentiment: there had been the arms deal with Russia; Britain would not supply arms to a country that described it as 'the enemy'. Eden then felt that Anglo-Egyptian relations had reached a crucial point. Russia had shown that it had intended to open a third front in the Cold War in the Middle East, and Britain faced by this threat had to defend its interests in the Middle East as energetically as it had in Europe and the Far East. The time had come for Egypt to declare itself: 'let him make a demonstrable effort to carry out the promises which he made to me, and he will not find me backward in coming to meet him half way'.[100] Ironically, Eden's approach had moved towards that of Churchill during his last premiership. Britain was on the road to Suez.

Throughout his peacetime administration Churchill dominated policy towards Egypt. He would not leave Eden to handle the matter alone. From the outset, however, the approach of the two men diverged radically on this subject. Churchill felt nothing but scorn for the Egyptians – they should be 'told' what to do – and so far as he was able, he kept control of British policy in this field. Eden's absences through illness or at conferences helped Churchill to play a decisive role and, when Eden was there, the Prime Minister fought against the policy of 'scuttle' being proposed by his Foreign Secretary. At the outset Eden wanted to involve the Americans, but the arrival of the Eisenhower administration made this difficult. Although Britain had responsibility for Western defence in the Middle East, Dulles soon concluded that it could not meet the obligation, and by July 1953 the National Security Council advocated 'greater independence and greater responsibility in the area by the United States vis-à-vis Britain'.[101] In January 1954 Sir Roger Makins, the British ambassador in Washington, mentioned 'a very understandable suspicion that the Americans are out to take our place in the Middle East'.[102] Furthermore, Eisenhower was not impressed with the idea of a fully-fledged English-speaking alliance. Churchill, like Neville Chamberlain and Ernest Bevin, saw this as crucial: the Prime Minister pointed to the importance of the Commonwealth's 80 million 'whites' in alliance with America's population, but it seemed that Eisenhower believed in treating Britain as one 'of a crowd'. Whereas Churchill was prepared to 'go it alone' on Egypt, Eden fought hard against this. The two men had a volatile relationship,[103] and at one point Churchill was apparently ready to accept Eden's resignation over the 'scuttle' policy.[104] By July 1954 it was Eden who was a little disenchanted with the United States and Churchill who wanted an Anglo-American agreement with Egypt, but in the end Eden's conciliatory policy prevailed, and Churchill finally gave way to the military arguments: ideas of a Middle East command or a Middle East Defence Organization based on the Canal Zone had little relevance with the development of the hydrogen bomb. Eden is often seen as Churchill's pupil, the man groomed as heir apparent. He acquired many of Churchill's habits including working from bed. Within a few months of becoming Prime Minister he had also acquired his master's view of Egyptians.

Notes

1. See R. Ovendale, *The English-Speaking Alliance: Britain, the United States, the Dominions and the Cold War, 1945–51* (1985), 118–42.
2. PRO, CAB 128/23, CC (51) 1.
3. PRO, PREM 11/92.
4. *Ibid.*
5. *Ibid.*
6. PREM 11/91.
7 *Ibid.*
8. E. Shuckburgh, *Descent to Suez: Diaries, 1951–6* (1986), 29.
9. See R. Ovendale, *The Origins of the Arab-Israel Wars* (1984), 137.
10. PREM 11/91.
11. *Ibid.*
12. *Ibid.*
13. *Ibid.*
14. CAB 128/24, CC (52) 18, 19.
15. PREM 11/91.
16. *Ibid.*
17. *Ibid.*
18. *Ibid.*

19. CAB 128/24, CC (52) 47.
20. PREM 11/392.
21. *Ibid.*
22. *Ibid.*
23. *Ibid.*
24. CAB 128/25, CC (52) 89.
25. CAB 128/25, CC (52) 91, 94, 101, 102, 107.
26. *FRUS, 1952–4*, IX (Washington, DC, 1986), 199–203.
27. *Ibid.*, 232–4.
28. *Ibid.*, 204–13.
29. See *ibid.*, 1931–4.
30. CAB 128/26, CC (53) 2.
31. PREM 11/392.
32. Shuckburgh, *Diaries*, 74–5; CAB 128/26, CC (53) 5.
33. CAB 128/26, CC (53) 9, 10.
34. CAB 128/26, CC (53) 12.
35. PREM 11/392.
36. *FRUS, 1952–4*, IX, 2020–1.
37. *Ibid.*, 2009–11; PREM 11/486.
38. PREM 11/486.
39. *Ibid.*
40. *Ibid.*
41. *Ibid.*
42. *Ibid.*
43. CAB 128/26, CC (53) 17.
44. CAB 128/26, CC (53) 20.
45. PREM 11/486.
46. *Ibid.*
47. *Ibid.*
48. *Ibid.*
49. *Ibid.*
50. PREM 11/392.
51. *Ibid.*
52. *Ibid.*
53. *Ibid.*
54. *Ibid.*
55. PREM 11/485.
56. *Ibid.*
57. *Ibid.*
58. *FRUS, 1952–4*, IX, 2061–2.
59. PREM 11/485.
60. *Ibid.*
61. *FRUS, 1952–4*, IX, 2065–9.
62. CAB 128/26, CC (53) 31.
63. PREM 11/485.
64. *FRUS, 1952–4*, IX, 379–80, 383–4.
65. PREM 11/485.
66. *Ibid.*

67. *Ibid.*
68. *Ibid.*
69. *Ibid.*
70. CAB 128/26, CC (53) 42.
71. CAB 128/26, CC (53) 43.
72. CAB 128/26, CC (53) 48.
73. CAB 128/26, CC (53) 51.
74. PREM 11/629.
75. CAB 128/26, CC (53) 72.
76. CAB 128/26, CC (53) 73.
77. PREM 11/484.
78. *Ibid.*
79. *Ibid.*
80. *Ibid.*
81. PREM 11/701.
82. *Ibid.*
83. *Ibid.*
84. Shuckburgh, *Diaries*, 137–9; A. Eden, *Full Circle* (1960), 257–9; S. Lloyd, *Suez, 1956* (1978), 14–23.
85. CAB 128/27, CC (54) 18.
86. CAB 128/27, CC (54) 21.
87. PREM 11/702.
88. CAB 128/27, CC (54) 29.
89. PREM 11/702.
90. Shuckburgh, *Diaries*, 203.
91. PREM 11/702.
92. *Ibid.*
93. N. J. Wheeler, 'British nuclear weapons and Anglo-American relations, 1945–54', *International Affairs*, 1986, 79.
94. CAB 128/27, CC (54) 37.
95. CAB 128/27, CC (54) 43.
96. PREM 11/702.
97. CAB 128/27, CC (54) 47.
98. Lord Moran, *Winston Churchill: The Struggle for Survival, 1940–65* (1968), 612–15.
99. CAB 128/27, CC (54) 63; PREM 11/702; Eden, *Full Circle*, 260–1.
100. PREM 11/859.
101. *FRUS, 1952–4*, IX, 394–8.
102. W. R. Louis, 'American anti-colonialism and the dissolution of the British Empire', *International Affairs*, 1985, 396.
103. See R. R. James, *Anthony Eden* (1986), *passim*.
104. Shuckburgh, *Diaries*, 75–6.

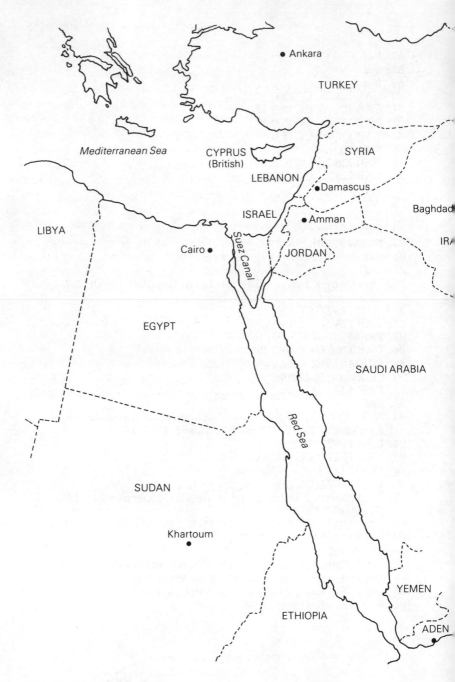

Map 1: The Middle East

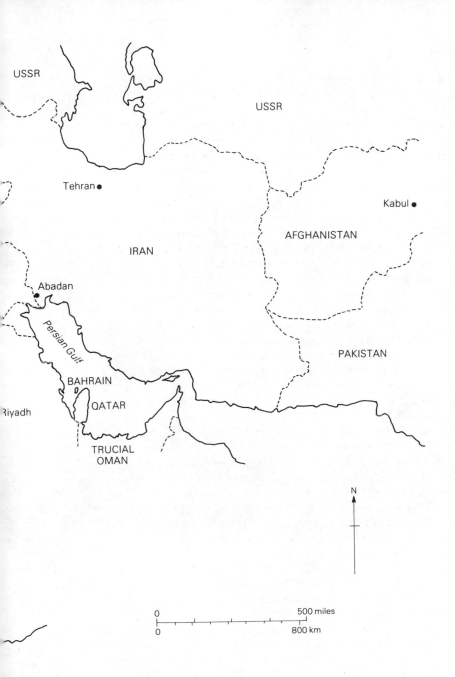

6   The 'Northern Tier' and the Baghdad Pact

Brian Holden Reid

The *imbroglio* surrounding the negotiation and failure of the Baghdad Pact has frequently been represented by British writers as an object lesson in how not to run alliance relations. In the memoirs of both Anthony Eden and Harold Macmillan a reluctant lesser ally, Great Britain, is represented as being encouraged to undertake extensive and expensive commitments in the Middle East in aid of the greater, the United States, and then, once these commitments had been made, the greater ally refusing to join the alignment created and offering reluctantly little more than moral encouragement. Indeed Eden in *Full Circle* adopted a tone of high indignation in criticizing the 'baffling' policy of the American Secretary of State, John Foster Dulles. He could not 'understand the prolonged coolness of American policy towards the Baghdad Pact in its most critical period, when the inspiration for the unity of the Northern Tier seemed to us to have been shared by Washington'. Eden put this alarming inconsistency down to 'sudden shifts' in American policy and the caprice of Dulles, a 'preacher in world politics' who frequently 'had little regard for the consequences of his words'; and Eden pointed out that the overriding lesson of the whole episode was that though it might be true that 'allies should subordinate their interests more closely to the opinions of their stronger partner . . . an alliance does not gather strength that way'.[1]

Eden's resentment at the unravelling of his handiwork was quite understandable as, at the time, the forging of the Baghdad Pact was considered a success for his patient and skilful diplomacy. In February 1955 Turkey and Iraq signed a mutual defence pact. Britain adhered to this on 4 April, Pakistan in July and Iran in September. There was every hope that other states friendly to the West, like Jordan, would also sign. Eden had demonstrated Britain's ability to construct a defensive alignment

– what the Americans called the 'Northern Tier' of Middle East states – willing to block Soviet expansionism towards the Persian Gulf. He had demonstrated that Britain was still a major power in the region and that, furthermore, a British rapprochement with Iran was possible after the nationalization of the Anglo-Iranian Oil Company in 1951. This chapter will assess the validity of these claims; explore the motives for Britain's adherence to the Baghdad Pact and her desire to organize a defensive pact in the region; and assess whether Eden's accusations of American inconsistency were justified. It will also examine the role of other Middle East states, not least Turkey, in the organization of the alliance system.

In considering the various motives why the British government sought to organize a defensive pact in this region, the attitude of Turkey was crucial. The Turkish government was anxious to show itself a loyal ally of Britain and the United States and sought an active role in halting Soviet expansionism. The Turks held that if the Middle Eastern states themselves showed a willingness to organize in their own defence, then the United States could be more easily persuaded to support them. Turkish initiatives were part of wider diplomatic aspirations to enlarge its role within Western spheres of influence, including membership of NATO and participation in the Korean War. An active foreign policy also helped divert attention from economic problems at home. In January 1955 the Turkish Prime Minister, Adnan Menderes, visited Baghdad with the intention of securing a bilateral defence agreement with the Iraqis. The attitude of Egypt, the leading Arab state, to this visit was hostile. The Turks were considered by Egypt as little more than American agents. The Turks were indeed agents of a kind, but of Britain rather than America; Menderes had made it abundantly clear to the British government that he understood the implications of the ending of Britain's 1930 treaty with Iraq, and the Turkish Secretary-General of Foreign Affairs had agreed that Turkey would work to create an agreement which would allow the United Kingdom to continue enjoying defence facilities in Iraq after the treaty lapsed in 1957. This was one major British reason for adhering to the Baghdad Pact which was to complicate relations with the United States. Britain wished to 'discreetly encourage' the pro-British regime of King Feisal in Iraq to join a defence grouping composed initially of Turkey, but joined later by other states. It was acknowledged that it was an 'important point for us . . . to provide without further delay an "umbrella" under which we can secure a satisfactory revision of the [Anglo-Iraqi] Treaty'. The 'umbrella' aspect was an important requirement because the defence facilities enjoyed by Britain – especially the RAF base at Habbaniya – would be gained not in her own right, as under the 1930 treaty, but under circumstances similar to those 'given to members of the North Atlantic Treaty Organization', of which Turkey had been a member since 1952. It was hoped that the Turks would convince the Iraqis that neighbouring countries could accept a Western military presence 'without any derogation of its national sovereignty and dignity'. They might also accept an assurance 'that the stationing of foreign troops in NATO countries . . . had not affected the independence of these countries' – and indeed that their independence had been strengthened because of an increase in their defensive strength. Eden noted in his memoirs that 'It was possible that the Pact could grow into a NATO for the Middle East . . . I was sure that the defence arrangements between ourselves and Iraq, which advantaged us both would be better placed in a wider agreement between equals.'

The British thus had two major motives for encouraging a Turkish-Iraqi agreement. First, certainly, they hoped to create a pro-Western grouping among the 'Northern Tier' states of the Middle East, bordering the Soviet Union. This would compensate in part for the earlier failure to create a 'Middle East Defence Organization' because of Egyptian opposition. But a more specific reason was to revise the Anglo-Iraqi treaty on a sounder footing than had been the case with the Anglo-Egyptian treaty (discussed elsewhere in this volume). Previously, in 1948, an attempt to renegotiate terms for the continuation of British bases in Iraq had been ruined by nationalist riots. The British were therefore keen to take advantage of the presence in power in Baghdad of the anglophile Nuri el-Said, victor of the September 1954 elections. Nuri was determined to make Iraq the leading Arab state with Western assistance (in contrast to Egypt's policy of radicalism and neutralism) and this made him particularly sympathetic to Menderes' ideas, based on co-operation with Britain and America, even though, historically, there were deep Iraqi suspicions of Turkey. Furthermore, given the temporary nature of so many Middle Eastern regimes, and the fluid and complex nature of the region's political scene, the British were keen to proceed *quickly*. As the British ambassador in Baghdad warned, 'if left much longer in suspense, [the proposed Pact] might turn rotten and simply become another of the many defunct projects of Middle East defence'. Unfortunately, however, as will be seen, by pushing matters to the proof so quickly the British also ensured that the Baghdad Pact did end as a failure.[2]

The discussions between Menderes and his Iraqi counterpart, Nuri, in January 1955, focused around four issues; staff conversations; free transit of troops and equipment through the ports and transport systems of both countries; the extension of these arrangements to 'other friendly powers'; and a duration of five years. In their meetings Nuri emphasized that he would not undertake commitments outside Iraq; also he expressed his disquiet that 'he still had the deepest suspicion of Turkish irredentism and would strongly oppose any arrangement involving Turkish troops entering northern Iraq'. However, the two premiers agreed to a treaty (signed the following month) following up the Iraqi-Turkish treaty of 1946, which would require the parties to co-operate in conformity with Article 51 of the United Nations Charter against outside aggression 'from any quarter, whether it comes from within the Middle East region or from outside'. The communiqué issued after the talks called for British and American support at the earliest opportunity.[3] The British government hurried to offer such support so that agreement in principle could be secured for 'the UK's participation in the new treaty and on some arrangement between the UK and Iraq for our continued enjoyment of defence facilities after the expiry of the 1930 Treaty'. Further staff talks were valuable as a means of 'convincing the Iraqis of our continuing [need] to enjoy such facilities and so prepare the way for an agreement . . . as Nuri is obviously not keen about them'. It is perhaps ironic in retrospect that, with such little confidence in their client, the British were assured by the Egyptian Prime Minister that Nuri was regarded throughout the Arab world as an 'Anglo-American stooge', and that any independent initiative such as the Baghdad Pact would postpone indefinitely any move towards Egyptian involvement with the West in defence matters. Nasser would not risk being tarred with the same brush. The Egyptians also warned that if other Arab states declined to be associated with Turkey and Iraq, the Northern Tier would lack substance, as 'the "linear" defence on the northern borders would be completely hollow'. This was a serious criticism. Evelyn Shuckburgh,

Under-Secretary for Middle Eastern Affairs, warned that any Middle East defence arrangement would fail without Egyptian support; Eden instructed that there should be less overt praise for the Turkish Prime Minister's visit to Baghdad in case it upset other Arab states.[4] Before going on to look at the completion and signature of the Turkish-Iraqi treaty in February, therefore, it is necessary to look at the wider range of considerations relating to it, particularly American, Iranian and Arab opinion. Taken together these factors both heightened British haste to see the treaty concluded, and fundamentally undermined the arrangement once it was made.

The American position on the Baghdad negotiations was perfectly consistent and clearly stated, contrary to the impression given in Eden's memoirs. Since the spring of 1953, following a tour of Middle Eastern and Asian states, the American Secretary of State, John Foster Dulles, had favoured building up co-operation in the area with such pro-Western regimes as Turkey and Pakistan, rather than Egypt and the Arab League. Though in January 1955 the Foreign Office detected that American thinking was not so positive as it had been, the factors on which American policy were based had not been modified substantially. The United States saw the Middle Eastern association developing along the lines of the 1954 Manila Pact, designed to defend South-East Asia, an agreement which only involved the Americans in the event of an act of aggression from outside. The Northern Tier was therefore aimed primarily at fighting the Cold War. Washington did not wish to see any further deterioration of relations with Egypt which would serve to weaken the defence potential of the region, but nevertheless did not think that further deterioration would be caused by the Turko-Iraqi Pact. In the event that the Arab League foundered, then the Northern Tier concept might provide an alternative 'centre of attraction' around which pro-Western Arab states might cluster. This was consistent with Eden's thinking at the time, when he minuted over Nuri's trip to Cairo in January 1955: 'I should not be bothered and did not mind whether Egypt left [the] Arab Collective Security Pact.'[5]

Although in January 1955 the Egyptians believed that it was the Americans, rather than the British, who had inspired the Turkish initiative, the Americans actually expressed a number of reservations about the Baghdad Pact from which they at no stage departed. Though offering 'strong support' for the Pact, they questioned the advisability of the United States joining it as an original signatory. After their experience with the ill-fated Middle East Defence Organization they concluded that they should avoid giving the impression (quite justified by Egyptian suspicions) that the Baghdad Pact had been imposed by the United States from the outside. All parties wanted a speedy signature – and here the State Department touched on a sensitive nerve – and the Americans reiterated that for them this was simply impossible. Indeed from the American angle, the problem was a far from urgent one. Her bilateral agreements with Pakistan and Turkey, combined with aid agreements with Iraq, Iran and Pakistan, 'prove US's interests in the area'. Dulles welcomed the Turko-Iraqi agreement at a press conference on 19 January 1955, but in private the United States continued to point out that it had no existing defence commitments to Iraq, and that if these were offered it would be further extending the scope of American obligations which would lead to all kinds of difficulties with Congress. It was also the case, moreover, that any agreement with an Arab state 'would be vigorously opposed by pro-Israeli opinion here'. If Turkey, Iraq and Britain signed initially, then 'the US would accede later'. These arguments continued to be ignored by the British and the nearer the presidential election of 1956 approached, the more inexplicable this attitude becomes. The main reason why the British chose to ignore the American position was of course that they realized that time was not on their side. The Turko-Iraqi agreement was considered a 'bird in the hand' which could lead to a favourable revision of the 1930 treaty; the alternative was an 'insidious Egyptian inspired' pause 'which would lose us what is possibly the last initiative of the ageing Nuri; discourage seriously the Turks and still offer us no real prospect of a satisfactory agreement through the Arab League'.[6]

A major outstanding problem which the Baghdad Pact seemed to help resolve was Iran. The dispute with Iran over the nationalization of the Anglo-Iranian Oil Company was a major confrontation with resurgent Middle Eastern nationalism which, after its experience with Palestine and Egypt, the Attlee government had been careful to avoid confronting directly. Since 1933 an agreement had been operated by which the Anglo-Iranian Oil Company (AIOC) had paid Iran royalties in proportion to the total amount of oil exported. Increasingly after 1945 this agreement was criticized, however, and a new agreement was reached in 1949 in which royalties were increased. But this did not prevent an increase in the number of voices calling for the nationalization of the AIOC. General Razmann, the Iranian Prime Minister, was assassinated for opposing them, and Dr Mossadeq succeeded as Prime Minister after a short interregnum. He introduced a nationalization law which was passed by the Iranian Parliament on 1 May 1951. Calls by the AIOC for arbitration to begin, as had been required by the 1933 agreement, were refused by the Iranian government. Despite some sabre-rattling, the British government referred the dispute to the International Court which initiated a prolonged legal wrangle. The most striking feature of the dispute was the intense American pressure not to use force. As F. S. Northedge observed, 'The licentious court of King Farouk did not commend him to puritanical America, whereas the hypochondriacal Mossadeq, highly visible on his sick bed on American television, seemed to symbolize yet another victim of British imperialism.' The Americans, who competed with the British for exploitation of the Middle East, were fearful that the use of force would trigger a communist coup. Attlee concluded in 1952: 'we could not afford to break with the United States on an issue of this kind'. Yet within three years Iran was pressing to accede to the Baghdad Pact and her government was pressing for closer co-operation with London; British relations with Iran had been transformed.[7]

How and why had this rapprochement been achieved? At an Anglo-American meeting held in Washington on 1 February 1952 the inevitability of an Iranian financial crisis was discussed. It was agreed that it was virtually certain that the left-wing Tudeh party would profit from the consequent confusion out of which 'would evolve a government either infiltrated with communists or dominated by communists'. It was feared that Mossadeq was 'soft on communism', that 'it was highly unlikely that he [Mossadeq] would do anything to check Communism in Persia'. This could only be checked by a strong, pro-Western government. Mossadeq had actually warned the State Department that Iranian financial resources would be exhausted by the middle of February 1952 but this warning was rightly considered an attempt to frighten the United States into offering Mossadeq assistance. The settlement of the outstanding oil dispute with Britain was the solution to the problem in both Britain and the United States' eyes. Once this problem was out of the way, the nationalist fervour which the dispute had aroused could be channelled away from attacking the British and directed preferably against the Tudeh, with its foreign contacts. The possibility existed that Mossadeq would turn to Moscow for financial assistance to force Britain to back down from its demands for compensation, but it was agreed that this was unlikely: Iran was traditionally suspicious of the Soviet Union, and an initiative by Mossadeq would only stir up anti-Soviet fears and add to his difficulties. It was agreed that a possible solution to the financial problem could be achieved through the International Bank which could also – importantly – provide the wherewithal for settlement of the compensation for the Anglo-Iranian Oil Company.[8]

Though they were agreed on the roots of instability in Iran, Britain and the United States disagreed as to how the problem should be solved. The Americans, fearful of a Communist coup in Iran or the spread of Soviet influence in the region, pressured Britain to make further concessions to settle the oil dispute. The British retorted that to do so would encourage nationalization of Western investments elsewhere; indeed they were quite content to demonstrate to the world the chaos that ensued after the nationalization of Anglo-Iranian Oil, 'and that it was unprofitable to follow Persia's example'. The State Department admitted that 'Mossadeq is not the man they would like to see Prime Minister of Persia. Nevertheless they feel that he will hold that office for some time to come and that they must accept him and do whatever is possible to encourage him to go along the right lines.' (These sentiments, as reported in London, now express a certain irony.) The British responded by claiming that Mossadeq was too much of an appeaser to stop the spread of communism. They agreed that Mossadeq would continue to survive – he was a nationalist symbol after all – but he would not resist communism. These views had little effect on Washington, however, and the Foreign Office was perplexed that whereas 'for strategic and for domestic reasons neither the United States Administration nor individual members of the State Department feel able to remain passive in the face of the risk of the spread of Communism', an American desire for action did not take the form of taking notice of British views.[9]

The Truman administration, with its forthright views on Iran, forced Britain to 'stand pat' over oil compensation. Britain tried to minimize these differences with the United States, acknowledging that Mossadeq would remain on the Iranian scene for many months at least and that the best course would be for Britain to work with the United States'in an attempt to keep him on the right lines'. Further developments, such as the success of the National Front over the Tudeh in the Tehran elections in 1953, supported the United States' view that progress could be made against possible communist penetration in Iran though the British remained sceptical that Mossadeq would take a hard line even if the communists tried to overthrow him. But the tactless way in which the Americans disregarded the British view is revealed in an entry in Evelyn Shuckburgh's diary when he was Eden's Private Secretary:

> We had a disagreeable couple of meetings with Acheson about Persia. He seemed to be quite out of sympathy with our position there . . . He seemed irritated by our experts . . . when they explained the damage which might be done to our interests . . . if we give the Persians a premium for having seized our installations. AE [Eden] was extremely calm and moderate but it certainly went very badly. Taking Acheson down the stairs afterwards, I said that we felt very depressed . . . He said 'You must learn to live in the world as it is', which I thought a very offensive remark, as it was no doubt meant to be.

These differences were accounted for by Shuckburgh's observation that 'For the United States the Cold War is paramount, whereas for the United Kingdom our economic strength is at the moment fundamental.' Regaining some semblance of economic strength by securing the maximum compensation from Iran was perhaps a more accurate way of putting it. Given its fear of the spread of communism, combined with a reluctance to move against Mossadeq, the State Department took the line that the oil dispute should be settled 'at any price'.[10]

At a meeting held at the Foreign Office on 14 February 1952, Paul Nitze declared that the only irrational element in Mossadeq 'was his anti-British attitude'. If an oil settlement could be attained which emphasized that it was the Iranian responsibility to make it work, the Americans were confident that Mossadeq would suppress the Tudeh. A. D. M. Ross of the Eastern Department observed 'that so much was incalculable in Persian politics. Forces which had remained dormant for a long time could . . . suddenly waken into action. It might be a mistake to give up all hopes of the Shah'; the Iranian economy was primitive, could sustain itself for long periods without strain and the standards of Western industrialized states should not be applied to it. At any rate, the Turkish government had already made an approach to Iran, and the American ambassador informed the Foreign Office 'that this had been quite favourably received, although the Persians had asked them that the Turkish Government should help them to obtain a satisfactory oil settlement'.[11]

The replacement of Truman and Acheson by the Eisenhower administration in January 1953 led to a greater degree of initial tolerance for the British viewpoint on the Iranian crisis. Iran was left to grapple with her financial difficulties and had refused to accept the jurisdiction of the International Court, whilst Britain was forced to let the crisis drift as the use of force had been ruled out. In May 1953 Mossadeq wrote to President Eisenhower asking for his support in removing British obstacles to the sale of Iranian oil. Eisenhower replied in a convoluted but not unambiguous style: 'I fully understand that the government of Iran must determine for itself which foreign and domestic policies are likely to be most advantageous . . . I am not trying to advise the Iranian government on its best interests. I am merely trying to explain why, in the circumstances, the government of the United States is not presently in a position to extend more aid to Iran or to purchase Iranian oil.' By the time this letter had been received in Tehran, however, a complete volte-face in American policy had occurred. Indeed, planning to mount a CIA coup, Operation 'Ajax' headed by Kim Roosevelt, had already reached an advanced stage. It had been decided that it was simply too great a risk to allow Mossadeq to remain in power. CIA money was used to bribe Iranian army officers to act against Mossadeq and ensure that a large crowd appeared in the streets of Tehran shouting support for the return to power of the Shah. In July Mossadeq dissolved Parliament and ruled by decree; Tudeh-inspired riots broke out and Eisenhower believed that Mossadeq was 'moving closer and closer to the Communists'. In August the Shah fled and the Soviet Union announced that it was beginning negotiations to provide Iran with financial aid, but a coup was finally launched on 22 August and was successful. Mossadeq was arrested by the Iranian army; the Shah returned to power; and a new oil deal was reached. Despite some support for Operation 'Ajax', the British lost their oil monopoly, only retaining 40 per cent of the total, Gulf Standard of New Jersey,

Texaco and Socony-Mobile also gained 40 per cent and the remaining shares went to Shell and the Compagnie Française des Petroles. Given American, and not British, intervention it was perhaps the best that could be hoped for.[12]

The British reaction to the overthrow of Mossadeq was prudent, concerned that 'we should avoid breaking the common front which we had at last succeeded in forming with the United States over Persia'. Therefore opposition should not be displayed to any American financial deal with Iran designed to secure stability. Lord Salisbury, standing in for both Churchill and Eden who were stricken with illness, urged a 'new look' on the proposals for an oil settlement to make them more attractive. Indeed the self-consciously cautious tone which indicated Britain's place on the sidelines of these events is revealed in a secret briefing Salisbury received before meeting the press:

> The word 'coup' is inexact as a description of the recent events. The initial attempt by the Shah to substitute Zahidi for Mossadeq was within his consitutional powers, although he was forced to have recourse to somewhat unorthodox methods. The events of 19 August were due to a spontaneous popular uprising in favour of the Shah ... We ... were surprised at the strength of Royalist feeling.

It was agreed that British aid could best come through a settlement of the outstanding oil issue. Dulles urged the resumption of negotiations with Iran on this matter to 'close the most dangerous gap in the line from Europe to South Asia'. Further, the United States required that the British government supported the Shah and would not seek to topple him; Churchill sent such an assurance to the State Department, but it was felt that there was no urgency to settle the oil question 'until a more or less definite Anglo-American line of approach has been decided upon'.[13] Neither Eden nor the British government could claim to have much credit for the isolation of Iran and the fall of Mossadeq. They helped in the intelligence operations but that is all: the CIA and US dollars were the most important factors. Eden was ill from April to October 1953 and completely absent from the scene. Churchill had a stroke in June 1953 and although by August he had started to make a recovery, he was protected by his staff. 'All this week', complained Evelyn Shuckburgh, 'we are trying to conduct foreign policy through the PM who is at Chartwell and always in the bath or asleep or too busy having dinner when we want urgent decisions.' As Mossadeq was overthrown on 19 August 1953 ('mysterious plottings in Persia', as Shuckburgh put it), it is significant that President Eisenhower donated $45 million on 26 August to rescue a bankrupt Iran, a sum of money that can be construed as providing the compensation that Britain demanded. Over the following months the main obstacle to solving the problems raised by what Shuckburgh called the 'horrors of Persian oil' was the Anglo-Iranian Oil Company. Shuckburgh's graphic diary entry is revealing:

> Hair raising comment by Dulles . . . about the iniquities of Sir W. Fraser and the A.I.O.C. If this consortium breaks down owing to his greed and folly, U.S.A. will leave us to stew in our juice, abandon co-operation with us throughout the Middle East etc. Everyone here [at Foreign Office] too is scandalized by Fraser, who seems to be quite unconcerned with the national interest and anxious to squeeze the utmost out of Persia for his already bloated company. A tough nut.

The eventual acceptance in October 1954 of £25 million compensation spread over ten years was the result of US pressure, and also the fear – that had dominated Britain's attitude throughout the crisis – that the United States would purchase Iranian oil regardless of the British claim that it was their property. This would do little to achieve that common front which Britain ought to secure with the United States in the Middle East.[14]

These developments also reveal that in Britain's calculations it was Turkey and not Iran that was considered to be the most important element in the founding of a pro-Western grouping in the Middle East. Though in March 1954 the rapprochement with Iran had been carried one stage further when Tehran expressed a wish to join the states of the Northern Tier, Britain was not over-enthusiastic. She wished to see Iran's economy recover first and was not impressed by the Iranian army. 'It would . . . be most wasteful to provide it with any significant quantity of modern heavy equipment.' American enthusiasm in this area was to be restrained, if possible, as the 'threat to Persia was from internal dissension, not external aggression'. Nevertheless a state visit by the Shah was arranged (during which he was disappointed to discover that he would not be staying at Buckingham Palace) and whilst in London he sought to trade adherence to Middle East alliances for arms. This approach was treated with caution:

> We want a regional defence pact which might be either the Turkish-Pakistani Pact plus Iraq and Persia or might include those from other Middle Eastern countries, but the last thing we want is some sort of Islamic Pact . . . It would prevent the original object of Middle East defence and become something with all the faults of the Arab League on an even larger scale.

The Turks themselves had already taken the initiative to merge a bilateral agreement with Pakistan, which they had made in April 1954, into a larger grouping. The Shah's approach really forced the British to declare their hand: whether they should pursue a policy which envisaged a defence arrangement covering the whole Middle East, or confine themselves to the American Northern Tier concept? The answer was, that given the intractability of the Egyptian problem and Egyptian opposition to a Middle East Defence Organization, the Northern Tier was preferable as a second best solution. In any case, the Turko-Pakistani Pact was not a very effective defence organization because its provisions only called for an exchange of information, mutual help in the provision of arms and 'joint studies' for meeting attacks against one or either party. There was no clause requiring either party to come to each other's support if attacked.[15]

Under these circumstances Iran was especially vulnerable, with a long land frontier with the Soviet Union, and would require the support of a mutual assistance clause in any treaty. The Shah envisaged Iran's association with the Baghdad Pact in two stages. The first was Iran's association with Pakistan and Iraq, her immediate neighbours; secondly, association with those other Arab states already aligned with Iraq, Iraq having membership of both groups and acting as a pivot. But the Shah's policy was a complex one which required working closely with Turkey, Iraq and possibly Afghanistan also. The Shah was perplexed by British lack of enthusiasm for building up the Iranian armed forces and could not understand why the United States instead provided Turkey with so much aid. He believed his own country to be of much greater strategic significance: 'Turkey merely protected the Eastern Mediterranean', the Shah averred, 'which Russia could reach by other means, whereas Persia stood between Russia and the Middle Eastern supply route, not to mention oil.' Iran would accede to any agreement, therefore, 'at a moment of her own choosing ... when she herself considers that she can be a stable and effective partner'.[16] In April 1955 President Bayar of Turkey visited Iran. The bed-ridden Turkish ambassador (who received visits from the Iranian Prime Minister, and not vice versa) had acquired a special position in Tehran, and the Turkish visit succeeded in persuading the Iranians to join the Baghdad Pact, a desire which was finally achieved in September. This process amply fulfilled the aims of British policy which also wished to see Iran associated in defence arrangements with her neighbours when she was strong enough: 'we leave the timing to her. It is not for us to judge whether Persian opinion is ready for such a step. The Secretary of State repeated this advice to the Shah when he was in London.' Turkey was once again therefore the all-important catalyst.[17]

It was all very well to draw non-Arab Islamic states, like Iran, Turkey and Pakistan, into a NATO-style defence arrangement. But of the Arab nations only Iraq ever became a member of the Baghdad Pact, and the fundamental reason for the Pact's later weakness must be sought in Arab, and particularly Egyptian, opposition to it. The strength of this opposition ought to have been clear to the British at the outset. It certainly affected the Iraqi position in the Baghdad talks in January, when Nuri tried to place limits on his commitments under a treaty with Turkey in an effort to avoid the impression that he was nothing more than a Western 'stooge'. Thus he was particularly keen to avoid a commitment to co-operate with Turkey in war, and on the key issue of British bases the original draft treaty put forward by Iraq did not even permit the continued use of defence facilities by Britain. Not surprisingly the British hoped that, in the final draft the 'Turkish Government will be able to bring [the] Iraqi Government to accept their text'. (The Turkish draft contained a commitment to wider defence co-operation to confront 'any armed aggression' in its two opening articles, where it spoke of setting up 'joint military plans and measures'.) Nuri's hopes of becoming the leading Arab statesman would, of course, come to nothing if he alienated other Middle Eastern states by precipitate action. In September 1954, on a visit to Cairo to meet fellow Arab leaders, he had vainly pressed for closer links to the West; he hoped that such links might be rewarded with American arms supplies. In fact such hopes were ill-founded. It was the declared policy of the Western powers (America, Britain and France) to maintain a balance of arms in the Middle East and forestall any Arab-Israeli arms race, so that the Arabs would get American arms only if they reached a peace settlement with Israel. Nuri was, therefore, clutching at straws – and doubly so since Nasser, in Egypt, had no intention of joining a pro-Western defence arrangement even if it did involve American arms supplies. In January 1955, with Nuri's undertakings to Menderes, the Egyptian leader became even more enraged with Iraqi pretensions to lead the Arabs into the Western camp. Nasser acted to isolate Nuri among the Arabs, and even threatened to break up the Arab League over Iraq's policy.[18]

Nasser's feelings towards the Turks at this time were scarcely less hostile. Turkey was clearly the catalyst, used by Britain (and, as the Egyptians believed, America) to bring about a Western defence arrangement. In fact the Foreign Office had decided some time before 'that the Turkish Government should take soundings about the possibility of [Iraqi] participation in a Middle East defence system and that if these soundings were successful further piecemeal approaches should be made'. The 'shock tactics' which Menderes employed, however, were increasingly resented in Cairo, from where the Turkish ambassador was actually expelled. Egypt's attitude was put down in the Foreign Office to 'pique at the prospect of losing the leadership of the Arab states'. There was doubtless an element of truth in this, but clearly Egypt's role was of vital significance, both for undermining Menderes' efforts and for instilling doubts in Nuri, and it was decided that Eden himself should discuss matters with the Egyptians, when he passed through the Middle East en route to a Manila Pact meeting.[19] Over dinner during his visit to Cairo in February 1955 Eden sought to placate Nasser. He deduced that Nasser was not 'entirely negative on the question of an ultimate settlement with Israel, though here he emphasised the importance of timing and a comprehensive settlement on which I personally agreed'. But Eden could not report any progress on the Baghdad Pact. Though Nasser made it plain 'that his interest and sympathy were with the West', he argued that the Turko-Iraqi Pact was badly timed 'and its unfortunate content, had seriously set back the development of effective collaboration with the West by the Arab states. We used every argument we could to persuade him at least to restrain his criticism and if the agreement was reasonable to cease his opposition.' But Eden argued in vain. 'I said that he should not treat this pact like a crime, to which he replied, laughing, "no but it is one".' Eden was correct in thinking 'that we had not made much impression' but, he reflected, 'I was impressed by Nasser who seemed forthright and friendly although not open to criticism on this Turko-Iraqi business. No doubt jealousy plays a part in this and a frustrated desire to lead the Arab world.'[20]

Eden was unwise to ignore the consequences of this hostility, for Egypt was increasingly to lead the Arab world; Iraq was increasingly isolated by her; and Turkey was, over the long run, no substitute. The short-sightedness of British policy was emphasized by the fact that in late 1954, in the wake of the Suez base agreement, Anglo-Egyptian relations had undergone a major improvement. Nasser may have rejected membership of any Western defence organization, he may have been sympathetic to the 'neutralist' movement among developing states (symbolized by the Bandung conference in April 1955), but he was not 'anti-Western', certainly not 'pro-Soviet'. The Baghdad talks, however, rekindled Egypt's grave suspicions about British aims in the Middle East and made Nasser determined to outbid Nuri for leadership of the Arabs – partly by toughening his stance against Israel, a move which (in contrast to British aims) could only cause greater tension in the Middle East. On 28 February indeed, four days after the Turkish–Iraqi treaty was signed, Egyptian and Israeli forces clashed at Gaza. The Egyptians were worsted. It hardly made Nasser better disposed to co-operate with the West. Instead, before the year was out, he had accepted the offer of arms from the Eastern bloc: British policy had thus helped in *precipitating* greater Soviet involvement in the Middle East, rather than preventing it.

Opposition to the Baghdad Pact in the Middle East went far beyond Egypt, however. Even if Nasser was never able to unite the Arabs under his leadership, the suspicions of Iraqi and Turkish ambitions in the region were sufficient to ensure that the hopes of Nuri and Menderes to draw other Arab states into the Pact were never fulfilled. Aside from any dislike of a pro-Western defence agreement, other Arab states did not look kindly on Nuri's ambitions for Iraqi predominance. Saudi Arabia was never likely to join closely in an agreement with Iraq because there was no love lost between the Saudi royal family and the Hashemites. Syria and Lebanon feared that one of the main objects of the Turkish–Iraqi treaty was to further Iraq's expansionist ambitions in the Fertile Crescent, threatening their own independence. Even the fellow-Hashemite monarchy in Jordan was reluctant to become too closely identified with Nuri for fear of being isolated alongside him, and because of Jordan's large Palestinian population. 'Shall we end up by annoying all these people?' queried Eden when these unpleasant factors became apparent. He was not far from guessing the truth.[21] Over the course of the year it became clear that Iraqi policy had achieved the opposite results to those Nuri had hoped for: in autumn Syria joined Egypt in taking arms from the Eastern bloc; in October Syria, Egypt and Saudi Arabia made bilateral defence agreements among themselves; and in December a British attempt to draw Jordan into the Baghdad Pact led to public demonstrations in Amman. And Turkish policy had a scarcely less negative effect on the Arabs than that of Iraq. Menderes' active policy reawakened fears that old Ottoman imperial claims might yet be revived. British officials were well aware that the Turks had to 'be careful of Arab opinion in carrying out the Pact ... There is a good deal of suspicion against Turkey in the Arab world, partly on account of her alleged designs to recover influence in the Middle East and partly because of her relations with Israel.' (On the latter point, Turkey sponsored Israel's application to the United Nations.) The primary reason for suspicion of Turkish territorial ambitions was the claim by Syria to Hatay (formerly the Sanjak of Alexandretta), which had been ceded by France to Turkey in 1939. Syria's claim was supported by all the Arabs. Even Nuri was deeply suspicious of Turkey on this point, fearing for Turkish claims to the province of Mosul. It was notable that the Baghdad pact agreements did not include any non-aggression clauses, and Nuri would not permit the stationing of Turkish troops in north-west Iraq, though the British thought the proposal 'makes good sense' militarily (and hoped to see South African forces drawn into the arrangement).[22]

Even Western powers were reluctant to associate with the Baghdad Pact. Apart from American reticence, the French proved critical of the new treaty. The French were historically suspicious of Britain's aims in the Middle East, and were keen to protect the independence of the former French mandates of Syria and Lebanon. The French argued that the Pact split the Arabs and forced the anti-Baghdad Pact Arabs to be even more hostile to Israel as an indication of the strength of their opposition.

'We must really try to get the French to stop messing everything up', wrote Evelyn Shuckburgh, and when France made representations against Turkish 'rough handling' of Syria, Eden observed, 'cheek'. Indeed Turkey went as far as to threaten that continued French opposition might result in a reconsideration of the previously benevolent Turkish attitude towards French colonial policy in North Africa. The Turks pointed out that 'French influence had been continuously used to encourage the Syrians to oppose the pact and align themselves with Egypt'. Though by March 1955 there were signs that the French position might change, and though Turkey did not object to eventual French accession, Paris was only likely to become more positive if Syria and Lebanon joined first.[23]

The Pact of Mutual Co-operation, finally signed by Iraq and Turkey on 24 February 1955, was to be the main axis along which the Baghdad Pact was maintained. A good deal of prevarication marked the signature of the treaty to the end. 'Indeed', observed the British ambassador in Ankara, 'it was never certain that the agreement would be signed, nor, if it were signed, what it would contain.' Nuri continued to be vague about the character of the agreement. ('Nuri is very diffuse – and it is always difficult to see precisely what he is getting at', was a typical complaint.) Menderes persuaded him to conclude a concrete agreement which answered the Turkish wish to see the British remain in Iraq. With regard to the updating of the 1930 treaty, British officials made clear that Menderes had 'always been remarkably receptive to any suggestions or proposals that ... [may] have had to [be] put before him or during the negotiations, and Her Majesty's Government are undoubtedly in his debt'. And it was eventually a bilateral agreement under Article 1 of the Turko–Iraqi Pact that permitted the 1930 treaty to be terminated and permitted Anglo-Iraqi military co-operation to continue. 'Nuri wants to do it in a hurry', wrote Evelyn Shuckburgh, 'and seems ready to give us the things we want. The idea of "joint training", which I think I cottoned on to ... is to be the basis of it.' Thus, at the same time that Britain adhered to the Baghdad pact on 4 April, an agreement was made with Iraq by which the RAF could continue to use bases in the country, though Iraqi sovereignty was nominally restored.[24]

The sense of haste on the part of the British and Turks was also clear to the end. Menderes 'considered the present moment critical'. He believed that Egypt 'was making a supreme effort to isolate Iraq, using every means including intimidation, bribery and falsehood, and Turkey, Britain and America together should do everything possible to frustrate it'. Anthony Eden minuted: 'I agree'. One of his officials, Sir Michael Wright, asserted 'that there has not for a long time been a political situation in Iraq so favourable to an agreement'. Nuri was calculated to be in a strong position with the Iraqi Parliament under his thumb. The all-important point so far as the British were concerned was that 'If we miss this occasion, we cannot expect it to recur.' Hence the note of ringing optimism that could be heard in the Foreign Office. Since 1953 'there has been a small perceptible movement . . . and the signing of the Iraqi-Turkish pact represents a significant staging-post in a journey westwards which will . . . end with a new defence arrangement with ourselves and perhaps the Americans and the active inclusion of Iraq . . . in the Western World'. The agreement was looked upon as a watershed: it was anticipated that the flow 'will henceforth be towards the interlocking of the Arab World with the Western World'. The Baghdad Pact would overcome Egyptian hostility and the preference in Cairo for 'an exclusive Arab defence organization to which Western powers would not be admitted, paying lip service to friendship with the West, but refusing to take the principal steps which should make that friendship a reality.'[25]

On Eden's accession to the premiership in April 1955, almost simultaneous with British accession to the Baghdad Pact, British policy towards the extension of the Pact was based on the following premises:

[That] we are not pressing these Governments [Syria, Lebanon and Jordan] to join the Turko–Iraqi Pact or any other pact. They are only concerned that these Governments should not commit themselves to exclusive groupings of another kind which underline and exacerbate the division of the Arab world, or limit their freedom of action for the future.

The indigenous character of the Pact should be maintained, but it was realized that there was no immediate prospect of any Arab state acceding: Syria, Egypt and Saudi Arabia 'were out of the question'. Jordan had given assurances that she would not join; and Lebanon preferred to remain neutral between the two blocs.[26] It was soon clear that the prospects for the Pact were not likely to improve much either, and that the British difficulties were largely of their own making. Anthony Eden's accusation that the United States, and the State Department in particular, did not enlighten the British government as to the difficulties it faced in acceding to the Baghdad Pact was exaggerated and unfair. Though the United States in general supported the British position in constructing a Northern Tier of pro-Western powers in the Middle East, it made clear the difficulties that it would encounter in joining this grouping as a presidential election in 1956 approached. The United States gave indirect support when it joined the military committee of the 'Central Treaty Organization' (as the Baghdad Pact became) in 1957, but the Pact was rendered virtually useless in July 1958, when Nuri and the Hashemite monarchy were overthrown in a bloody coup. Iraq, under new, radical and nationalist leaders, left the Pact in 1959 and it thus became exclusively non-Arab. For Britain the Pact was a convenient vehicle for renewing her use of defence facilities in Iraq, and it was largely created by an ambitious Turkish leader, Menderes, pressuring an equally ambitious (but also fearful) British client, Nuri. It was always excessively optimistic to believe that other Arab states would join the arrangement. The Pact was never likely to prosper because of a series of difficulties: Egyptian and Saudi hostility; French doubts; American reticence; suspicion of Iraqi ambitions; and fears that increased Turkish influence would lead Ankara to harass Syria. (When the Pact was extended, in July, to Pakistan – already a member of the Manila Pact and closely linked to America – it also succeeded in enraging Indian ill feeling.) Thus, in return for an agreement to maintain defence facilities in Iraq, which was itself dependent on the vagaries of Middle Eastern domestic politics, British encouragement of the Turkish-Iraqi treaty only helped to exacerbate tensions in the region in the year before the Suez crisis. Like many of the schemes laid after 1945, and founded on the belief that Britain remained a great power in the Middle East, the Baghdad Pact was akin to a house built on sand.[27]

Notes

1. A. Eden, *Full Circle* (1960), 64; H. Macmillan, *Tides of Fortune, 1945–55* (1969), 630–1.
2. PRO, FO 371/115484 and 110997; Eden, *Full Circle*, 219–20.

3. FO 371/115484.
4. *Ibid.*.
5. FO 371/115485, 115469 and 109998.
6. FO 371/115486.
7. F. S. Northedge, 'Britain and the Middle East', in R. Ovendale, ed., *The Foreign Policy of the British Labour Governments* (1984), 173–6.
8. FO 371/104662.
9. FO 371/109998.
10. E. Shuckburgh, *Descent to Suez: Diaries, 1951–6* (1986), 27.
11. FO 371/98608.
12. S. E. Ambrose, *Eisenhower: The President* (New York, 1984), 111–2, 129–30; D. Carlton, *Anthony Eden* (1981), 359.
13. FO 371/114577.
14. FO 371/114813; Shuckburgh, *Diaries*, 150, 235–6, 299. Britain originally demanded £30 million.
15. FO 371/109998.
16. *Ibid.*
17. FO 371/114816.
18. FO 371/115489.
19. FO 371/114816.
20. FO 371/115495.
21. FO 371/115486.
22. FO 371/115498 and 115499.
23. FO 371/115499; Shuckburgh, *Diaries*, 290.
24. FO 371/115492 and 115495; Shuckburgh, *Diaries*, 252.
25. FO 371/115486 and 115497.
26. FO 371/115500 and 115504.
27. I am most grateful to my research assistant, Raymond Cave, of Corpus Christi College, Cambridge for his hard work in seeking out the relevant documents for my use.

7 South Africa and the Simonstown Agreements

G. R. Berridge and J. E. Spence

The orthodox interpretation of the Anglo-South African Simons-town Agreements, signed in June 1955, is that the balance of advantage lay with Britain rather than South Africa.[1] According to this view, South Africa was compelled to make three major concessions in order to secure sovereignty over the Simonstown Naval Base: first, that Britain would retain the right to use the Base in both peace and war even if South Africa remained neutral; second, that South Africa would purchase naval capability worth £18 million from British shipyards in order to enhance its contribution to the defence of the sea lanes round the Cape and, incidentally, reduce the defence burden on Britain; and third, that South Africa would not subject the coloured workers on the Base to the rigours of apartheid laws applying elsewhere in the Union.

The orthodox view also emphasizes that the South Africans failed to achieve their objective of incorporation in a multilateral defence arrangement of the kind enjoyed by New Zealand, Australia and Canada via their membership of ANZUS and NATO respectively. To this extent, the Simonstown Agreements certainly were a second-best alternative to South Africa's grander strategic vision.[2] Nevertheless, they gave it 'a degree of quasi-formal association within the Western alliance'[3] by virtue of 'British acceptance of the view that Anglo-South African security in the Southern oceans was indivisible'.[4] This qualification of the traditional interpretation of Simonstown has been emphasized in earlier writings by the authors,[5] when analysis lacked the advantage of access to official documents describing the course of the negotiations. The account that follows makes use of this material in testing the validity of the standard view still further, with particular reference to the 'concessions' that

South Africa was allegedly compelled to make as the price of British signature.

The origins of the Simonstown Agreements must be sought in the closing years of the Attlee administration.[6] Far from pushing for republican status and isolation from the mainstream of international politics, South Africa's newly elected Nationalist rulers were enthusiastic proponents of an anti-communist NATO-style defence pact for Africa,[7] and were anxious to build up the Union Defence Force by arms purchases from Britain and – if possible – America. Although both the British Foreign Office and the government's military advisers were, for different reasons, sceptical about Pretoria's strategic pretensions – the Cape Route, for example, was not regarded as a major priority for the deployment of Western naval capability – they were strongly in favour of a South African contribution to the defence of the Middle East which, after Western Europe, appeared the most likely area for Soviet military intervention. The consequence was that British policy-makers aimed at tempting South Africa into a formal bilateral military commitment to the defence of the Middle East by promising arms (then in very short supply) and above all by holding out the prospect of eventual integration into a multilateral Western alliance.

It was during a visit to London in July 1949 by F. C. Erasmus, South Africa's Minister of Defence, that the British first emphasized the need for a South African contribution to Middle East defence. However, faced with prevarication by Erasmus and a need to offer some more precise inducement, A. V. Alexander, the Minister of Defence, suggested that the Union might welcome the transfer of the Royal Naval Base at Simonstown (with the proviso that Britain would have 'joint user' rights in time of war), an arrangement which in any case appealed to the Admiralty and the Ministry of Defence for reasons of economy. However, the proposal foundered: the Commonwealth Relations Office (CRO) objected that, if implemented, transfer would strengthen the Nationalist government in its political contest with General J. C. Smuts, the leader of the pro-Commonwealth United Party opposition. Nor would there be any guarantee that Dr Malan's successors would honour assurances about the future of the Base.

On his return to London in September 1950, however, Erasmus was sufficiently encouraged by Britain's attitude towards his own defence priorities that he gave the firm undertaking to Middle East defence to which London now attached even more importance. (The Korean War had just broken out and Britain had begun to support the idea of a 'Middle East Defence Organization', into which the South African contribution would be integrated.) Hitherto the details have remained secret, but the records indicate that South Africa – provided it could purchase military equipment from Britain – undertook to contribute the following capabilities to joint defence of the Middle East: '1 Amoured Division; 1 Fighter Group of 9 Squadrons; Personnel for 1 Air Transport Squadron; [and] Such Naval Forces as could be spared from their primary task of protecting South African waters'. Emmanuel Shinwell, now Minister of Defence, accepted this *quid pro quo* and agreed further that the two governments should jointly sponsor a conference on defence facilities in Africa to which other interested parties should be invited. This agreement had all the hallmarks of a genuine anti-Russian entente between the two governments with respect to Middle East defence, but two obstacles to its implementation soon appeared. The first related to the Union's reluctance to find the money for the expeditionary force (estimated at between £40 million and £50 million); the second concerned a request by Erasmus for transfer of the Simonstown Base to South African sovereignty. This provoked disagreement between the Admiralty and Patrick Gordon Walker, the Secretary of State for Commonwealth Relations, who was against any discussion of transfer, and it was eventually agreed that Britain should 'play it long'. Rather surprisingly, Erasmus raised no profound objection and the question of transfer was postponed.

In February 1951 Gordon Walker paid his first official visit to the Union, having previously stressed to his Cabinet colleagues the importance of good relations with South Africa, particularly because of the value of Simonstown in time of war and the significance of the Union's gold for the Sterling Area. However, he found the South Africans still unwilling to pay for the Middle East expeditionary force and still insisting on transfer of the Simonstown Base. In June/July 1951 further discussions took place, in London, but little progress was registered and a new difficulty arose when Erasmus made clear for the first time that his government was not prepared to give an unqualified promise of the availability of Simonstown to Britain in wartime. By now distracted by the imminence of their own general election and beginning to nourish the hope, forlorn as it turned out, that the United Party would soon supplant the Nationalists in office in the Union, the British continued to prevaricate on Simonstown. At this difficult stage the issue of the African Defence Facilities Conference (promised by Britain in September 1950) came to the fore. The British feared the South Africans would use the conference to raise contentious issues such as 'internal security', and, worse still, attempt to create an African Defence Pact linked to NATO by the back door. However, it was agreed that the talks should be confined to 'practical and technical questions' and the principal outcome of the conference, which was held in August 1951 in Nairobi, was agreement on the freest use of transportation and comunications in time of war. The South Africans returned home having failed to secure the establishment of any 'continuing organisation'. In effect, their delegation had been out-manoeuvred by the British, who had been content to sit back and witness the torpedoing of the Union's ambitions by other conferees: the French, Belgians and Portuguese.

Two months later the Attlee government gave way to the Conservatives, leaving many issues in Anglo-South African defence discussions unresolved. Yet it is clear that the protagonists had moved a long way towards establishing the main lines of the package deal which was struck in June 1955. The South Africans had already delivered their formal commitment to Middle East defence, while the British had already delivered Nairobi. But the Nationalists were not yet prepared to compromise their neutrality in any agreement over Simonstown; nor, in regard to the Middle East, were they yet prepared to put their money behind their rhetoric. As for the British, they remained anxious about the political – as opposed to the strategic – implications of surrendering sovereignty over Simonstown, and were less than keen to provide scarce armaments to a drastically politicized Union Defence Force whose masters they did not yet trust.

When the Conservatives entered office in October they found the South Africans initially no more keen to spend sufficient money on equipment for the expeditionary force to the Middle East than they had been under Labour. The Minister of Finance, N. C. Havenga, was now personally convinced that the Russians had no intention of precipitating war,[8] while the new Chief of the General Staff, General C. L. De Wet Du Toit –

regarded by the British as uncompromisingly obtuse – had convinced himself that if war did come 'equipment would be provided at once out of the hat for the Union's Expeditionary Force
. . . and that the finance for the transaction would be settled on
some completely new basis'.[9] In consequence, there was now a
real danger that no provision would be made for it in the budget
for 1952–3 either. By December, however, there had been a
considerable shift in South Africa's attitude, which may well
have been prompted in part by strong domestic criticism over
the state of the Union's defence forces and the approach of a
general election. Erasmus and Havenga not only agreed that
earlier estimates of the expenditure required for new military
equipment were too low but accepted that payment would have
to be made in the normal way as deliveries came forward.
Furthermore, they agreed to establish a fund to cover the expenditure into which would be paid almost £3 million of un-
spent moneys voted for defence in 1951–2, £5 million in 1952–3
and yet larger sums in later years, depending on requirements.[10]

Encouraged by this development, and influenced by 'general
considerations' which argued for the preservation of good
relations between Britain and South Africa, officials in the CRO
submitted a paper to the new minister, Lord Ismay, which
showed that their thinking had moved decisively towards the
South African position on the transfer of the Simonstown Naval
Base. Britain, said this paper, could not in the present climate
sustain its case for unqualified user rights at the Base. This was
inconsistent with the position relative to bases in Canada and
Australia, and had been specifically rejected by Britain itself in
negotiating American rights at air bases in the United Kingdom.
In any case, it added, even if the existing user rights could be
retained by Britain, 'it would probably be impracticable to make
efficient use of Simonstown' in a war in which South Africa did
not side with Britain, since, unlike Gibraltar for example, the
Base was highly dependent on its hinterland, not least for its
landward defence. Finally, since the Union had publicly declared
its co-belligerency with Britain in the event of a war against the
Soviet Union, the Base was in practice likely to be available to
the United Kingdom when needed.

The CRO paper therefore recommended that discussions with
the Union should be reopened. Britain should accept the principle of transfer of the Base to Union control on the basis of the
qualified user rights already promised, provided that the South

African Navy (SANF) could be transformed into 'an efficient naval organisation' – the 'practical issue of major importance' – and that the process of transfer 'would be a lengthy one'. Britain should also agree to an early public statement on these lines, including – if absolutely necessary – reference to Britain's qualified user rights.[11]

Ismay endorsed the CRO paper, and on 2 January 1952 Sir Percival Liesching, Permanent Under-Secretary at the CRO, informed Sir John Le Rougetel, Britain's new High Commissioner in the Union, that they hoped that 'firm decisions should be reached as soon as possible after the Prime Minister's return from America'.[12] However, on 12 March the CRO paper was rejected by the Defence Committee. This decision was taken against the background of a mounting political crisis in South Africa and was prompted by the Conservative government's desire to avoid giving any encouragement to the Nationalist government at the expense of its English-speaking rivals. In this Churchill played a decisive role, arguing that Simonstown was 'an essential link in Imperial communications' to which 'there was no obvious alternative', and that it was not necessary to reopen the question of Simonstown as the Union was not pressing for an answer. If the South Africans did insist on raising it again, he said, then he would resist on the basis of Britain's legal rights any proposal for transfer without 'an unqualified assurance that facilities would be available to us in both peace and war'.[13]

Between March 1952 and early 1954 there was little movement in Anglo-South Arican defence relations. On the military equipment side, Britain's optimism of December 1951 proved to have been misplaced. A year later Havenga and Du Toit, having been convinced that the risk of war had receded, believed that if Britain was slowing down the pace of its rearmament then there was no reason why South Africa should not do the same. This conclusion was reinforced by the Union's current shortage of overseas capital for major civil projects to which it was committed and its consequent need for rigid economy in public expenditure – including the defence vote – if these projects were to be financed from revenue without major increases in taxation in a general election year.[14] The upshot of this was that on 2 January 1953 Erasmus asked the British government to slow down deliveries of arms already ordered by the Union.[15] In London this South African announcement was received with disappointment, though it was not felt that any strong objection could be lodged since the Union was ahead of both Australia and New Zealand in the placing of orders for British arms.[16] By the end of April agreement was reached on the slowing down of deliveries,[17] but not even the new schedule was met by the South Africans. A substantial order had been placed for Centurion tanks and these were being delivered but – partly because Eric Louw, as Minister of Commerce and Industries, was resisting arms expenditure as well[18] and partly because American firms were now actively canvassing for arms orders in the Union – by March 1954 the CRO was complaining that the South Africans had not spent anything like the amount which had been agreed, especially in regard to army trucks and fighter aircraft.[19] The latter failing was regarded as particularly serious because the Union had undertaken to have a fighter wing in readiness for the Middle East by the end of 1953.[20]

As for Simonstown, with Churchill's hostility to its transfer unabated, and the South Africans preoccupied with internal politics (including a general election in 1953), the whole issue remained dormant until early in 1954. The Admiralty, it is true, risked reopening it in 1953 when, forced to suggest cuts in the first round of the 'Radical Review of Defence Expenditure', it once more proposed that Simonstown, together with the facilities at Trincomalee and Colombo, be closed down.[21] However, this had provoked an explosion from the new Commonwealth Secretary, Lord Swinton. Swinton, an elder statesman of the Tory Party, had a deep and unashamed affection for the 'old' Commonwealth. According to one of his senior officials at the CRO, Joe Garner, he also had 'great prestige with the public and carried weight in the Cabinet'[22] Swinton thought that it would be a tragedy to hand over Simonstown to someone as anti-British as Du Toit, especially since Malan himself was 'sound' on the Commonwealth defence relationship and there was currently no fuss over the Base.[23] Not to be outdone, Churchill remarked to Swinton that he was 'amazed' at the Admiralty suggestion, adding that 'it would be more reasonable to shut down Portsmouth'.[24] Shortly afterwards, the Prime Minister minuted to Swinton: 'I entirely agree with you. The savings from massacring these two vital fuelling stations would only be half a million a year. With the Suez Canal almost certain to be blocked in war, it would hardly be possible to make two worse suggestions. It would be interesting to ask the Admiralty how much more their staff costs now than it did before the war. I am sure it would be possible to save half a million on them.'[25] Not surprisingly, the Defence Committee rejected the proposal and nothing more was heard of it.

However, at the beginning of 1954 Erasmus let it be known that he would like to be invited to London for defence discussions. He had not, he indicated, visited Britain since 1951 and was unacquainted with present ministers; moreover, he wanted to make sure that he was up to date on current strategic thinking about the Middle East. He also wanted to resume negotiations on Simonstown.[26] In London it was soon concluded that Erasmus should be welcomed. Such a visit would enable Britain to put pressure on him to rescue South Africa's forces from their present 'deplorable state' (not least by equipping them properly), to send an air force squadron to the Middle East in *peacetime* following the ending of its commitment in Korea, and accept the sensitive demand of the Royal Navy that the SANF should be placed under its command in war. The prospect of further discussions on Simonstown should also forestall the possibility that the Nationalists would raise an embarrassing public fuss about this question (as they had recently done over British-controlled Bechuanaland, Basutoland and Swaziland – the 'High Commission Territories'), and would help to compensate for the very negative line which the Commonwealth Secretary had felt it necessary to take towards the Union over this last issue.[27] There were also encouraging hints that there was more sympathy in the South African government for the British point of view on the availability of Simonstown in war – at least amongst service personnel and officials – than there had been in 1951.[28]

This last point was of some importance because during the 'Radical Review' in 1953 Swinton had shown himself to be almost as old-fashioned on Simonstown as Churchill, while opinion in the Admiralty had also hardened against the terms on which the CRO had finally been prepared to settle in 1951–2. The Admiralty certainly remained in favour of transfer of the Base, the more so since the Navy was now being threatened with a further round of severe economies,[29] but it was now more inclined to insist once more on an unqualified user guarantee. This was partly because it recognized the depth of Churchill's feeling on this question, partly because it seemed as if the South Africans themselves were moving towards acceptance of it, and partly because it now felt that while an unqualified legal right to use Simonstown in war might be of little practical significance in the face of determined South African neutrality, the existence of such a right would give Britain a 'moral' advantage urging the Union to make any such neutrality benign.

The stiffening of Admiralty resistance, however, was also a result of a change in the general strategic climate. First, the Naval Staff had concluded in 1953 that more importance should be attached to the Cape Route in war, especially a war against Soviet Russia, now that a 'broken-backed' stage of conflict following an indecisive nuclear exchange was foreseen; and that, although it remained likely that the ships on the South Atlantic station would be withdrawn at the start of war, Simonstown, with its important communications facilities, would be the most appropriate location from which to control ocean convoys and shipping in the South Atlantic and South Indian Oceans.[30] Secondly, the feeling had developed that the advent of thermonuclear weapons had increased the vulnerability of bases in the United Kingdom itself and thus 'greatly' increased the importance of 'all our overseas bases'.[31] And thirdly, the 'latest Chiefs of Staff thinking' laid 'more stress on preparations for cold war and on the maintenance of our position as a World power than on hot war', which implied 'a greater emphasis on the importance of Simonstown in peacetime'.[32] Churchill accepted the view that Erasmus should be invited and it was agreed that he would arrive in London in mid-August. However, if it were to contemplate transfer of the Simonstown Base, London would not only require of him an unqualified user assurance, but also satisfactory guarantees concerning its efficient maintenance, and adequate safeguards for the future of its coloured workers.[33]

Erasmus, to the subsequent surprise of the British, had arrived at the conclusion that the wording of the guarantee to Britain concerning user rights at Simonstown was of secondary importance 'because of the friendship between the two countries and the knowledge that they would be together in any foreseeable war'.[34] As a result, he arrived in London prepared – with the full authority of the Nationalist Cabinet – to give Britain and its allies the *unqualified* assurance about their right to use the Base in war as well as in peace, the withholding of which had been a major stumbling block in 1951. He was thus hopeful that he would be able to return to South Africa with a decision in principle to transfer the Base to Union sovereignty, his major aim.[35] Unfortunately for the South African defence minister, however, Churchill remained extremely loathe to oblige him, the more so in consequence of the recently negotiated surrender of the Suez Canal Zone base and the hostile Tory backbench reaction to it. Even as the negotiations were about to begin, the Prime Minister had minuted to the interested departments that 'To weaken our rights over Simonstown as settled in Treaty by me and Smuts in 1921 and in 1930 is a very serious step. To do so at the same time as we are giving up the Suez Canal in fact is cutting off the remaining link between Britain and Australia and New Zealand.'[36]

In Cabinet on 27 August Churchill reiterated his doubts, claiming that Simonstown had 'always been of first-rate strategic importance' and that 'its value appeared to be even greater now in the light of the reduced importance of the Suez Canal and the greater uncertainty about the degree of co-operation in defence matters which was to be expected of the South African Government in the future'. Therefore, announced the Prime Minister, in the face of only mild qualifications from Swinton and the Minister of Defence, Alexander, 'before any encouragement was given to him [Erasmus] to think that the United Kingdom Government might be ready to re-open the question of transfer, the matter must be brought again before the Cabinet. World conditions', Churchill concluded, 'had substantially changed even since 1951, and it was by no means certain that conditions for transfer of the base which had been considered sufficient at the time would prove on examination to meet adequately the conditions of to-day.'[37]

On the eve of the formal negotiations, during an 'informal' discussion without officials, requested by Erasmus, the Union defence minister gave Swinton and Alexander all of the assurances which had been set by London as conditions for handing over Simonstown (with the exception of that pertaining to coloured workmen, which does not appear to have been raised), together with a reaffirmation of the military commitment to the Middle East.[38] As a result, the issue was immediately returned to Cabinet, where Alexander proposed that, in the light of this advance, 'they should, while avoiding any commitment, try to obtain a clear picture of what he had in mind about the future of the base; and he would then bring the matter again before the Cabinet'. Alexander was supported strongly by Swinton, who presented the case for relinquishing sovereignty, but once more Churchill dug in his heels, observing that 'he was reluctant to contemplate any transaction which would be presented as yet another surrender of the rights and responsibilities of the United Kingdom'. Nevertheless, the Prime Minister at least agreed to Alexander's guarded proposal,[39] and over the next few days more detailed negotiations took place in which some progress was made. The Admiralty, however, was less enthusiastic about the results of these discussions than the Minister of Defence, remaining anxious that Erasmus's assurances were too vague.[40]

In any event, the issue of Simonstown was brought back to Cabinet for a third time, on 8 September, in what Alexander and Swinton clearly saw as a war of attrition on Churchill's position. Alexander, whose statement was endorsed later in the meeting without qualification by the Parliamentary and Financial Secretary, Admiralty, began the discussion by outlining all of the points on which the South Africans had met British anxieties, in particular on the guarantee of unqualified user rights in peace and war, on the position of the Commander-in-Chief, South Atlantic (who would be permitted to fly his flag over a new headquarters in the Cape Peninsula), on the position of coloured workers at the Base, and on the secondment to the SANF of Royal Navy officers in order to maintain the efficiency of the Base until the South Africans could cope on their own. Having omitted mention of any points of remaining disagreement with Erasmus, Alexander next told the Cabinet that the Union had also once more confirmed its commitment to Middle East defence, and he concluded by observing that 'The fullest possible co-operation of the South African Government in all these matters was of great importance and a comprehensive agreement in which the transfer of Simonstown would take its due place might be greatly to our advantage.'

Following this, the Commonwealth Secretary added that South Africa once more seemed keen to promote a regional pact in Africa and that 'Such a development might not be unwelcome to us as representing a move by South Africa away from neutrality.' And he threw in a new point, namely, that 'he had now received legal advice to the effect that it was by no means certain that, in a future war in which South Africa remained neutral, we should, in fact, be able to rely on the 1921 Treaty to ensure our continued use of the facilities of the Base'. Nevertheless, conscious of Churchill's hostility, Swinton hastened to indicate that at this stage he was not suggesting that any decision should be taken 'even in principle' about the future of Simonstown. Instead, he merely sought authority 'to bring the current discussions with Mr Erasmus to a conclusion on the general basis that they had achieved substantial progress towards agreement between ourselves and South Africa on defence matters but that much further work and discussion would be required before any final agreements could be reached'.

Since Churchill had been personally responsible for negotiating the 1921 treaty, it was not a good idea of Swinton's to suggest that it would be worthless in the event of South African neutrality in a future war. At any rate, in his reply Churchill immediately latched on to this, simply asserting that it was an argument which he 'could not regard as valid'. However, with no vocal support in Cabinet at all on the general question,[41] and clearly aware that he was losing the argument, the Prime Minister retreated to the core of his position. 'He recognised', record the Cabinet minutes, 'that the significance of Simonstown was largely symbolical; but he would find it hard to reconcile himself to its surrender, which would dishearten those elements in South Africa who remained steadfast in their loyalty to this country and were sadly in need of encouragement at the present time.' Consequently, this Cabinet discussion concluded by authorizing Alexander and Swinton to proceed with Erasmus along the cautious lines suggested by the Commonwealth Secretary.[42]

Following this Cabinet, Swinton and Alexander had to tell Erasmus when they met him for a concluding discussion on 10 September that they could make no commitment even in principle to the transfer of Simonstown. Turning upside down the emphasis of the report which they had made to the Cabinet on the course of the detailed discussions, they both stated that though progress had indeed been made, many practical difficulties remained and that no plan for transfer had been produced which they could recommend to their colleagues. Erasmus expressed extreme disappointment at this announcement, remarking that his government 'would take a very poor view of it', especially since it had backed down completely on the question of availability of Simonstown to Britain in war. Nevertheless, he saw no alternative to accepting the only gesture that Swinton and Alexander could make to him: that 'a joint committee on the spot [that is, in South Africa] was the best way of advancing the matter'. However, he made it plain that if the joint committee produced 'a workable and acceptable plan' for the transfer of Simonstown to the Union which was then rejected by the United Kingdom government, South Africa would resort to public attack.[43] This threat was taken seriously by the British ministers, who reported in a Cabinet memorandum of 15 September that any such rejection 'would jeopardise the whole range of South African cooperation with us'.[44]

Erasmus had also raised once more during these discussions the old Nationalist idea of an African Pact, or African Defence Organization, though now he emphasized that what the Union was thinking of was 'the security of the hinterland of the Union, i.e. Africa south of the Sahara'. This obliged Swinton and Alexander to reiterate London's belief that the defence of Africa lay well to the north, and they agreed to look at his plan only on condition that it was 'complementary to sound arrangements in the Middle East'.[45] As for South Africa's commitment to this region (following the major strategic reappraisal occasioned by development of the hydrogen bomb, the defence of the Middle East was now to be made in the Zagros Mountains in western Iran rather than in Egypt),[46] the gap between what Britain wanted the Union to do here to make this a reality and what Pretoria was prepared to do seems to have remained as large as ever after the conclusion of these talks.

Conscious of the need to proceed urgently in order to reduce Erasmus's disappointment, terms of reference for the Admiralty mission were swiftly worked out,[47] and approved by Churchill himself on 15 September. Swinton also drew up a Cabinet paper in which he presented the case for a comprehensive defence agreement with the Union, concluding that 'a settlement with the South Africans, apart from immensely improving our position in the defence field, would be of definite value in promoting the improvement of our general political relations with the Malan Administration. On this', he added, 'we must not forget that our industrial future may be bound up with our ability to obtain South African uranium.'[48]

In mid-October the Admiralty mission left for South Africa. On arrival it found that Commodore H. H. Biermann, head of the SANF, proposed to move his staff and all of his existing ships (two destroyers, two frigates and two minesweepers) to Simonstown and also base there new vessels acquired under a major programme of naval expansion which would be complete by 1958: six additional frigates and eight coastal minesweepers.

The mission was sceptical that the Union had either the men or the money to carry out this expansion programme but had no alternative but to base its planning with the Union's experts on the assumption that it would. In a little over three weeks the Joint Working Party produced its report. This, claimed C. G. Jarrett, the senior Admiralty official who led the British side, contained 'a plan capable of achieving the objects set and "practical" in the sense that it should work without a disastrous decline in efficiency given willing and honest performance of the various undertakings proposed for acceptance by the Governments concerned'. There remained small disagreements but the South Africans had made the major concession sought by Swinton: they would place the SANF under the command of the Commander-in-Chief, South Atlantic, in time of war. When Jarrett commended the report to the Admiralty on his return, however, he added two important caveats: first, the question mark which hung over the SANF's capacity to run Simonstown after transfer; and secondly, and more particularly, the question mark which hung over the good faith of the Nationalists: 'All that the Admiralty delegation can say is that they are unable to exclude the risk that the present enthusiasm of the Union Government would wane once they had secured possession of the base, a prize of great value to them for internal political reasons, but one which may mean little to them for its own sake.'[49]

Having moved quickly with the Admiralty mission, London was content to allow the South Africans to make the next move. This they duly did on 17 December, when their High Commissioner in London, Gerhardt Jooste, indicated that they would like to resume negotiations 'on the basis of the tentative proposals contained in the report' and that Erasmus was prepared to return to London for this purpose.[50] If Britain was to accept resumed negotiations on the basis of the report, it was clear that it would be indicating a willingness to settle, and on the suggestion of Harold Macmillan, who had recently become Minister of Defence, it was agreed that Churchill's approval should be sought before a reply was dispatched. 'If there is going to be a mild explosion over this', he said, 'it is better to have it over now.'[51] On 23 December, in a minute formally supported by both Macmillan and J. P. L. Thomas, the First Lord, Swinton therefore put to the Prime Minister the case for further talks at the ministerial level with the South Africans, albeit not until after the Commonwealth Prime Ministers' Conference in early February. Were a settlement to be reached along the lines recommended in the Joint Working Party Report, Swinton emphasized to Churchill, 'It would not be a question of getting out of Simonstown, but of sharing it with an enlarged South African Navy.'[52]

Churchill accepted this powerful démarche and the South Africans were invited to return to London. However, shortly after this the Admiralty began to get cold feet over the row which the proposed deal with the South Africans would be likely to precipitate in the House of Commons. 'So far as the Conservative Party is concerned', Thomas told Macmillan, 'it is likely to be a repetition of the row on Egypt but on this occasion we shall also have the Socialist Party against us on the grounds that we should have no truck with the present South African regime and its native policy.' Such an alliance 'would be dangerous if it came to a vote', and such an eventuality, the First Lord added, should be avoided in a year which was likely to see a general election.[53] Macmillan and Swinton – and their officials – were not quite as nervous as Thomas but were by no means complacent about domestic political problems. As a result, on 4 March Swinton put it to Jooste that the signature and publication of any agreement – though *not* its negotiation – should be postponed until after the general election, which, he informed the High Commissioner, he was 'practically certain' would take place 'sometime this year'. Jooste readily agreed that it was not in South Africa's interests to jeopardize the electoral fortunes of the Conservative government[54] –a point subsequently confirmed by the new Union leader, J. G. Strijdom.[55] If Swinton, Macmillan and Thomas were concerned to minimize domestic political problems by getting their timing right, they were also alive to the importance in this respect of the *presentation* of any agreement with the South Africans to the House of Commons. Hence both in the negotiations themselves and in the publicity attending the signature of any agreement the transfer of Simonstown would have to be *linked* to all of the other issues on the agenda of Anglo-South African defence talks – in particular, Middle East defence – as part of 'a package deal'.[56]

In the event the procedure suggested by Swinton was never needed. In April 1955 Churchill resigned and Anthony Eden, who had at last replaced him as Prime Minister, called the general election for May. It was thus agreed that Erasmus should come to Britain in June. Eden also made some changes in the Cabinet which would affect the side fielded against Erasmus. Harold Macmillan took over from Eden at the Foreign Office and was replaced at Defence by Selwyn Lloyd, while Swinton had been retired from the CRO and succeeded by the diffident but quietly determined Earl of Home.[57] In May the government was returned with an enlarged majority and its earlier anxieties about the domestic repercussions of the emerging deal with the South Africans were thus much reduced.

In extending its invitation to Erasmus, the CRO had made clear that he would be expected to discuss South Africa's contribution to the Middle East, though not without some apprehensions since fresh grievances had been added to the financial and other reasons which ever since 1951 had prevented the Union from putting flesh on its commitment. Not only had Australia and New Zealand's undertakings to the area been switched to South-East Asia but Britain's own commitment had been drastically scaled down; moreover, London had been slow in informing the South Africans of these changes.[58] Nor was London encouraged by reports coming from its defence representatives in Pretoria on the current state of strategic thinking in the Union Defence Ministry, where Du Toit was now making no secret of his belief that, in view of British weakness, the dispatch of a Union Expeditionary Force to the Middle East in the event of a Soviet assault would be not only to invite its destruction but to leave the Union defenceless against a communist-inspired native rising.[59] And Liesching, in reference to recent statements by Erasmus on the fading of the Middle East Defence Organisation plan, told the CRO on the eve of the London negotiations that 'At the present time Mr Erasmus certainly regards the Middle East commitment, if not as having lapsed, at any rate as being in a state of suspense.' (He added that the condition of the South African forces was so deplorable that it was a moot point as to whether any South African commitment to the Middle East was worth having anyway.)[60]

Of course, London was well aware that the return of Simonstown was going to be the focus of the negotiations for Erasmus, who, finding himself in a weakened position in the new Cabinet of J. G. Strijdom (Malan had retired in December 1954), badly needed the fillip to his prestige which this would provide.[61] As a result, much of the disussion in London preparatory to the negotiations centred on whether or not handing over the

Simonstown Base should be 'linked' to a fresh Union commitment to the defence of the Middle East. Such a commitment,
said the Chiefs of Staff, was now of more importance than ever
in view of the shortage of land and air forces to hold the anticipated Russian advance along the line of the Zagros Mountains
and would need to provide for 'a contribution by South Africa to
arrive within at most a few days of D-day', in contrast to the
leisurely programme written into the 1950 agreement. This contribution, the Chiefs of Staff indicated, should be a minimum of
one armoured brigade and a wing of three fighter squadrons, to
be followed by the remainder of the armoured division and two
more fighter wings as soon as possible. The South Africans
would also need to undertake a major re-equipment and training programme, which should include peacetime exercises in
the Middle East itself.[62]

The Admiralty, however, was strongly opposed to the linkage
proposal, holding that the nearly completed Simonstown agreement contained better terms than Britain was ever likely to get
from the South Africans in the foreseeable future, and was more
important than any forces which the Union might provide for
the Middle East. Moreover, if linked to the Middle East commitment, this agreement was likely to be lost, since it was considered highly unlikely that Erasmus could make this commitment firm enough, timely enough or substantial enough to
satisfy the Chiefs of Staff. Nevertheless, outside the Admiralty
there was strong support for the linkage proposal and the upshot was agreement – suggested by the First Sea Lord himself
(Lord Mountbatten) at the Chiefs of Staff Committee on 3 June –
that this should initially be put to the South Africans but that if
they refused to go along it should be abandoned and a separate
agreement made on Simonstown. The corollary of this, of course,
was that the South Africans would not get even the neutered
African Defence Organization which London was now prepared
to consider.[63]

At the meeting of the Cabinet Defence Committee on 10 June,
chaired by Eden, the Admiralty's tactical compromise was diluted somewhat by the Prime Minister but seems to have held
basically intact. Like the Admiralty, Eden was 'doubtful whether
it would be wise tactics to link the Simonstown agreement too
closely with South African assistance in Middle East defence',
though there was general agreement in the committee that
Erasmus 'should be strongly pressed to accept a firm commitment'

on this. The Prime Minister was particularly anxious to improve the agreement's provisions on coloured workers in order 'to protect ourselves from the criticism that we were conniving at discrimination against coloured peoples'. As a result, said Eden, he would 'prefer that Mr Erasmus's anxiety to reach a settlement on Simonstown should be used to obtain a more satisfactory agreement on that issue'. At the end of its discussion, the Defence Committee accepted Eden's priorities. Thus, said the Prime Minister, 'our first aim should be to obtain a satisfactory agreement on the future of the naval base at Simonstown ... Our second aim should be to obtain some assurance of South African participation in the defence of the Middle East, though this should not at this stage be pressed to the point of jeopardising our chances of obtaining a satisfactory agreement on Simonstown. On the third subject', he concluded, 'we should decline to enter into an African Defence Organization but should explore the possibility of holding further conferences on communications and logistics in Africa, in continuation of those already held.'[64]

Certain key files bearing on the June negotiations, including minutes of the disussions, remain classified, so it is not possible to be absolutely certain of the sequence of events. However, it is clear that, as proposed, the British side pressed Erasmus for a fresh Middle East commitment as a *quid pro quo* for Simonstown, and that – as feared by the Admiralty – he was prepared to offer vague assurances but not to give the sort of firm and specific commitment which the Chiefs of Staff wanted.[65] This was in spite of also being offered British support for a functionally limited African Defence Organization. For this reason, on 22 June Lord Home suggested to Selwyn Lloyd, 'very reluctantly', that Erasmus should be told that 'the whole subject of the Middle East and defence facilities in Africa should await further discussion'. The present negotiation, said the Commonwealth Secretary, should now be confined to finalizing settlements on the transfer of Simonstown, on naval co-operation and on secret military staff talks with regard to the defence of Africa and the Middle East. (On all of this considerable progress had already been made, though there was deadlock on the timetable of the transfer of the Base and disagreement on the application of a colour bar in the Dockyard.)[66] 'If Erasmus jibs at this', said Home, 'we could indicate that unless he is agreeable to further staff talks on the military side the Simonstown settlement would be jeopardised.'[67]

With the negotiations at a critical stage, on 23 June the interested minister reported their progress to the Cabinet and sought advice on how to proceed. As presented to his colleagues by the Minister of Defence, the choice was between either 'concluding an agreement on Simonstown and on naval co-operation, together with a promise of military staff talks on the Middle East', which was his personal preference, or, 'in default of a firm South African promise to co-operate in the defence of the Middle East', breaking off 'the whole of the discussions' (the strong linkage proposal). Anthony Eden immediately endorsed his defence minister's line, observing in its support that he 'would not put too high a value on a South African undertaking to contribute towards the defence of the Middle East' – an attitude which gave off a strong whiff of sour grapes. The Prime Minister appeared more exercised (albeit, on the face of it, mainly for reasons of efficiency and 'presentation') by the inadequate safeguards offered by Erasmus for the future recruitment of 'coloured workers' into the Simonstown Dockyard. As a result, the Cabinet decided that the British side should 'press strongly' for further safeguards for them and that, subject to satisfaction on this point, 'it should continue to be a primary objective in these discussions to obtain a satisfactory agreement on the transfer of the naval base at Simonstown and on naval co-operation generally, and that attainment of that objective should not be prejudiced by insistence on a firm South African promise of co-operation in the defence of the Middle East'.[68]

Following this Cabinet the negotiations were resumed and on 28 June the Cabinet had before it their results. The main developments were that the South Africans had met the British on the coloured workers, and the two sides had split the difference between them concerning the date of transfer of Simonstown, which would be no later than 31 March 1957. Furthermore, Erasmus had agreed to sign a secret letter to Selwyn Lloyd (see Appendix), expressing South Africa's willingness to take part in staff talks relating to Union participation in the defence of the Middle East, which, said the memorandum circulated by the three interested ministers on 25 June, 'goes a good deal further than anything which Mr Erasmus has previously been prepared to accept'.[69] In the light of these South African concessions, the defence minister, the Commonwealth Secretary (clearly having changed his mind) and the First Lord of the Admiralty asked the Cabinet to endorse the draft agreements which they had produced.

Formally, these provided for the transfer of Simonstown to Union sovereignty in return for an unqualified user guarantee for the Royal Navy (and, in war, for allied navies as well), the promise of an increased Union contribution to the defence of the Cape Route by a South African Navy substantially enlarged through £18 million worth of purchases from British shipyards, and South African agreement to place this navy under the command of the Royal Navy Commander-in-Chief, South Atlantic in war (though this was now only implicit, as was pointed out in Cabinet on 28 June). The draft agreements also announced Britain's acceptance *in principle* of the need for a limited African Defence Organization and an undertaking to help the Union establish it, together with a spiritually related provision whereby other governments might be invited to join the new Anglo-South African naval command structure; and, in return, provided for South Africa's commitment *in principle* to the 'defence of Southern Africa, Africa and the Middle East gateways to Africa', and staff talks to give this substance. These drafts, the Cabinet was informed, would take the form of exchanges of correspondence between Selwyn Lloyd and Erasmus and while the first three, on Regional Defence, Defence of the Sea Routes and the Simonstown Base, would be published, the fourth, on staff talks relating to South Africa's contribution to the defence of the Middle East, would, on the insistence of Erasmus, remain secret.

The drafts on Simonstown and Defence of the Sea Routes provoked no serious debate in the Cabinet but the other two did. Indeed, Lord Reading, the Minister of State for Foreign Affairs, was of the view that it might be possible to extract a 'firm promise' of South African help in the Middle East if and when the United States had made 'a definite military commitment' to the region. As a result, he argued for 'holding . . . over for further discussion at a later date' the draft agreements on regional defence and staff talks. However, against this was presented the view that 'postponement might jeopardise the prospect of making effective progress through Staff conversations'. The opinion of the Chiefs of Staff (now echoing Eden) 'that these conversations might offer an opportunity for a more practical approach to this problem' was also reported, and the possibility was thrown in 'that closer contact between the military staffs might pave the way for a further effort to overcome the political difficulties which now stood in the way of a firm

South African promise to co-operate in the defence of the Middle East'. On these arguments, which in the light of the known strategic as well as political prejudices of Erasmus and his service chiefs were optimistic, to say the least, Reading was defeated, and with only insignificant amendments the Cabinet authorized a settlement with Erasmus on the basis of the four draft agreements.[70] On 30 June they were signed and on 4 July, with the exception of that providing for staff talks, they were published simultaneously in Britain and the Union.

The real deal between Britain and South Africa over Simonstown was, of course, quite different from that presented to the public in both countries in this exchange of correspondence. In the first place, the promise of unqualified user privileges at the Base about which the British government made so much was not a major South African concession because both sides had come to accept that in the Cold War co-belligerency was implicit in their relationship. In the second place, neither was South Africa's naval expansion programme a major concession by the Union, though less because it was needed in Pretoria's own interest than because few people in Westminster, less in Whitehall and none in Portsmouth seriously believed that the South Africans had either the will or the personnel to carry it all through – as subsequently proved to be the case.

In reality Simonstown was returned to the South Africans because the Admiralty knew that it was *in practice* worth little in the absence of Union goodwill and because it wanted to spend its limited resources on more important things. It was also returned because the *symbolic cost* to the Empire and to the relative political strength of English-speakers in the Union which the sacrifice of sovereignty over the Base would entail, and which in the end Churchill alone had not been prepared to incur, was now believed to be less important. Outweighing it was the wish to avoid, for the sake of Britain's other interests in the Union, 'putting a needless strain on friendship [with South Africa] in the future', as *The Times*, a lone voice in questioning the official and public justification for the Simonstown Agreements, pointed out.[71] The broader picture – as earlier documented in *Economic Power and Anglo-South African Diplomacy*[72] – included Britain's economic interests in the Union, especially in gold and uranium, and it is clear from the record that the two Commonwealth Secretaries who did most to shape the parameters of the Simonstown Agreements – Patrick Gordon

Walker and Lord Swinton – were sensitive to this point. The broader picture also included the future of the High Commission Territories: Swinton feared that his refusal to surrender them would lead to a deterioration in relations with Pretoria. And it had also lately come to include a desire to prevent South African opposition to the inclusion of independent black states in the Commonwealth.[73]

It is now apparent, however, Eden's sour grapes and Admiralty reservations notwithstanding, that the British interest 'in' South Africa which had carried London furthest towards a settlement with Pretoria over Simonstown was its *continuing hope for the creation of an effective fighting force in the Union firmly committed to the defence of the Middle East*. It is also now apparent that the failure to make much ground with this had been, despite the superficial cleverness of Eden's argument in Cabinet, the great disappointment to Britain of these negotiations, though it had not been a great surprise. This, as well as the slenderness of South Africa's formal concessions (perhaps its biggest was excepting 'coloured workers' from apartheid laws at the Naval Base), gives the lie to the orthodox view – cleverly inspired by the British government – that even in its formal terms the Simonstown Agreements were very favourable to Britain.[74]

Appendix

The secret agreement on Anglo-South African staff talks with regard to the defence of the Middle East

It is clear that the conclusion of the Agreements which have now been signed by us, providing for co-operation between the Union of South Africa and the United Kingdom in matters relating to the security of Africa, require as a logical consequence an effective form of consultation between our respective Service Staffs on all relevant questions.

This essential aim can most effectively be reached by the development of the existing procedures for exchanging information in a manner which would ensure the frankest form of collaboration on matters falling within the purview of the Agreements.

While the Union's participation in the Middle East would

depend on the formal arrangements arrived at after negotiations between the Governments primarily interested, I would be happy to authorise the South African Service Staffs to include, in their discussions with your Service Staffs, matters relating to South Africa's participation in the defence of that area. This would of course have to be on a provisional basis and without commitment.

I should be glad to learn whether the suggestions contained in this letter meet with your concurrence.[75]

Notes

1. See J. Barber, *South Africa's Foreign Policy, 1945–70* (1973), 89; W. C. B. Tunstall, *The Commonwealth and Regional Defence* (1959), 51.
2. J. E. Spence, *The Strategic Significance of Southern Africa* (1970), 15.
3. *Ibid.*, 15.
4. *Ibid.*, 13.
5. See *ibid.*; G. Berridge, *Economic Power in Anglo-South African Diplomacy: Simonstown, Sharpeville and After* (1981), ch. 4.
6. This section is based on G. Berridge, 'The Attlee government and South African defence', article forthcoming.
7. See R. Ovendale, 'The South African policy of the British Labour government, 1947–51', *International Affairs*, 1982–3, 41–58.
8. PRO, DEFE 7/176.
9. *Ibid.*
10. DEFE 7/177.
11. PRO, DO 35/2369.
12. *Ibid.*
13. PRO, ADM 116/5969; CAB 131/13, D (52) 1st.
14. DEFE 7/177.
15. *Ibid.*
16. *Ibid.*
17. *Ibid.*
18. DEFE 7/178.
19. *Ibid.*
20. *Ibid*
21. For background see E. J. Grove, *Vanguard to Trident* (1987), 90–2.
22. J. Garner, *The Commonwealth Office, 1925–68* (1978), 284–5; and on Swinton see J. A. Cross, *Lord Swinton* (1982).
23. ADM 116/6050.
24. *Ibid.*
25. *Ibid.*
26. DEFE 7/178.
27. CAB 128/27, CC (54) 34.
28. DEFE 7/178.

29. ADM 116/5979.
30. *Ibid.*; Grove, *Vanguard to Trident*, ch. 3.
31. *Ibid.*
32. *Ibid.*
33. *Ibid.*
34. DO 35/5479.
35. *Ibid.*
36. ADM 116/5979.
37. CAB 128/27, CC (54) 57.
38. ADM 116/6050.
39. CAB 128/27, CC (54) 58.
40. ADM 116/5979.
41. CAB 128/27, CC (54) 59.
42. *Ibid.*
43. DO 35/5479.
44. CAB 129/70, C (54) 291.
45. DO 35/5479.
46. DEFE 13/36.
47. DO 35/5479.
48. *Ibid.*
49. DEFE 13/36.
50. *Ibid.*
51. *Ibid.*
52. *Ibid.*
53. *Ibid.*
54. *Ibid.*
55. *Ibid.*
56. *Ibid.*
57. Garner, *Commonwealth Office*, 285.
58. DEFE 13/36; ADM 116/6049.
59. ADM 116/6049.
60. *Ibid.*
61. *Ibid.*
62. *Ibid.*; DEFE 4/77 (COS meeting, 3 June).
63. *Ibid.*
64. CAB 131/16, D (55) 3rd.
65. ADM 116/6050.
66. ADM 116/6049.
67. *Ibid.*
68. CAB 128/29, CM (55) 17.
69. CAB 129/76, CP (55) 54.
70. CAB 128/29, CM (55) 18.
71. *The Times* , 7 July.
72. Berridge, *Economic Power*, ch. 4.
73. DO 35/7139.
74. The authors gratefully acknowledge the financial assistance of the

Nuffield Foundation and Leicester University Research Board in the research for this chapter.
75. CAB 129/76, CP (55) 54, endorsed by the Cabinet on 28 June, CM (55) 18, and almost certainly signed with the other agreements on 30 June – see subsequent reference in CAB 129/78, CP (55) 170.

8 The Settlement of the Korean War

Peter Lowe

When the Conservatives assumed office a military stalemate existed in Korea and discussions were taking place between the American-dominated United Nations Command (UNC) and the communists to secure a cease-fire. The failure of the last Chinese offensive launched in April 1951 had marked the end of attempts by each side to obtain a military victory.[1] Whilst it suited both sides to open discussions over terminating the war, however, neither was desperately anxious to end it. The Chinese and the North Koreans suspected that the Americans would tire first and allow them to secure concessions; so far as can be inferred, the Soviet Union was embarrassed at the prolongation of the war but was not willing for it to be concluded on terms that were disadvantageous. The United States held that it would take a considerable time to reach agreement and was prepared to pursue a waiting game. The principal issues involved in the truce talks were the line of demarcation, arrangements for supervising a truce and for ensuring compliance (including the appointment of a neutral commission) and the disposal of prisoners of war. The communists insisted at first that the demarcation line should be the 38th parallel, the original line of division between the zones of Soviet and American dominance adopted in August 1945. Since UN forces occupied territory to the north of the 38th parallel, however, this was unacceptable. Progress was slowly made in resolving the differences over the demarcation line and inspection arrangements but the problems associated with prisoners of war proved extremely intractable.

Concern was already felt in the British Foreign Office that the UNC was unduly inflexible and that the correct balance of diplomacy and tenacity had not been achieved. One official wrote to a colleague in Washington:

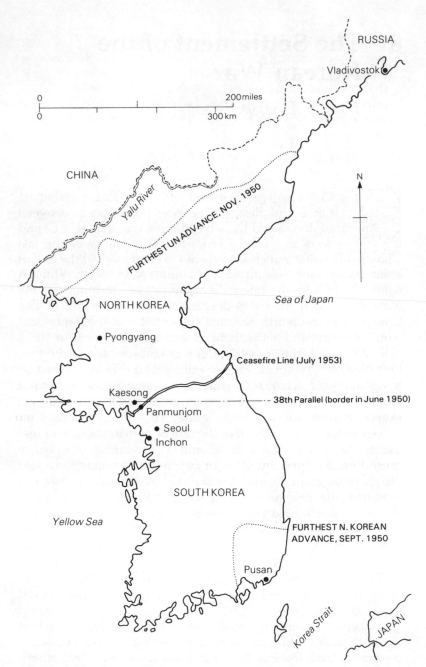

RUSSIA

Vladivostok●

0 ____ 200miles
0 ____ 300 km

CHINA

Yalu River

FURTHEST UN ADVANCE, NOV. 1950

N

NORTH KOREA

Sea of Japan

● Pyongyang

Ceasefire Line (July 1953)

Kaesong ●

- - - 38th Parallel (border in June 1950)

Panmunjom

● Seoul
● Inchon

SOUTH KOREA

Yellow Sea

FURTHEST N. KOREAN
ADVANCE, SEPT. 1950

Pusan ●

Korea Strait

JAPAN

Map 2: The Korean War

The purpose of this letter is merely to repeat what I am sure you already know, i.e. that we attach very great importance to securing an armistice in Korea, that we are less pessimistic than the Americans about the chances, that we attach importance also to the way the talks are conducted and to the impression left on world opinion as regards responsibility for the outcome.[2]

Churchill took a personal interest in the Korean talks as a result of his preoccupation with maintaining close Anglo-American relations while simultaneously modifying the more abrasive features of American policy. The Prime Minister contributed characteristically trenchant minutes at regular intervals between November 1951 and July 1953. On 16 November he addressed Anthony Eden emphasizing:

No one knows what is going on in Korea or which side is benefiting in strength from the bombing and grimaces at Panmunjom. We must try to penetrate the American mind and purpose . . . The other side clearly do not want an agreement. It is important to think out how prolonging the deadlock can benefit them. Obviously it diverts United Nations resources. But what do they hope for?[3]

Eden replied that it had been extremely difficult to follow the complex developments at Panmunjom but he thought that matters were becoming clearer.[4] The UNC proposed on 17 November 1951 that the demarcation line should be the existing line of contact if an armistice was signed, and agreement was reached on 23 November on this basis. On 27 November approval of the location of the demarcation line was ratified by the two delegations. The UNC feared, however, that the communists might then delay indefinitely in settling remaining items on the agenda with the consequence that there might be a secret build-up of communist forces for a subsequent attack. In the first phase of his return to office Churchill was inclined to share this suspicion, as did Eden (and a settlement was indeed long delayed), but later a more critical attitude towards the American approach developed.

In Washington the State Department and the Joint Chiefs of Staff devoted much thought to the repercussions of an armistice agreement in the sense of ensuring that China did not violate its terms. The Americans were contemplating such sanctions as a complete economic blockade of the Chinese coast; agreement for a UN naval blockade of China; further military action against China including air bombardment, but without land operations; no possibility of admitting the Peking government to the Chinese seat in the UN; and for Britain to accept at least its present commitment of forces in Korea pending clarification following an armistice.[5] The Secretary of State, Dean Acheson, told Sir Oliver Franks, the ambassador in Washington, that it was important to agree on a statement to be issued after the announcement of an armistice, although this would not necessarily stipulate the precise sanctions to be applied if the armistice broke down.[6] Acheson and Eden discussed Korean developments in the presence of certain of their colleagues during talks in Rome in November 1951 when Acheson made clear that he was considering an Anglo-American statement, or an American declaration supported by Britain, rather than a statement to be issued through the UN. Eden was told that he must understand how violent a reaction there would be from American public opinion in the event of the communists breaking an armistice agreement. Eden responded that he would consult Churchill but British public opinion also had to be borne in mind. Of the retaliatory measures envisaged against China Eden thought, as a personal reaction, that UN bombing beyond the Yalu would be less awkward for the British government to handle than a naval blockade.[7]

Churchill chaired a meeting of defence ministers and the Chiefs of Staff on 30 November 1951. The British believed that the Chinese and North Koreans would probably respect an armistice agreement and that if a warning statement was issued it should be in general terms. A naval blockade was regarded as highly dangerous and capable of precipitating a third world war. Soviet ports would have to be excluded in which case a blockade would not be effective enough. Bombing of Chinese ports and centres of communication would be less dangerous. Churchill's view was recorded as being

> that Russia would start World War III when she wanted to; she certainly would not do so merely to honour her pledge to China. He was, therefore, not unduly worried about bombing targets in Manchuria. As regards a war with China he considered that China was not a country against which one declared war; rather a country against which war was waged.[8]

British views were communicated to Washington and Eden informed Acheson that the negotiators at Panmunjom should press for the most effective supervision arrangements attainable. These could be obtained through joint inspection teams at key points or through supervisory teams led by neutrals, but some trust would have to be put in communist good faith. The British government further agreed that a warning statement against a breach of the armistice would have to be approved by other allied states, and felt that it should be adopted by as many as possible from those countries contributing forces to the military campaigns in Korea. The statement should be couched in suitably general terms. As regards a naval blockade of China and bombing operations north of the Yalu, the Admiralty believed that a blockade would take years rather than months to have full effect; excluding the Soviet Far Eastern ports would render a blockade futile, and including them would raise the danger of a third world war. The chiefs of staff were doubtful over what would be accomplished through bombing north of the Yalu, but it would be wiser than a blockade.[9]

President Truman believed that the conduct of the talks at Panmunjom had been too conciliatory but was persuaded, after a meeting with the Joint Chiefs of Staff, on 10 December, that the right tactics were being pursued. A form of words for the latter part of the warning statement suggested by a British official, Robert Scott, was considered too weak by the State Department,[10] but Eden underlined the dislike of the proposed American wording because

> the warning in the draft statement communicated to the
> Foreign Office is too positive and menacing. It states that
> aggression after the armistice will result in hostilities outside
> Korea; whereas in the view of His Majesty's Government the
> warning should rather be in the form that it might not be
> possible to avoid the extension of hostilities.[11]

There should be no commitment at this time to specific action in hypothetical circumstances in Eden's view, and decisions that might precipitate global war should be adopted only after meticulous consideration.[12] In the end, appreciating the strength of feeling in Washington, Eden reluctantly accepted the proposed American wording in the final part of the statement. But he held that the warning should relate not to 'another act of aggression' but to 'a major breach of the armistice'. In addition the UN must be associated with the statement in appropriate terms.[13] Eden further deemed consultation with India to be wise given the role played by Indian diplomats in communicating Chinese opinions and because of India's developing ambition in the UN. The State Department did not welcome the suggestion: the Indian ambassador in Peking, K. M. Panikkar, was intensely distrusted and India's refusal to support the UN militarily in Korea was condemned.[14]

The British view regarding the problems of securing a long-term settlement in Korea and of resolving broader Far Eastern matters was that a conference should be convened comprising either five powers (United States, Britain, France, the Soviet Union and China) or seven powers (as previously with the addition presumably of India and Egypt) with provision for associate membership for South Korea and North Korea. Such a conference could handle Korean and general Far Eastern problems. The United States was opposed to the proposal, however, because UN participation was not provided for and neither was involvement by other countries interested in the region, as with Australia, New Zealand and the Philippines. Furthermore, it was impossible for the impression to be conveyed that the United States might recognize Peking.[15] The State Department was contemplating, in December 1951, a conference including the two Korean states, America, the Soviet Union and China. A new UN commission was also required and in Washington's view should include the United States, the Soviet Union, Australia, Thailand and Turkey; only if Britain and France strongly wished to participate could they do so. This is of interest for revealing that Britain was not considered to be essential, underlining the decline in British status.[16]

At the beginning of 1952 the outstanding issues in the talks at Panmunjom mainly concerned inspection arrangements and the disposal of prisoners of war. On 16 February the communists proposed Poland, Czechoslovakia and the Soviet Union for membership of the neutral nations inspection teams but the UNC opposed the Soviet nomination. On 19 February it was agreed that a political conference to produce a Korean settlement should be convened within three months of an armistice being signed. It was not too difficult to perceive a compromise on these issues as part of a package deal, but the prisoner of war issue proved far more difficult to resolve than originally anticipated. The UNC (without consulting Britain) proposed, on 2 January 1952, that repatriation should proceed on a *voluntary* basis. The assumption in the Geneva convention of 1949 was that prisoners would be returned to the country for which they had fought at the time of capture. It had not been expected that significant numbers would be unwilling to return and (as in the case of prisoners taken by the UNC) might wish to go elsewhere. The United States had approved but not ratified the Geneva convention; the Chinese communists had not been involved in negotiating the convention. Thus North Korea had not accepted the application of the convention at the beginning of the war, but had done so in July 1950 after General MacArthur had announced that the UNC accepted it. (Notwithstanding some of the complexities it was embarrassing for the UNC to be accused by the communists of not applying the convention.) The problems inherent in the dispute were extremely complicated and it took at least the first half of 1952 for the British government to comprehend the full range of factors. As throughout the Korean conflict consultation between Washington and London was poor; various relevant aspects came to light gradually, and on occasions after Eden had given assurances to the House of Commons in good faith which turned out to be inaccurate or erroneous. The White House, the State Department and the Pentagon did not grasp all the important features either: in particular, it was not understood how the prisoner of war camps functioned. It remained true, however, that information could have been sent to London more promptly.

John Addis of the Foreign Office reviewed the state of the armistice talks in late January 1952. On the credit side the communists had conceded the principle of inspection and proposed inspection by neutral teams, which had been accepted by the UNC on 11 December. On 14 December the communists accepted rotation of troops after an armistice was signed: they had also agreed that they could not bring in more aircraft or arms. Addis criticized the negotiating technique of the UNC:

> The manner in which the United Nations Command have conducted the negotiations – rapid and unexplained changes of front on the main questions, and a policy of sometimes stepping up demands after concessions have been offered by the other side – has not contributed to removing the suspicion which undoubtedly exists on the Communist side that the Americans do not sincerely want an armistice. An offer is now necessary from our side to convince the Communists that the negotiations are genuine and to make progress possible.

Addis contended that the concessions made by the communists, together with the warning statement, should give adequate security. On the prisoner of war question, he believed that this should not be allowed to prevent the conclusion of an armistice, and found it surprising that the Truman administration was prepared to jeopardize the prospects of American prisoners by pursuing the principle of voluntary repatriation. He attributed the American decision to the potency of emotionalism and thought it unlikely that such an attitude would be adopted in Britain.[17]

Truman had actually taken the decision to oppose forcible repatriation for powerful moral reasons reinforced with political considerations. It would be wholly wrong to send back Chinese or North Korean prisoners who repudiated communism: to do so would condemn many to death or torture. Furthermore, the 'free world' would gain from such an open reverse for communism.[18] It was true that the American and British governments had sent back Russian prisoners in 1945 and many had perished but Truman was not influenced by this precedent and viewed the matter in clear-cut terms of right or wrong. Dean Acheson concurred despite the presence of doubts of the kind indicated by Addis. Furthermore, Churchill firmly agreed with Truman, and so did Eden. The Foreign Office explored the legal complexities and deduced that the grounds for refusing to return prisoners were weak owing to the terms of the Geneva convention, so that Sir William Strang, the Permanent Under-Secretary, informed Eden on 20 March 1952 that a ministerial decision was required. Eden wrote, 'I did not know that our legal grounds were so poor; but this doesn't make me like the idea of sending these poor devils back to death or worse',[19] and Churchill reiterated in a minute to Eden that there must be no question of forcible repatriation.[20] Rumours reached American ears in April 1952 that the Foreign Office was contemplating retreat over the principle,[21] but an indignant reply was sent to Washington maintaining that the truth was the opposite of the allegation.[22] In reality there was a division of opinion among officials, but the decisive reactions of Churchill and Eden and the importance of preserving some harmony in Anglo-American relations put an end to internal debate.

In initial discussion of the number of prisoners who might refuse repatriation, it had not been anticipated that the problem would be as large as it was. At the beginning of 1952 it was estimated that between 10 and 25 per cent would refuse: American officials thought that approximately 116,000 (out of 132,000) prisoners and 18,000 (out of 38,000) civilians would go back; about 28,000 prisoners and 30,000 civilians would not wish to return; but only around 16,000 prisoners and 20,000 civilians would *forcibly* resist repatriation. The screening process in April 1952 revealed a radically different picture: apparently only 70,000 prisoners wished to return. Subsequently, after rescreening of some prisoners, the figure of those accepting repatriation was raised to approximately 82,000, and the ultimate figure of those accepting repatriation was 82,500, so that about 50,000 chose not to return.[23] The Chinese and North Korean reaction to the American stand over voluntary repatriation was vitriolic: it could hardly be expected that those who had emphasized the superiority of their status and the invincibility of their ideological beliefs, could accept that many of their soldiers did not wish to return.

It was not originally understood in London that the procedure for ascertaining the wishes of prisoners was as murky as it turned out to be. Revelations concerning procedures and revolts in certain camps shook confidence in the competence of the administration of the camps. It was assumed in London that the camps were run in an orderly fashion without excessive pressure having been used to influence prisoners. On 1 March 1952 Robert Scott observed that the Americans were worried over the danger of the communists rehabilitating airfields so as to accommodate jet aircraft and might be willing to compromise if the communists would reciprocate over prisoners of war. Scott described the latter, however, as most probably the hardest issue to resolve. He believed that the Americans had erred in notifying the International Red Cross of holding certain categories of prisoners which would have been better defined in another way. More seriously, use had been made of Kuomintang (Chinese Nationalist) agents from Taiwan in implementing 'reindoctrination' in the camps, and pressure had been brought to bear with the encouragement or connivance of some camp commanders to secure propaganda successes for the West through prisoners condemning the political systems from which they had escaped. Scott thought that while one could sympathize with the American wish to support voluntary repatriation, the point might be reached eventually where the Americans would have to contemplate an element of forcible repatriation. This might be acceptable to the communists and could break the deadlock. In Scott's judgment the American public would be prepared to pay this price to achieve the return of American prisoners.[24]

Concern was voiced within Britain over the duration of the talks in Panmunjom. Relatives of British prisoners understandably protested and anxiety was frequently expressed in the House of Commons. Eden wrote to the leaders of the Labour and Liberal parties on 1 May 1952, stating that all prisoners held by the UNC had been fairly treated and had been clearly notified of their rights regarding repatriation; that no pressure had been brought to bear and Kuomintang agents had not been employed as interpreters; and that it was impossible for the UNC to compel 60,000 prisoners to return against their wishes. Eden added that he was well aware of the plight of the approximately 1,000 British and Commonwealth prisoners held by the communists but the overriding principle of voluntary repatriation must be sustained.[25] Unfortunately Eden's letter was unintentionally misleading for he had believed that the screening process had been completed: he stated so in Parliament. Shortly afterwards it became clear that the American figure of 60,000 prisoners was an estimate and that significant numbers had still to be questioned. A stiff protest was sent to Washington in late May 1952 with emphasis on how vital it was that parliamentary statements be accurate.[26]

Even more alarming were the revelations resulting from the serious mutiny in the camp on Koje island on 8 May 1952, when the American commander was kidnapped by communist prisoners who threatened his life unless his deputy signed a statement admitting that force had been used against prisoners. The acting commander signed and grave embarrassment was caused to the UNC. The two offending American officers were demoted and a long overdue investigation into the running of the camps took place. The State Department was already pursuing discreet enquiries of its own and disturbing reports were forwarded. It emerged that certain camps were controlled by a hierarchy of pro-Kuomintang prisoners who used torture and physical coercion including murder against those opting for repatriation to China instead of choosing Taiwan.[27] In other camps communist prisoners dominated the functioning of the camps and employed similar methods against prisoners not wanting to be repatriated. The riots on Koje showed unmistakably that the operation of the camps had been carried out with considerable ineptitude. Insufficient thought had been given to administration and some of the personnel were not of appropriate calibre. Eden was upset and irate with the situation, which included complaints in the Commons, and he told the State Department that he was greatly disturbed at the riots and the aftermath: the evidence in the report of the International Committee of the Red Cross and in press accounts were bound to foster doubts as to the validity of the screening; and it would be difficult for the British public to grasp how within ten days 170,000 men were satisfactorily interrogated 'individually and in reasonable privacy'. He recommended that a second screening be carried out; the British government adhered to the principle of voluntary repatriation but public opinion must be satisfied on the screening process.[28]

In the course of further exchanges with the United States, in late May 1952, it appeared that approximately 40,000 prisoners had not been screened in the first place. But Churchill continued to believe that Britain must work as closely as possible with the United States and he dictated a minute on 12 July 1952 saying that there could be no question of compelling Chinese prisoners to return to China against their will – 'These are the ones, above all others, who carry with them the moral significance, as the ones who had opted for us would certainly be put to death or otherwise maltreated.'[29] John Addis, more inclined to envisage an element of forcible repatriation, observed that any North Koreans returned forcibly were more likely to be victimized than the Chinese but he wisely concluded that there was no point in replying to the Prime Minister at this juncture. His colleague, C. H. Johnston, ironically commented that he would not relish forcible repatriation to China if in the predicament himself.[30]

In the summer of 1952 the United States urged that preparations be made to apply more pressure to China. In part this began when UNC planes bombed hydroelectric plants on the Yalu on 23 June. Intensified bombing had been under consideration for some time: the Labour Foreign Secretary, Herbert Morrison, had assented to it in September 1951 on the understanding that a new Chinese offensive would be launched in Korea. When the bombing occurred in June, India was promoting discussions in the UN to secure a breakthrough in handling the issue of the prisoners of war. The Truman administration distrusted the Indian government and particularly distrusted

Panikkar, the ambassador in Peking, and Krishna Menon, the peripatetic spokesman at the UN. (The British view was that Panikkar and Menon had their uses, provided information derived from Panikkar was utilized cautiously and that no encouragement was given to Menon's more impulsive inclinations.) The timing of the Yalu bombings was embarrassing to London, since the accusation was made by Labour MPs that it had been timed so as to frustrate Indian efforts at mediation. More embarrassing to Churchill and Eden was the fact that the Minister of Defence, Lord Alexander, and the Minister of State at the Foreign Office, Selwyn Lloyd, were in Washington when the bombing took place and had not been consulted. Churchill made clear in the Commons however that the Labour front-bench spokesmen did not differ fundamentally from the government.[31]

Consideration was being given within the American government again at this time to the application of intensified pressure on China through the Additional Measures Committee of the UN General Assembly. The standard British reaction to suggestions of further pressure on China was to cite the exposed position of Hong Kong: the political and economic viability of the colony must not be threatened because of British participation in additional pressure on China. This usually gave the Americans cause for reflection since they, too, regarded Hong Kong as a vital symbol of resistance to the Peking government.[32] Eden and his officials still deemed the possibility of a blockade of China to be too dangerous on the grounds that it could bring about a general war. However, the Prime Minister was sceptical and thought the Foreign Office was exaggerating the Chinese menace. He dictated a sardonic minute on 26 August 1952:

> I think we take a great responsibility considering our
> relatively small contribution in taking too stiff a line with the
> United States who are bearing practically all the burden ... I
> do not regard Communist China as a formidable adversary.
> Anyhow you can take it that for the next four or five years 400
> million Chinese will be living just where they are now. They
> cannot swim, they are not much good at flying and the Trans-
> Siberian railway is already overloaded. I do not see how they
> can get at us except in South-East Asia and Hongkong ...
> When you think how much the Chinese are costing us and
> costing the Americans twenty times more ... I cannot feel that

the measures proposed by the United States should be incontinently turned down. I think the Chinese might well be made to feel as uncomfortable as they make us.[33]

Eden replied on 1 September that the American proposals would cause grave difficulty: a general embargo on trade with China would be contrary to the economic interests of Britain and would connote the ruin of Hong Kong; an effective blockade would affect Port Arthur, Dairen and Vladivostok as well as Soviet and satellite shipping, which would be to threaten a world war. The American suggestion of severing diplomatic relations with China would not worry the Chinese but mean the loss of the listening post in Peking, whilst the draft resolution for the forthcoming UN General Assembly envisaged by the Americans would handicap the UNC negotiators at Panmunjom through giving maximum publicity to the prisoner of war issue: the Foreign Office believed the latter could only be settled through averting the glare of excessive publicity and allowing delicate negotiations to be completed. There was strong opposition in the General Assembly, and the Australian and South African governments shared British anxiety. Eden fully recognized, however, that Britain should not fall out with the United States.[34] Churchill concurred with Eden's analysis and added 'don't let's fall out with U.S. for the sake of Communist China'.[35]

The British delegate at the UN reported that 'of all the contentious items coming up at next Assembly, Korea is the most important.[36] Debate late in the year at the UN centred on the Indian attempt to secure acceptance by both sides of the functions of a neutral commission, which would supervise arrangements for dealing with those prisoners refusing repatriation. The United States was hostile to the Indian initiative, since Truman and Acheson did not wish to consider any weakening of the stand adopted, and viewed India with suspicion. Eden, Selwyn Lloyd and their advisers felt that India could play a valuable role, however, given the independent policy pursued by Nehru within the UN and the relatively good contacts between New Delhi and Peking. The dilemma was that progress in resolving the prisoner of war controversy was, in the British judgment, unlikely to be accomplished without Indian assistance: yet the Americans were unhappy to follow this path and it was essential to avoid a serious clash with Washington. The tensions and strains stretched the diplomacy and patience of Eden, Lloyd and Acheson to the limit; ironically a rift in Anglo-American relations was to be averted through the action of the Soviet Union.[37] When Eden was in New York, in early November 1952, he became engaged in a hectic round of consultations principally involving American, Canadian and Indian representatives. The Canadian external affairs minister, Lester Pearson, was President of the General Assembly and was sympathetic to Indian efforts. Krishna Menon was regarded as well meaning but characterized in his approach by what one British official described as a 'typical example of Hindu political compromise, including emphasis on non-violence, verbosity, and a general woolliness of conception'.[38] Undoubtedly Menon tried to be *too* clever, but Eden and Selwyn Lloyd believed that with firm British guidance undue woolliness could be eradicated and Menon's activities would bear fruit. Menon's ideas in early November centred around release and repatriation in accordance with the Geneva convention; classification of prisoners, according to nationality and domicile, would be handled by a repatriation commission; force should not be used against prisoners who would be entitled to make representations to the repatriation commission.[39] British thinking ran along the lines of releasing all prisoners with facilities for immediate repatriation; both sides should accept that no force should be used against prisoners after an armistice, thus ensuring that no prisoner was forcibly repatriated or detained; inspection teams of neutral nations (assisted by joint teams from respective Red Cross societies) should be responsible for the fulfilment of the terms.[40]

When Eden and Selwyn Lloyd met Acheson on 9 November[41] Acheson stressed how important it was to avoid disagreement and to obtain detailed execution of the terms decided upon after conclusion of an armistice agreement. He was worried at possible Pentagon opposition to armistice terms and pointed out that Truman was now a 'lame duck' President following the recent election; it would not help if Truman approved terms only to have the Pentagon encouraging the President-elect, General Eisenhower, to think along different lines. The Americans disliked the idea of any Soviet satellites belonging to the commission, but Eden and Lloyd remarked that in reality the presence of satellites could not be avoided.[42] Andrei Vyshinksy, the Soviet foreign minister, showed little flexibility in a speech to the UN other than wishing talks to be continued: he reiterated the communist view that an armistice agreement should be signed and the prisoner of war issue settled subsequently.[43] (Eden notified Vyshinksky that he was willing to meet him for a private talk but he was sceptical as to the outcome.)[44]

On 14 November Eden met Acheson again in the presence of Robert Schuman, the French foreign minister, and Lester Pearson. Eden noted that various drafts of an Indian resolution had been circulated informally, adding that none met the essential requirement of clarity over the principle of non-forcible repatriation. It was imperative to avoid a situation in which deadlock might arise after signature of an armistice agreement owing to divergent interpretations of it, and Acheson emphasized that he could not accept a situation in which pressure could be applied to individual prisoners refusing repatriation.[45] Eden commented that if Menon could meet this central point a resolution would meet with extensive support. But, when Menon produced a draft which proved acceptable to Eden, Acheson still opposed it – a move which Eden attributed to Pentagon pressure. Acheson argued that there could be some uncertainty over the fate of prisoners refusing repatriation (this could provide the communists with a pretext for breaking an armistice agreement while accusing the UN of non-compliance) but Eden remarked that the real difficulty was the weakness of Acheson's political position. Importantly, moderate Republicans, including Eisenhower, felt that there were opportunities which should not be rejected, and that if the war could be ended this should be done.[46]

Eden returned to London for a time and Selwyn Lloyd headed the British delegation. Lloyd and Pearson saw Acheson on 16 November when he persisted in opposition to an Indian proposal. At a meeting of twenty-one countries convened by Acheson on 17 November, Lloyd advocated supporting the Indian initiative and enjoyed general support, but Acheson argued vigorously in the opposing sense (supported only by Greece and Australia).[47] In private Acheson applied considerable pressure to try to induce a change in British policy and warned that Eisenhower would be surrounded by advisers favouring expansion of the war.[48] When Eden returned to New York, the American attitude, far from softening, seemed to have hardened. Eden observed that 'Acheson himself could not have been more rigid, legalistic and difficult ... At times it almost seems as if United States Government were afraid of agreement at this time. This is what some of their own countrymen are beginning to suspect.'[49] The American press gave prominence to the Anglo-American differences on 24 November, and Eden was obliged to issue a statement denying that Britain was moving away from the principle of opposing forcible repatriation.[50] Just as it looked as though the divergence could become a serious one, however, help came from an unexpected quarter. Vyshinsky launched a mordant attack upon the Indian resolution in the First Committee debate. This afforded Acheson a splendid opportunity of which he took full and skilful advantage. He spoke warmly of the Indian initiative to which he had hitherto been hostile, adding that the purpose of the resolution needed to be sharpened, but that a suitable form of words should not be hard to devise. Eden and Lloyd rejoiced and hastened to consult Menon.[51] Acheson was still somewhat difficult in his discussions with Lloyd but the worst was over. China endorsed the Soviet approach that there should be a cease-fire first with the prisoner of war problem to be decided later, but the United States supported the amended Indian resolution, and this was accepted in the plenary session, in a vote in which the minority comprised the Soviet bloc.[52]

There was still a long way to go but Eden had acted positively and assisted in dissuading Acheson from an unwise course. In a memorandum for his Cabinet colleagues the Foreign Secretary made clear how awkward Acheson had been: Acheson had come to one meeting the worse for drink and verbally assailed Selwyn Lloyd. Eden paid Acheson the doubtful compliment of having been more difficult to deal with than the American military, 'more royalist than the royalists'.[53] Here Eden's dislike of Acheson emerged, but there appeared to be no doubt of Acheson's testiness, which could be attributed to prolonged strain and disappointment at the Republican victory in the election. While Eden was in New York he had met Eisenhower and exchanged views with the President-elect. Churchill and Eden welcomed Eisenhower's victory, feeling that he was well placed to restore Anglo-American relations to a basis of amity. Eisenhower was under some pressure to endorse the attitude of the Truman administration over the Indian initiative but he was reluctant to do so before acquainting himself more fully with the facts. Eden dispelled some of Eisenhower's doubts and he became more sympathetic to Indian efforts. Eisenhower confirmed, when he met Eden on 20 November, that he would fulfil his pledge to visit Korea in the near future and that he would assess the military situation. He supported the stand taken against forcible repatriation, but he did not want prisoners refusing to return to be imprisoned indefinitely. If these aspects could be resolved he would be satisfied. 'He said that we ought to realise that we could not maintain our position in Asia without the help of the Asians. That was why he considered the Indian initiative so important.'[54] Eisenhower even requested Eden to send a message to Nehru thanking him for the role played by India. The discussions between Eden and Eisenhower were cordial and augured well for the future.[55]

The Eisenhower admininistration assumed office in January 1953. There appeared to be little likelihood of an armistice agreement being attained in the immediate future, and Eisenhower and his Secretary of State, John Foster Dulles, began to consider methods of applying pressure on China so as to terminate the war. Eisenhower genuinely wished to improve consultation with Britain but the exasperation felt in Washington over the war quickly gave rise to renewed tension. Consideration was given in Washington to a military push north so as to occupy the 'waist' of Korea; this would place important industrial areas of North Korea within the Republic of Korea and would bolster the morale of its army. Dulles discussed this with Eden on 5 March but conceded that he had no idea of the military cost of pursuing such a campaign. According to Dulles's account Eden showed some sympathy but warned that Britain must be fully consulted before action was taken.[56] Between April and June 1953 the Prime Minister moved to a central position in dealing with Korean developments. Eden was absent for a lengthy period for a major operation and Churchill took over as acting Foreign Secretary. It was a period of much interest, for . 'hurchill followed a more independent approach driven on by his determination to secure an improvement in Western-Soviet relations before the Cold War became a hot one of disastrous global dimensions. Korea was significant because Soviet assistance in achieving an armistice could lead to greater developments. On 15 April Churchill informed the Commons of the agreement reached at Panmunjom for the exchange of certain sick and wounded prisoners.[57] He now doubted whether it would be wise to issue the warning statement, prepared fifteen months earlier, immediately after the signing of an armistice agreement, since such a statement could be counter-productive when attempts were being made, after Stalin's death, to improve relations with

Moscow. The State Department was deeply disturbed when informed on 4 May and one official, Alexis Johnson, reminded the British embassy that the UNC placed great reliance upon the 'Greater Sanctions Statement'. He held that the Pentagon would not take kindly to the British proposal.[58]

The American administration was now pessimistic at the chances of agreement being reached in Korea and, at a meeting of the National Security Council held on 13 May, the possible use of atomic weapons was discussed. Eisenhower showed interest in employing atomic weapons in order to dislodge the Chinese from their present positions in Korea, but the military representatives doubted the efficacy of such weapons given the circumstances in Korea. The likely responses of America's allies were discussed and it was held that the consequences would be grave, possibly involving the temporary disruption of NATO. Fresh from his experience in Europe Eisenhower referred eloquently to European apprehension and deplored the fact that relations with Britain were now so bad:

> To many of them [Europeans] there was simply nothing worse than global war for the reason that it would amount to the obliteration of European civilization ... We were already in considerable difficulties with these allies and, it seemed to the President, our relations with Great Britain had become worse in the last few weeks than at any time since the end of the war.

(Relations between Washington and London had in fact been worse in December 1950 and January 1951, after Chinese entry into the war but Eisenhower had not then been involved.) The deductions from the discussion over atomic weapons was that it would be too high a price to pay for possible success in Korea if relations with America's allies were disrupted.[59] Meanwhile, on 4 May in the Commons Churchill had, in the words of John Addis, 'cut across the hesitations and delays which have caused so much adverse comment here recently. It has to some extent forced the hands of the U.N. Command and their directors in Washington. This was no doubt done quite deliberately; and if I may be allowed to say so, I think it was a very good thing it was done.'[60] Within the Foreign Office there had been dissatisfaction at the way in which the head of the UN negotiating team, General William Harrison, handled the negotiations at Panmunjom, and in his remarks in the Commons Churchill made obvious his own doubts, saying that it should be feasible (the principle of not accepting forcible repatriation having been approved) for progress to be made in determining the arrangements for holding and supervising the prisoners opposed to repatriation.[61]

In a minute written on 18 May for Strang and Selwyn Lloyd, Churchill stated: 'Evidently the obstacle is Syngman Rhee. Let me have in outline what you think I might send to encourage [US Under-Secretary of State] Bedell [Smith] to buck him up.'[62] Rhee, the South Korean leader, did indeed emerge, between the middle of May and the signature of the armistice agreement in late July, as a major obstacle. Rhee was profoundly dedicated to securing the reunification of Korea under his own leadership: he was hostile to anything that would cut across this objective and deployed his not inconsiderable range of tactics to cause as much trouble as he could. Ultimately he was only persuaded to co-operate through a combination of conciliation and coercion from Washington. There was a tendency in Britain to underestimate the challenge posed by Rhee, however, and, as a corollary, to underestimate the political difficulties facing Eisenhower and Dulles. After consultations with a wary Eisenhower Churchill moved to open his contacts with Russia. On 2 June he sent a personal message to Molotov, the new Soviet foreign minister, recalling their wartime co-operation and hoping that they could re-establish contact so as to diminish world tension. Churchill added that it would 'help if this Panmunjom prisoners-of-war business were got out of the way'.[63] Churchill was following a strategy of encouraging each element and of balancing criticisms with praise.[64] In the Commons on 9 June he commended General Mark Clark, the head of UN Command, who had been described by some as too unyielding, and Sir Esler Dening, the ambassador in Tokyo, reported that Clark deeply appreciated the Prime Minister's remarks. Clark also told Dening, on 10 June, how difficult it was to cope with the prisoners in camps where many of the guards were South Koreans who could be manipulated by Rhee:

> While not wishing to exaggerate the situation, General Clark considers Syngman Rhee could, if he wishes, incite the prisoners to break out . . . [and] the guards to desert. There is no move the General can now make to alter the situation. He is thinking in terms of asking his Government that United

Nations officers other than American should assist in the administration of these camps and if the South Korean guards deserted he would have to replace them by United Nations units. He is very conscious of the fact that the Communists will accuse us of a breach of faith if the prisoners escape.[65]

Dening thought that criticism of Clark should be tempered through appreciation of the problems he faced. Dening also pointed out that American military circles in East Asia reflected right-wing Republican attitudes: 'In consequence if things go wrong after an armistice, I have no doubt that the blame will be put on us and the other Powers who are generally held to have influenced the U.S. Government to amend their proposals.'[66]

On 4 June the communists accepted the UN Command's proposals to transfer prisoners to the neutral nations repatriation commission, comprising Czechoslovakia, Poland, Sweden, Switzerland and India, with Indian troops to act as guards. Prisoners wishing to be repatriated were to be sent home within sixty days of the armistice; non-repatriates were to be retained for an additional period of between 90 and 120 days and attempts could be made to persuade them to go back by the countries for which they had originally fought. Non-repatriates would eventually be freed or the UN General Assembly would determine their fate. Clark and Dening were in agreement that Rhee was likely to cause increasing trouble before and possibly after the armistice agreement was signed. Rhee was extremely unhappy at the approach of the armistice but was shrewd enough to realize that if he had to tolerate an agreement he could exact a high price for so doing: this meant a mutual security pact with the United States and further economic assistance. Rhee became involved in an exchange of correspondence with Eisenhower and Dulles of an acrimonious nature, and contingency plans were devised in Washington for countering Rhee which included the possibility of removing him. There were grave risks in going thus far, however, and it was decided to buy Rhee off through the offer of a mutual security pact, while indicating that if Rhee persisted in obstructiveness action of an unspecified character would be taken. Within Britain there was distinct impatience at what seemed to be the irresolute policy of Eisenhower and Dulles. This was unfair and in retrospect it may be stated that the President and his Secretary of State handled a most challenging situation as successfully as was feasible.

Rhee's principal act of sabotage was the release on 18 June of 25,000 North Korean prisoners which (as Clark had warned) threatened to prevent the signing of the armistice. Churchill's ire and his anxiety was revealed in a surprisingly frank personal message to Molotov sent on 20 June: 'I am sure the United States Government are deeply angered by Syngman Rhee's outrage and so are we. We must not let our thoughts on dangerous issues be unduly disturbed by this sinister event',[67] whilst one British official, Sir Gladwyn Jebb, wrote: 'I myself find it quite intolerable that this elderly brigand, who represents everything that we, for our part, detest, should presume to enrol ... the Western World in a crusade against Communism ... [He] should simply be arrested and deported'[68] Churchill was taken seriously ill with a stroke on 23 June and Salisbury assumed temporary charge of the Foreign Office. Once Churchill began to recover, however, he communicated his opinions through his inimitable minutes. His anger at Rhee was conveyed on 2 July graphically if unrealistically:

> The first question is whether the United States can afford to leave Rhee to his fate and accept a Communist subjugation of Korea. It is purely a question of American sentimental pride ... Myself, I think the United States are so powerful that they can afford to be indifferent to a local Communist success. They could afford to let Rhee be squelched and Korea communised and spend the money saved on increasing their armaments ... If I were an American, as I might have been, I would vote for Rhee going to hell and taking Korea with him and would talk to Russia direct on a heavily armed basis.[69]

In reply Salibury wrote on 3 July that he disliked the idea of fighting both Rhee and the communists. Rhee's antics could produce a situation combining tragedy and farce which would 'cause complete bewilderment to those whose sons are fighting in Korea and also to earnest supporters of the United Nations'.[70]

Rhee wanted to attract as much attention as he could and hoped to induce Dulles and perhaps Eisenhower to visit Korea. Instead Walter Robertson, Assistant Secretary of State for Far Eastern Affairs, was sent to negotiate with him.[71] Robertson's task was a thankless one: Rhee was extremely difficult to pin down and had a habit of going back on assurances given. The familiar complaint was voiced in the Foreign Office of inadequate consultation over the progress of the Rhee–Robertson talks,[72] but renewed communist offensives in June and July demonstrated that Rhee could pursue an independent policy only to a limited extent. He was forced to accept that he could not afford a fundamental rift with the United States. Grudgingly Rhee concluded that an armistice was inevitable and, in return for an American promise of a mutual security treaty and economic aid, he agreed not to obstruct an armistice agreement. At 10 a.m. on 27 July 1953 the armistice was signed and came into operation twelve hours later, thus bringing to an end the military conflict after two years of negotiations. Despite strong British doubts over making the warning statement (aimed at China) public, the statement was signed on 27 July and published in the joint policy declaration by the allies on 7 August.

The armistice provisions included the recommendation that a political conference should be held within ninety days to achieve a full settlement. Rhee was profoundly suspicious of any development that might weaken his hold and the United States had to extend further assurances to him. The Eisenhower administration wished to secure a unified Korea on a basis ensuring the survival of the Rhee regime but in effect this amounted to South Korea assimilating the North. The Churchill government, with Eden resuming his work at the Foreign Office in the autumn of 1953, believed that a solution could not be found if Rhee remained, but this belief had to be subordinated to the practicalities of co-operating with Washington. The prospects for unification were bleak therefore. Rhee was opposed to neutralization and the communists would not contemplate concessions that would jeopardize Kim Il Sung's regime in the North. From the British viewpoint developments have to be seen in the light of the efforts of Churchill and Eden to reduce tension between East and West. In addition, developments in Indochina came to overshadow Korea at the end of 1953 and in 1954. Discussions began at Panmunjom on 26 October in considering preparatory arrangements for the peace conference but enjoyed little success. Further problems were encountered in disposing of prisoners of war with bitter accusations hurled by both sides; these were at last resolved in January 1954. The Berlin conference of Soviet and Western foreign ministers agreed in February that a peace conference would assemble in Geneva on 26 April charged with producing a settlement for Korea and Indochina, but again the preoccupation was with

Indochina. Failure to secure progress over Korea was admitted by the powers in June and Korea remained divided.

Churchill and Eden saw the British role in Korean developments, between October 1951 and July 1953, as encouraging conciliation while standing firm on basic principles. As with the Attlee government there were frequent complaints at poor consultation between Washington and London. Britain's declining power and economic difficulties meant that America attached less significance to discussions with British leaders than formerly. The principal contribution of Churchill's government to the termination of the Korean War lay in the pressure exerted in support of Indian initiatives in the UN in November–December 1952 and in Churchill's advocacy of conciliation from April to July 1953, including his messages to Molotov. Where the prisoners of war issue was concerned, Churchill and Eden decided that Britain must support the United States unequivocally in sustaining the principle of voluntary repatriation. It is clear that some officials in the Foreign Office felt less strongly, and that certain of them would have accepted a degree of forcible repatriation in order to end the war and to obtain the return of UN prisoners. Churchill and Eden were determined to avoid a rift with America, although both were prepared to act independently at times and if necessary to rock the boat, as in November 1952 and April to June 1953. The British view of the Korean situation was that it was right to oppose the original North Korean aggression in June 1950, but Britain stayed in Korea in order to preserve friendship with the United States and maintain the moral authority of the UN, not to prop up the rotten regime of Syngman Rhee. Churchill and Eden thus concurred with their Labour predecessors in the essential characteristics of British policy towards the Korean War.

Notes

1. For a discussion of the circumstances leading to the Korean War and to Chinese intervention in October 1950, see Peter Lowe, *The Origins of the Korean War* (1986). For developments during the first year of the war, see Lowe, 'Great Britain, Japan, and the Korean War, 1950–1', in J. Chapman and D. Steeds, eds, *Proceedings of the British Association for Japanese Studies*, IX (1984), 98–111, and M. L. Dockrill, 'The Foreign Office, Anglo-American relations and the Korean War, June 1950–June 1951', *International Affairs*, 1986, 459–76.

2. PRO, FO 371/92795/841.
3. PRO, PREM 11/112.
4. *Ibid.*
5. *FRUS*, 1951, VII (Washington, DC, 1983), 1221–3.
6. *Ibid.*, 1157–8.
7. *Ibid.*, 1191–3.
8. PREM 11/112.
9. *FRUS 1951*, VII, 1221–3.
10. *Ibid..* 1297.
11. *Ibid.*, 1318.
12. *Ibid.*, 1319.
13. *Ibid.*, 1432.
14. *Ibid.*, 1448.
15. *Ibid.*, 1362.
16. *Ibid.*, 1360–2.
17. FO 371/99564/34.
18. For a valuable account of American policy during the lengthy truce exchanges, see B. J. Bernstein, 'The struggle over the Korean armistice: prisoners of repatriation', in B. Cumings, ed., *Child of Conflict: The Korean-American Relationship, 1943–1953* (1983), 261–307.
19. FO 371/99569/151.
20. FO 371/99570/176.
21. FO 371/99570/183.
22. *Ibid.*
23. Bernstein, in Cumings, *Child of Conflict*, 284–6, 307.
24. FO 371/99568/123.
25. FO 371/99572/215.
26. *FRUS, 1952–4*, XV (Washington, DC, 1984), 249.
27. *Ibid.*, 192–3.
28. FO 371/99573/254.
29. FO 371/99581/409.
30. *Ibid.*
31. For interesting exchanges in the debate, see *502 HCDeb. 5s*, 2247ff., and *503 HCDeb. 5s*, 269ff.
32. FO 371/99582/438.
33. PREM 11/301.
34. *Ibid.*
35. PREM 11/301.
36. FO 371/99584/488.
37. For a useful account of the Indian initiative and its repercussions, see R. Bullen, 'Great Britain, the United States, and the Indian armistice resolution on the Korean War, November 1952', in I. Nish, ed., *Aspects of Anglo-Korean Relations* (1984), 27–44.
38. FO 371/99589/621.
39. *Ibid.*
40. FO 371/99589/622.
41. Philip Jessup (ambassador-at-large in the State Department) and

Ernest Gross (the deputy American delegate to the UN) were also present.
42. FO 371/99589/627.
43. FO 371/99589/637.
44. FO 371/99589/633.
45. FO 371/99589/636.
46. FO 371/99589/644.
47. FO 371/99589/646.
48. FO 371/99589/654.
49. FO 371/99590/665.
50. FO 371/99590/671.
51. FO 371/99590/674.
52. FO 371/99592/732.
53. PRO, CAB 129/57, C (52) 441.
54. FO 371/99591/713.
55. PREM 11/323.
56. *FRUS, 1952–4*, XV, 806.
57. FO 371/105486/148.
58. *FRUS, 1952–4*, XV, 968–9.
59. *Ibid.*, 1016.
60. FO 371/105489/212.
61. FO 371/105489/196.
62. FO 371/105494/329.
63. PREM 11/406.
64. Molotov replied cordially to Churchill's message. As regards Panmunjom the outcome did not depend on Soviet action, 'Nevertheless, we can state with satisfaction that the path to a successful conclusion of the negotiations has already been marked out.' PREM 11/406.
65. FO 371/105499/416.
66. FO 371/105502/487.
67. PREM 11/406.
68. FO 371/105511/737.
69. FO 371/105508/626.
70. *Ibid.*
71. FO 371/105506/568.
72. FO 371/105509/686, 692.

9   The Settlement of the Indochina War

Geoffrey Warner

> Of all the countries in South-East Asia, Indochina is the most directly menaced through the Communist victories in China, and it is important that a friendly democratic regime should be in control . . . a Communist-dominated Viet Minh Government under the Communist Ho Chi Minh . . . would have grave repercussions throughout South-East Asia, and greatly increase the threat to the internal security of [British] Commonwealth and foreign countries in the area.[1]

These are the sentiments one might expect to read in an American policy statement at the end of 1949. In fact, the document is British, a brief on Indochina prepared in December 1949 and approved by the Cabinet's China and South-East Asia Committee as a statement of goverment policy. A comparison with NSC 64, drafted by the American government on 27 February 1950, although not approved by President Truman until 24 April, shows just how close British and American thinking was on Indochina. Thus, NSC 64 concluded:

> Indochina is a key area of Southeast Asia and is under immediate threat . . . The neighboring countries of Thailand and Burma could be expected to fall under Communist domination if Indochina were controlled by a Communist-dominated government. The balance of Southeast Asia would then be in grave hazard.

NSC 64 advocated 'all practical measures . . . to prevent further communist expansion in Southeast Asia', especially Indochina,[2] a policy echoed by a British policy paper of 31 March 1950, which declared that 'everything possible . . . should be done to support the French in Indochina',[3] although this did not include the dispatch of troops. The China and South-East Asia Committee decided on 16 December 1949 that 'there could be no

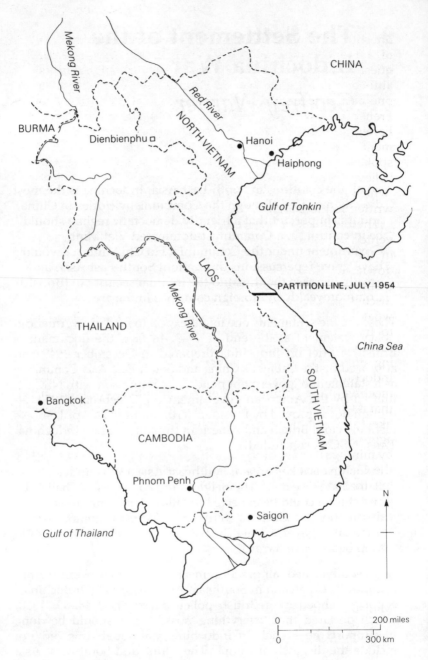

CHINA

Mekong River

BURMA

Dienbienphu □

NORTH VIETNAM

Red River

Hanoi ●

● Haiphong

Gulf of Tonkin

LAOS

PARTITION LINE, JULY 1954

THAILAND

Mekong River

China Sea

SOUTH VIETNAM

● Bangkok

CAMBODIA

N

Phnom Penh ●

● Saigon

Gulf of Thailand

0   200 miles

0   300 km

Map 3: Indochina

question of United Kingdom troops being drawn in' in the event of a French withdrawal from Indochina.[4] This was partly a question of resources: Britain was heavily committed in its own anti-communist guerilla war in South-East Asia, in Malaya. But one also suspects that there was no great enthusiasm for the French-backed regime of Emperor Bao Dai in Vietnam. In a Foreign Office brief for a parliamentary debate on the government's decision to recognize the Bao Dai regime, the ministerial spokesman was informed: 'It is the administration which is believed to command the greatest support there.' The words 'which is believed' were underlined and 'faut[e] de mieux' was written in the margin.[5]

The outbreak of the Korean War in June 1950 probably prevented Indochina from becoming the focal point of the Cold War in the Far East. Nevertheless, after the Korean War bogged down into stalemate in 1951, and as the Conservative government came into office in London, there was a great deal of discussion between the United States and its allies about what should be done if the Chinese turned their attention to Indochina and sought to win a major victory there. The British, however, displayed no more enthusiasm about becoming embroiled in a major war with Communist China over Indochina than they had done over Korea. It was explained at a meeting of the Cabinet's Defence Committee on 19 March 1952 that if China did intervene in Indochina, '[t]he Americans would like to extend the area of conflict beyond the actual point of aggression by bombing ports and communications, and possibly by mining rivers in China, and by instituting a naval blockade of the China coast'. The British Chiefs of Staff, on the other hand, felt that this 'might lead to total war, and that in any event it would increase our own difficulties and dangers in Asia, especially in Hong Kong and Malaya'. They therefore wanted to restrict the bombing of Chinese communications to 'areas immediately adjacent to the battle-front, though this might, if necessary, include the bombing of Chinese territory'. The politicians agreed with the military men. 'It would be silly to waste bombs in the vague inchoate mass of China', said Prime Minister Winston Churchill, 'and wrong to kill thousands of people for no purpose.'[6] There was also a discussion of what would happen if the French withdrew from Indochina altogether, a contingency which Churchill thought quite likely. It was pointed out that '[t]he loss of Indochina to Communism would probably result sooner or later in the establishment of Communist regimes in Siam and Burma. That would bring the Communist threat to the borders of Malaya.' The Chiefs of Staff argued that this threat could be countered by occupying the Songkhla position on the Kra Isthmus, which was in Siamese territory. It is interesting to note that the Chiefs of Staff believed that they could hold Malaya against a full-scale Chinese attack in these circumstances. The Prime Minister said that it was 'too early to assume the worst' and it would therefore be a mistake for the British government to commit itself at this stage. 'It would, however, be prudent to make plans, without expenditure of money or resources, on the lines suggested by the Chiefs of Staff'.[7]

By the end of April 1953 the Defence Committee had reached the conclusion 'that H. M. Government must seize and hold the Songkhla position immediately if the security of Malaya on the landward side was in danger as a result of events in Indochina or Siam'.[8] A special Cabinet committee had even been set up to watch over the situation.[9] There were, in fact, two separate military plans: Operation RINGLET, which dealt with the situation which would arise in the event of a non-military threat (such as the collapse of the Siamese government as a result of developments in Indochina); and Operation IRONY, which dealt with a fully-fledged military threat.[10] It is quite clear, therefore, that fully one year before Dien Bien Phu the British government had not only considered the possibility of a French collapse in Indochina, but also produced contingency plans for that eventuality which it was felt would preserve the integrity of Malaya. At the same time, it would be misleading to imply that the British government was indifferent to what was going on in Indochina. Simply because plans existed for coping with a French collapse, this did not mean that the prospect was viewed with equanimity. As a brief for the Prime Minister put it on 25 June 1953:

> The threat to United Kingdom and other Commonwealth interests in South East Asia, notably Malaya, increases as the position in Indochina deteriorates. With their present policy the French are drifting towards an eventual collapse ... A new lead from Paris and resolute decisions by the French Government are indispensable. ... The present indications are that, so far from facing the necessary decisions of policy and

making the required increased effort, the French may wish to cut their commitments and possibly liquidate them altogether by negotiation with the Communists.[11]

The French foreign minister, Georges Bidault, confirmed his country's interest in a negotiated settlement at a meeting in Washington on 13 July 1953. Alluding to the imminent truce in Korea, he told his British and American colleagues 'that we might soon have a situation in which the fighting had stopped in Korea but was still going on in Indochina. French opinion would find it very hard to accept this and some solution must be found.' Although he made no specific proposal, Bidault implied that any political conference which followed the Korean armistice might also deal with Indochina.[12]

Ho Chi Minh's statement of readiness to negotiate with the French, published in the Swedish newspaper *Expressen* on 29 November 1953, provided further grist to the mill of the peace party in France, but the British did not believe that the time was ripe. A good indication of their thinking is provided in a letter from Denis Allen, the Foreign Office official in charge of Far Eastern affairs, to the British chargé in Peking, Humphrey Trevelyan, which was sent on 8 January 1954 in response to a request for guidance from the latter. Allen reminded Trevelyan that the Foreign Secretary, Sir Anthony Eden, had described Indochina as the 'strategic key' to South-East Asia in the House of Commons on 5 February 1953. He went on:

Its loss to Communism would constitute a grave threat to the remainder of South East Asia and would seriously endanger our position in Malaya. We therefore hope that the French will maintain their efforts to build up the strength and independence of the Associated States [Vietnam,Laos and Cambodia] both politically and militarily, so that when French forces are eventually reduced or withdrawn the States will be able to survive on their own and to resist Communist attempts at penetration.

The best way of ensuring this, Allen believed, was for the French to inflict 'a decisive military defeat' on the Viet Minh. 'A negotiated settlement would only be tolerable if the outcome was such as to safeguard the independence of the Associated States. In our opinion such negotiations can only be carried out from a position of political and military strength, and we do not

consider that such a position has yet been reached.' Nevertheless, Allen recognized that, in adopting this position, 'we are
already entering something of a vicious circle', and conceded
that 'a Communist offer of Five-Power talks baited with a
promise of an Indochina settlement would be difficult for any
French Government to resist'. He thought that the forthcoming
Berlin conference between Britain, France, the United States and
the Soviet Union, which had been convened mainly in order to
discuss the German problem, but at which other matters would
no doubt be raised, would be 'worth watching from this point of
view'.[13]

If we are to believe Sir Anthony Eden's memoirs, the Foreign
Secretary did not entirely share these opinions:

> at the beginning of 1954 my thoughts began to turn to the
> possibility of some form of partition as a solution which might
> bring hostilities to an end and effect a settlement which would
> hold. My chief concern was for Malaya. I wanted to ensure an
> effective barrier as far to the north of that country as possible.
> I thought it possible that the Western powers might guarantee
> Laos and Cambodia and part of Vietnam. More important
> still, I hoped that matters might be so contrived that India,
> and perhaps some other eastern nations, would join in the
> guarantee. This would buttress the agreement. I was
> convinced that the longer negotiation was delayed, the more
> difficult the situation would become for the French.[14]

For Eden, therefore, the Berlin conference offered an opportunity
to get the ball of negotiation rolling, and not a dangerous temp-
tation for the war-weary French. Eden made ample use of the
opportunity and the communiqué issued at the end of the Berlin
conference on 18 February 1954 announced the convening of
another conference at Geneva on 26 April to which, in addition
to representatives from the four powers, those from Communist
China 'and other interested states' (including the Viet Minh
and the Associated States) would be invited to discuss the
problem of ending the war in Indochina. Predictably, the Viet
Minh sought to use the interval between Berlin and Geneva to
strengthen their already powerful negotiating position. On 13
March 1954 they launched the first assault against the French-
held fortress of Dien Bien Phu in the far north-west of Vietnam.
Between them the decision to summon the Geneva conference
and the battle for Dien Bien Phu were to precipitate one of the

gravest international crises since the end of the Second World War and one of the deepest rifts in the Western alliance.

The United States administration had not been at all happy about a conference to discuss a negotiated settlement of the war in Indochina, still less one to which Communist China was invited. Indeed, according to the Secretary of State, John Foster Dulles, he had only agreed to it on condition that the French government would bring the treaty for the establishment of the European Defence Community (EDC), the elaborate scheme for rearming West Germany and integrating it into the Western alliance, before the French National Assembly by Easter, thus bringing the two-year delay in its ratification to an end.[15] Even before the Berlin conference ended, a number of indications reached London from Washington that, on account of the deteriorating military and political situation in Indochina, the US administration was contemplating some kind of increased involvement in the conflict in order to stiffen French resolve. On 8 February 1954 the Under-Secretary of State, General Walter Bedell Smith, confirmed to the British ambassador, Sir Roger Makins, that a reappraisal of American policy was indeed in progress. Bedell Smith confessed that he did not find either the military or the political outlook encouraging and felt 'that the French were not aiming so much to win the war, as to get into a position in which they could negotiate'. The Americans, on the other hand, 'were doing all they could to persuade the French that their negotiating position would be pretty hopeless unless they negotiated from strength'. To this end the United States was 'ready to give as much assistance as possible', although Bedell Smith emphasized that this would not include the dispatch of American troops, which '[t]he President would not do ... even if he had the power'.[16] Less than a week later, however, another member of the British embassy staff reported that this was not the view of everyone in the administration. In particular, Admiral Arthur Radford, the Chariman of the Joint Chiefs of Staff, 'holds firmly the view that the defence of Indochina – or rather Tonking – is essential: and that if necessary American troops should go in'.[17]

Makins became sufficiently concerned to request guidance from his superiors in London as to what the British reaction to greater American involvement in Indochina would be. It came in the form of another personal letter from Denis Allen, which showed a marked shift in attitude from that expressed in his letter to Humphrey Trevelyan some seven weeks earlier. Although restating the dangers inherent in a communist take-over of Indochina and the desirability of a Viet Minh defeat, Allen went on:

> It is, however, becoming increasingly doubtful whether the all out defeat of communism is possible ... the French ... are clearly only playing for time, while doing their utmost ... to contain the war within Indochina. It is still not certain that time is on the French side. More massive United States intervention would not necessarily help the military situation, if its only result was to bring about a corresponding increase in the scale of Chinese intervention. ... Any negotiated settlement is bound in present circumstances to involve leaving behind in Indochina a considerable degree of communist influence ... Nevertheless, the obvious risks of any such settlement might have to be accepted if the only alternative seemed to be the enlargement of the war through increased intervention from outside.

Allen concluded 'that at any rate until the Geneva Conference has met this country would be reluctant to see the United States involve themselves further in Indochina on a scale which seemed to increase the risk of Chinese intervention and thus of extending the war'.[18] Although it was sent on 24 February 1954, more than a fortnight before the onset of the siege of Dien Bien Phu, Allen's letter was a remarkable summary of what British policy was in fact to be throughout the crisis which developed at the end of March. It was also, of course, much closer to the position which Eden claimed had been his since the beginning of the year.

By the end of March the Foreign Office had produced a briefing paper on 'Policy towards Indochina', which was in-tended to guide British policy up to and including the Geneva conference. It began by pointing out that, although the defence of Indochina was so important to free world interests that every effort should be made to induce the French to press on with the dual policy of resisting the Viet Minh and building up the Associated States, recent developments did not encourage the belief that this would be successful.

> *Politically*, the conditions necessary to inspire all-out popular support for the national struggle have not yet been created in

Vietnam . . . In France, war-weariness is increasing . . .
Militarily, despite massive American material aid, the
despatch of French reinforcements to Indochina and the rapid
expansion of the Vietnamese army, the initiative remains with
the Vietminh and the French Commander-in-Chief has been
able to make no better claim than that the present campaign
has been a 'dead heat'.

On the subject of possible increased American involvement, the
briefing paper noted that this could take a number of forms:
even more material aid, the provision of instructors and advisers
as in Korea, intervention by American air or naval forces, intervention by Formosan or South Korean troops, and intervention
by American ground forces. It was felt that although the provision of more material aid and instructors would not provoke
Chinese intervention, it would be some time before this could
produce results. On the other hand, '[a]ny direct intervention
by the armed forced of any external nation . . . would probably
result in Chinese intervention, with the danger that this might
ultimately lead to global war.' The briefing paper went on to
draw the gloomy conclusion that if its assumptions were correct,
'there may no longer be any prospect of a favourable solution to
the Indochina problem and the most we can do is to strive for
the adoption of the least disadvantageous course'. After examin-
ing a number of possible solutions (a cease-fire in place, a coalition government, free elections and partition), the briefing
paper came down in favour of the last on the grounds that 'it
might salvage more from the general wreck than any other'.
Such partition would have to be effected in such a way, however, as to leave the whole of Laos and Cambodia outside
communist control.[19] At their meeting on 31 March 1954 the
Chiefs of Staff, while reiterating their former view that '[t]he
only really acceptable solution to the present situation in
Indochina was a decisive defeat of the Viet Minh by the French',
nevertheless approved the Foreign Office briefing paper on the
grounds that such a defeat was 'very unlikely'. On the following day the briefing paper was also endorsed by the Foreign
Secretary.[20]

In the meantime, however, the United States administration
had publicly sounded its clarion call for 'united action' to save
the situation in Indochina in Dulles' speech to the Overseas
Press Club in New York on 29 March 1954. On the following

day the Secretary of State told Sir Roger Makins 'that the key sentence in his speech about united action . . . was based on a report of the Joint Chiefs of Staff which had been approved by the National Security Council and the President'.[21] On 2 April, however, he admitted that '[w]hen he had spoken of united action he had not had any specific plan in mind. Many courses were open. Much depended on the views of the Allies and how far they were ready to go in joint action.'[22] Nevertheless, it seemed clear from the rest of the conversation that the Americans were intending, first and foremost, to try to force the Chinese to stop helping the Viet Minh. As Makins reported to London:

> Dulles said the Administration had concluded that if it was made plain to the Chinese that continuation of aid to Viet Minh was dangerous for China, they would desist . . . The American Chiefs of Staff believed that the Allies had a military superiority in the Far East which they would not have in three or four years' time; that the threat of action would be a sufficient deterrent; but that if not we should be in a strong position to carry it out. This involved risks, but the risks would be diminished if a group of countries joined in the warning.[23]

Makins clearly saw the gap which had opened up between British and American perceptions of the situation in Indochina. 'Hitherto we have agreed pretty well with the Americans on the day-to-day handling of policy in the Far East', he reported on 4 April 1954, 'in spite of longer range differences of political appreciation. But though we may continue for a time to agree on tactics, a decision to range ourselves with the fundamental American decision or dissociate ourselves from it cannot be long delayed and will have a profound effect over the whole field of Anglo-American relations.' The embassy's view was that, despite the risks involved, the British should go along with the United States. 'If we align ourselves with the Administration we shall be able to bring our influence continually to bear upon them. We now have an opportunity to retrieve the damage to our world position and to Commonwealth solidarity which the ANZUS Pact has undoubtedly caused and to work for a security system in the Far East in which we shall have our rightful place. The Americans will certainly desire our cooperation and would, I believe, be ready to listen to our views as well as support us elsewhere even though our contribution in resources is small.'[24] On the same day that Sir Roger wrote this, President Eisenhower dispatched an urgent personal letter to Churchill. Among other things, this confirmed Makins's prediction that if Britain sided with the United States over 'united action' in Indochina, the latter would support British interests 'elsewhere'. His letter also contained, however, an ominous addition to the possible consequences of 'united action'. Whereas both Dulles and Bedell Smith had strenuously denied any intention of using ground troops, Eisenhower wrote: 'I do not envisage the need of any *appreciable* ground forces on you or our part.'[25]

The question of British support for the American proposal in favour of 'united action' in Indochina came before the full Cabinet on 7 April 1954. The Prime Minister read out Eisenhower's letter to him and the Foreign Secretary summarized a paper setting out his views which he had previously tabled for his colleagues:

> The proposal to organise the collective defence of South East Asia . . . is to be welcomed. It could remove the anomaly of our exclusion from ANZUS and contribute to the security of Hong Kong and Malaya. At the same time, with the Geneva Conference in prospect, I have grave misgivings about the timing of the proposed arrangement. There appears to be no likelihood of a French military collapse in Indochina between now and the Geneva Conference, by which time the rains should have started, making large-scale campaigning impossible for several months . . . In the circumstances, to proceed with the United States proposal in all haste before Geneva would impair the prospect of any sucessful negotiation at Geneva . . .
> . . . The fundamental weakness of the United States proposal is its assumption that the threat of retaliation against China would cause her to withdraw aid from the Vietminh . . . If I am right in [my] view, the joint warning to China would have no effect and the coalition would then have to withdraw ignominiously or else embark on warlike action against China. Neither blockade nor the bombing of China's internal and external communication, which the United States Government appear to have in mind, were considered by our Chiefs of Staff to be militarily effective when these were discussed in connection with Korea. They would, however,

give China every excuse for invoking the Sino-Soviet Treaty and might thus lead to a world war.

The time to consider a warning against China, argued Eden, was later, possibly after a settlement had been reached at Geneva, when the Chinese could be warned not to breach it. Since American ideas were still not fully formed and since a proposal to organize some form of collective security in South-East Asia was attractive, the Foreign Secretary proposed to accept President Eisenhower's suggestion that Dulles should come to London in order to put Britain's views directly to him. The Cabinet accepted Eden's view.[26]

The Foreign Office briefing paper for the talks with Dulles repeated the objections to the American proposals for 'united action' and stressed the advantages of a British counter-proposal. In view of the controversy which subsequently erupted over this issue, it is important to note that the Foreign Office brief stated unequivocally:

> Her Majesty's Government accept the principle that South-East Asia defence should be organised on the basis of a coalition of interested nations *and agree that the necessary exchanges with the Governments concerned should begin at once. However, no announcement regarding the proposed coalition should be made until the Geneva Conference has begun and we have some idea of how the negotiations there may be going.*[27]

During the conversations with Dulles on 11 and 12 April 1954, Eden carefully distinguished between two aspects of the American proposals. The first was the question of forming a lasting collective security system for South-East Asia, which the British government welcomed. The second was the question of Indochina itself, where the Foreign Secretary was not prepared to go beyond 'a warning that we should not allow the prospects of the Geneva Conference to be prejudiced by military action'. Dulles on the other hand made it clear that his main interest was the present situation in Indochina, although he agreed that an *ad hoc* coalition to deal with this 'might eventually develop into a defence organisation for South East Asia on the ANZUS or NATO model.' Referring to an American draft of the communiqué to be issued at the end of the meeting, Eden stated bluntly that 'it would be difficult for HMG to give an undertaking in advance of the Geneva Conference regarding action to be taken subsequently'. Dulles replied that a situation might still arise in South-East Asia in which intervention was necessary. He went on: 'The United States Government was convinced that Indochina was the place for such intervention, provided two requirements could be met: (1) an unequivocal declaration by the French Government of independence for the Associated States, and (2) the placing of the conflict on an international basis.' Eden could not accept this. He explained 'that British public opinion, with the Geneva Conference in prospect, would be firmly opposed to any present commitment to become involved in what was an unpopular war in Indochina'.[28]

At a ministerial meeting on the evening of 12 April, Eden submitted a redraft of the communiqué and explained that he had managed to insert 'an expression of hope that the Geneva Conference would lead to the restoration of peace in Indochina, and . . . had excluded from it any statement which might commit us to provide direct military assistance in Indochina'. After some amendment, the Foreign Secretary's colleagues accepted his draft.[29] So did Dulles when the two men met with their advisers for the third time on 13 April. The only problem which remained was which countries should be invited to any discussion on the collective defence of South-East Asia. Throughout the discussions Eden had urged upon the Secretary of State the importance of involving India. Dulles, on the other hand, argued that to invite that country might prompt demands in the United States that Formosa and South Korea should be included as well, a position which (it was well known) the British strenuously opposed. It was finally agreed, according to the British record of the meeting, 'that in any statement to the House of Commons, Mr Eden should explain that the whole question of membership was a matter for further consideration and that it would be discussed with the Goverment of India as with the Government of Pakistan and others'.[30] This did not, however, settle the question of the next steps. The Foreign Office brief for the visit had stated that preliminary exchanges between interested governments could begin at once, provided no public announcement was made before the Geneva conference, and in a telegram to the State Department Dulles reported that after he had returned to Washington, 'we would get in touch with [the] British to see how best we might proceed in organising united will to resist aggression in S[outh] E[ast] A[sia]. One possibility was to establish a formal working group in Washington. Eden thought this [a] good idea and said Makins would be available.'[31] There is nothing corresponding to these two sentences in the British record.

Dulles acted according to his understanding of the agreement that had been reached. On 16 April Makins reported that the Secretary of State was convening the Ambassadors of the United Kingdom, New Zealand, Australia, the Philippines, France, Thailand and the Associated States on the 20th, partly in order to establish a working group to look into the question of establishing some form of collective defence for South-East Asia. Makins said that he assumed he could agree to this proposal.[32] An indignant Eden replied that he most certainly could not. In a series of telegrams he expressed his strong disagreement with the secretary of State's action. 'According to my understanding', he wrote, 'we reached no definite agreement in London on either (i) the procedure for the "examination of the possibility of establishing a collective defence" or (ii) a definite list of states to be approached.'[33] The unfortunate Ambassador duly saw both Bedell Smith and Dulles, but reported on 18 April that the invitations to the meeting on the 20th had not only already been issued, but also the fact of its being held had been published in the press. In the circumstances, both Dulles and Makins thought that the best solution would be to 'convert' the meeting into a larger and more general one which would provide some background briefing in advance of the Geneva conference. Although Dulles did not say so to the British, it is clear from American sources that he was furious about the whole incident, firmly believing that Eden had gone back on his word. In this he seems to have been correct. A precious item of testimony from the diary of Evelyn Shuckburgh reveals that on 3 May 1954 Denis Allen told him and another Foreign Office official that 'we are getting very near having cheated the Americans on this question of starting talks on S.E. Asian security ... [W]hen Dulles was in London A[nthony] E[den] *did* indicate that we should be willing to start such talks at once, provided we were not committed to any action in Indochina. The American record showed that, but ours was obscure on the point and A[nthony] E[den] has always denied it.'[34] What *may* have happened, as Eden explained to Dulles when the two men next met in Paris on 22 April, was that when he had agreed to the informal working group, he had forgotten about a meeting at the end of April between the so-called 'Colombo powers' (India, Pakistan, Burma, Ceylon and Indonesia) and felt the proposed meeting would create problems there.[35] If this really was the case, it is surprising that the British Foreign Secretary did not admit it beforehand. It may also be that what upset Eden was the public nature of the proposed meeting. It will be recalled that the Foreign Office brief for the Dulles visit had specifically stated there should be no publicity. Here, the Americans were undoubtedly to blame.

Later in the month, in Paris Dulles made one more attempt to propel Eden into 'united action' in Indochina before the opening of the Geneva conference. On 23 April he told the British Foreign Secretary that Bidault 'had indicated that . . . the French were all but determined to quit the fight in Indochina altogether'. Dulles commented 'that he was afraid we are confronted with the collapse of France as a great power . . . A vacuum would be created not only in the Far East, but in Africa and other parts of the world, and this would confront the Western alliance with many very grave problems.' Eden was not prepared to take Dulles' word for this and wanted to see for himself what Bidault thought. He saw the Frenchman later that evening and found him much less pessimistic than Dulles.[36] In the meantime, however, a telegram had reportedly arrived from the French commander in Indochina, General Navarre, in which he claimed 'that only a powerful strike by the American air force in the next 72 hours could save the situation at Dien Bien Phu . . .' When confronted with this information by Dulles, Eden replied that he did not see how aerial intervention could have much effect on the situation at this stage and that 'it might have far-reaching consequences'. The Secretary of State seemed to agree, but said that if Eden felt able to stand by him, 'he was prepared to recommend to the President to ask for "war powers"'. Eden was now so concerned by the gloomy predictions of a collapse of French morale and even a possible lapse into neutralism propounded by Dulles and the NATO Supreme Commander, General Gruenther, that he offered to hold secret talks in Washington about the possibility of going to the assistance of Siam.[37]

On the following day the British found themselves confronted by the most belligerent member of the US administration, Admiral Radford, as well as Dulles. Shuckburgh's account of the meeting conveys the essence of the meeting in a fraction of the space taken up by the official telegram:

> Dulles ... proceeded to tell us, in effect [he wrote], that the
> US Government are ready to give immediate military help to
> the French in Indochina provided we will do so too, and
> subject to Congress giving the President the necessary
> powers. Radford, whom we did not think very intelligent,
> and who is obviously raring for a scrap, said that the only
> thing to do, to stop French and Vietnam morale collapsing
> when Dien Bien Phu falls (as it must in a day or two), is for
> US/UK more or less to take over the conduct of the war, push
> the French into the background and hope that the locals will
> be so inspired by this spectacle that they will rally against the
> Communists. He was not specific as to the military action
> required, but it involved sending RAF squadrons from Malaya
> to Tongking and an aircraft carrier if we can. We were deeply
> disturbed by this[38] ...

What the Americans were now envisaging was, of course,
something much wider than intervention at Dien Bien Phu.
Indeed, Dulles told Eden that 'there was no (repeat no) possibility
of United States participation in the ... battle, both because
the President had not the power to act with such speed, and
because it was perfectly clear than no intervention could now
save the fortress'.[39] The American request, as Shuckburgh
noted, placed the British on the horns of a painful dilemma. 'If
we refuse to co-operate with the US plan', he wrote, 'we strain
the Alliance. If we do as Dulles asks, we certainly provoke
the bitterest hostility of India and probably all other Asiatic
states and destroy the Commonwealth.' Moreover, 'a war for
Indochina would be about as difficult a thing to put across to the
British public as you could find.'[40]

Eden returned to London that night and briefed the Prime
Minister at the latter's country residence, Chequers. At 11 a.m.
on 25 April (a Sunday), the Prime Minister presided over an
emergency ministerial meeting at No. 10 Downing Street to
which the Chiefs of Staff were also invited. Eden explained what
had taken place in Paris and relayed the American request for
this latest form of 'united action'. Then, basing himself on a
document drafted by Shuckburgh, he

> said that ... his recommendation to his colleagues was that
> they should decline to give any immediate undertaking to
> afford military assistance to the French in Indochina. It now
> seemed inevitable that large parts of Indochina should fall

under Communist control, and the best hope of a lasting solution lay in some form of partition. Our object should therefore be to strengthen the negotiating position of the French at the Geneva Conference. Their position would not be strengthened by a premature military intervention which would soon be seen to have been ineffective. On the contrary, he thought that France's Allies could at the moment make a better impression on the Chinese if they left them to guess what action they might subsequently take to help the French in Indochina.

The meeting endorsed the Foreign Secretary's recommendation that Britain should not accede to the American request, together with an eight-point statement of principles (drafted by Allen which would guide him in further discussions on the subject at Geneva. Among other things, these provided an assurance that, if a settlement were reached at Geneva, Britain would be prepared to take part in guaranteeing it and in setting up some form of collective defence in South-East Asia. If no settlement were reached, Britain would be ready to consider with its allies what action should be taken. It was, in any event, 'ready to join with the United States Government now in studying measures to ensure the defence of Siam and the rest of South-East Asia including Malaya in the event of all or part of Indochina being lost'.[41]

The crisis, however, was still not over. In the afternoon the French ambassador in London, René Massigli, asked urgently to see Eden. Despite what Dulles had told Eden in Paris the previous day, the Americans were now saying that if the British and the other powers would sign a declaration of intention to stop the expansion of communism in South-East Asia, the administration could obtain a congressional resolution which would enable a carrier-based strike force to go into action at Dien Bien Phu in three days' time.[42] In the light of this new information, ministers and Chiefs of Staff were hastily recalled for another meeting at 4 p.m. Eden criticized what he called 'this indirect approach [by the Americans] to the United Kingdom Government through the French'. Although the administration had spoken to the French ambassador in Washington, it made no corresponding communication to his British counterpart. The Foreign Secretary made it clear that he believed that the proposal for a strike at Dien Bien Phu was a red herring, and that the real objective would turn out to be China. Ministers had no authority from Parliament to support such action and it would not be approved by the United Nations; it might, moreover, 'be the first step towards a third world war'. The Prime Minister and his colleagues were of the same opinion and reaffirmed their earlier decision against intervention.[43]

Although Admiral Radford sought in vain to persuade both Churchill and the British Chief of Staff of the folly of their ways when he came to London on 26 April 1954, it is clear that the ministerial meetings of the 25th marked the end of any prospect of 'united action' before the Geneva conference.[44] The reasons for the British government's reluctance to embrace it are also clear. First, there was the very real fear that involvement might escalate into a third world war. Secondly, there was considerable doubt that the French, for both military and political reasons, would stay the course in Indochina, whatever was done on their behalf. Thirdly, there was concern about the effect on public opinion. Finally, there is no doubt that the majority of Commonwealth countries, especially in Asia, would not have supported Britain if the latter had agreed to 'united action'. Whether any of the fearful possibilities envisaged by the British government would in fact have come about if 'united action' had been implemented is, of course, a matter for speculation. In the light of what we now know from communist sources, it seems unlikely that either the Russians or the Chinese would have risked a world war for the sake of the Viet Minh. One thing, however, is certain: the crisis over 'united action' had subjected the Anglo-American relationship to the gravest strain. This was not a good omen for the Geneva conference.

The Geneva conference with Eden and the Russian, Vyacheslav Molotov, as co-chairmen, began on 8 May 1954 in the most inauspicious circumstances, for Dien Bien Phu had fallen to the Viet Minh the previous day. The British idea of a negotiated settlement had been spelt out as early as March 1954 and comprised the preservation of the whole of Laos and Cambodia from communist control and the partition of Vietnam,[45] but it was of course recognized that the United Kingdom had very little control over the situation. The most it could do was to seek to exercise influence, not least over its own allies. In this connection, Eden recorded on 12 May that two things were essential: the French should make up their minds what they would accept; and the Americans should not press them to hold out for more than they could hope to get.[46] Unfortunately, the French government under Joseph Laniel seemed completely unable to reach a firm decision on anything. On 13 May it survived a vote of confidence in the National Assembly by only two votes; from then on it was living on borrowed time until its eventual overthrow on 12 June. It was only when Pierre Mendès-France took over as Prime Minister a week later that France seemed to enjoy firm leadership. As for the United States, it still seemed to the British that they did not really want a settlement at all. Twice, on 30 April and again on the evening of 1 May, Dulles sought to convince Eden of the need for some sort of action in Indochina. During the final conversation he said that he was not asking for any material assistance, but only for 'moral support' and alluded to the possibility of holding a bridgehead for perhaps two years until Vietnamese troops had been trained in order to defend their own country.[47] It was no wonder that Eden felt that whereas his concept of a South-East Asian defence organization was one which would guarantee a possible settlement, the Americans seemed to be thinking in terms of one which would help to reconquer Indochina.[48]

The British Foreign Secretary did, however, give Dulles a memorandum on 30 April 1954 in which he expressed his readiness to begin secret talks about a collective defence organization for South-East Asia, and by 5 May this had been expanded into an offer of discussions within the framework of the Five-Power Staff Agency (a military co-ordinating body originally set up in 1952 and comprising representatives of Britain, France, the United States, Australia and New Zealand). After Eden and Bedell Smith agreed on the terms of a public statement about the talks on 10 May, Shuckburgh noted in his diary: 'We are getting into line again.'[49] Alas, the apparent harmony was not to last long. On 8 May the United States had dropped what Bedell Smith called 'a broad and unmistakable hint' to the French that it was still ready to proceed to an examination of the internationalization of the war. In the wake of the disaster at Dien Bien Phu the French were ready to clutch at any straw, and bilateral negotiations began.[50] The British knew nothing of these Franco-American discussions until news of them appeared in the press on 15 May. Armed with this information a furious Eden confronted Bedell Smith on the following day. The hapless American could only admit what was going on. He did, however, deny that the matter was anything like as serious as the newspaper headlines had suggested. 'What was contemplated', he explained, 'was American help in training', a remark which was as disingenuous as his denial that the United States had taken the initiative in the talks. Eden explained that in the circumstances the British could not possibly proceed with the Five-Power Staff conversations.[51] An assurance from Bidault, on 17 May, that there was no question of the French requesting any intervention until the Geneva conference was over, fortunately led Eden to reconsider his refusal, but he remained suspicious and critical of American intentions.

Eden explained to his Cabinet colleagues on 24 May 1954 that he felt that there was 'a fair chance' of agreement at Geneva and would continue to work for one. When Churchill suggested that even if the United States were to intervene militarily in Indochina, Britain need not necessarily dissociate itself politically from such action, Eden said that, as things stood, 'he saw little prospect that a Western military intervention ... would command sympathy or support, either in the other countries of South-East Asia or in the United Nations or from any substantial body of opinion in this country'.[52] For Eden this disagreement must have seemed all the more serious because of the Prime Minister's insistence on the need for an early visit to Washington for discussions with President Eisenhower. The subject had been broached in April and it seems clear from the available documentation that Indochina was not to be the main item on the agenda. Nevertheless, Eden was deeply concerned at the possible consequences of Churchill's frequently expressed desire for a meeting of minds with the Americans upon the developing situation at Geneva. The day after the Cabinet discussion Eden, who had returned to Geneva, cabled Churchill that it would be a grave mistake in his view if the visit to Washington (arranged for 18 June) were to be announced before the position at the conference had become clearer. Any announcement, the Foreign Secretary warned, would be assumed to be connected with Anglo-American differences over Indochina and it would be felt 'that these differences had attained such serious proportions that you felt it necessary to visit the United States yourself in order to compose them.'[53]

On 29 May Eden heard to his surprise that the French and the Americans had agreed on a plan for intervention in Indochina. On the following day he warned Field-Marshal Sir John Harding, the Chief of the Imperial General Staff, who was representing Britain at the forthcoming Five-Power Staff conversations, that he should not allow himself to be manoeuvred into a position in which the only option under discussion was intervention, and on 1 June he told Churchill that he was becoming increasingly worried at the situation which might develop at the time of the Washington visit. The French predicted it would be the danger period for a possible Viet Minh attack on Hanoi and, in addition, there was 'only too much evidence ... that the main American concern is not now, if it ever has been, for the success of the conference, but with preparations for intervention.' He feared that, in the circumstances, he and the Prime Minister might arrive in the US capital at the precise moment when the French were in deep trouble and the American desire for intervention at its height. 'The call for us to take part in such an adventure would then be intensified and the strain on Anglo-American relations, when we had to decline, could be all the worse.'[54] The issue came before the Cabinet on 5 June 1954 when Churchill emphasized that the opportunity for personal discussions with President Eisenhower should not be missed. Eden, who had once more returned from Geneva to take part in the Cabinet meeting, said that it would be difficult for him to accompany the Prime Minister if the conference had not been concluded. This did not mean he was against the Prime Minister going on his own but, at the same time, he warned, 'an embarrassing situation might arise if, while the Prime Minister was in Washington, the Geneva Conference broke down and strong political pressures developed in the United States in favour of military intervention in Indochina'. Eden's reservations clearly carried a great deal of weight. Several ministers felt it would be 'unfortunate' if he were unable to accompany the Prime Minister, and the Cabinet agreed to defer a decision.[55]

Soon after he returned to Geneva, Eden sent a gloomy report on the prospects to the Prime Minister. There were, he said, three clear issues on which the conference was divided: the form of supervision of any agreement, the composition of the supervising authority and the independent status of Laos and Cambodia. 'All that can be said', he continued, 'is that if we have to break these are clear issues which world opinion should be able to understand.' In the event of a breakdown, he suggested that Laos and Cambodia should both appeal to the United Nations on the grounds that they had been invaded by the Viet Minh.[56] Bedell Smith, to whom Eden had also communicated his thoughts, delightedly cabled Washington that it was now clear that the British Foreign Secretary believed that negotiations had failed and was ready 'to move ahead quickly in Southeast Asia coalition which would guarantee Cambodia and most of Laos under umbrella of some U.N. action'.[57] This was putting it too strongly. The British position with regard to the military consequences of a defeat in Indochina and the formation of a South-East Asian defence organization had not altered. The Five-Power Staff talks had begun in Washington on 3 June and Field-Marshal Harding's proposal that, if necessary, he would record specific UK dissent from any argument that Malaya would be indefensible in the event of the loss of Indochina, Burma and Siam, was endorsed by the Chiefs of Staff. And when the State Department requested that Thai and Philippine military representatives be invited to take part in some of the discussions, a Foreign Office official commented that this looked like 'a fresh attempt on the part of Mr Dulles to get his pre-selected South-East Asia Pact going on a basis unacceptable to us'.[58]

In any event, there were soon to be signs of a breakthrough at Geneva. On 10 June, when Eden (on advice from London) gave a public warning that the conference was on the verge of failure, he was told 'that things were possibly beginning to move' in the bilateral conversations between French and Viet Minh military representatives.[59] Six days later, Chou En-lai asked to see him and admitted for the first time that the situation in Laos and Cambodia was different from that in Vietnam. He added that, provided there were no American bases in either Laos or Cambodia, both the Viet Minh and the Chinese would be willing to recognize the existing royal governments after the latter had reached internal agreements with the 'resistance' forces. Finally, Chou said that he thought it would not be difficult to persuade the Viet Minh to withdraw their forces from the two countries as part of a general agreement concerning the withdrawal of all foreign forces. Eden concluded his report to London by saying that he had received a strong impression that Chou En-lai favoured a negotiated settlement in Indochina, although it remained to be seen how much influence he exercised over the Viet Minh.[60] In the meantime the proposed visit to Washington by Churchill and Eden had at last been arranged for 25 June.

Whatever the reason for the shift in the communist attitude at Geneva – a continuing fear of possible US intervention or the belief that the fall of the Laniel government in France would lead to a more congenial successor – it succeeded in dissipating the atmosphere of gloom which had enveloped the British Cabinet's deliberations on 5 June. When Eden reported to his colleagues on the 22nd, he felt able to say that he now believed a negotiated settlement 'was not beyond reach', and set out his objectives for Washington in the following terms:

(a) We must persuade the Americans to give the French at least a chance of reaching a settlement in the next few weeks.

(b) We must continue to make it clear that we cannot consider intervening in Indochina and we must do our best to restrain the Americans from doing so . . .

(c) We must again make it plain that we can accept no further commitments in regard to 'united action' in South-East Asia until the outcome of Geneva is known.

(d) But we can express willingness to examine at once and in secret how best we can proceed to strengthen our common defences.

(e) We should discuss how the principal Asian powers in that area can best be associated with this work.

But we should not agree, before Geneva is over, to any wider and more publicised meeting, at which Siam and the Philippines would be the only Asian countries present, to plan and proclaim an anti-Communist alliance.[61]

When Churchill and Eden arrived in Washington, they found that the Americans had modified their policies to a considerable extent. On 26 June Dulles told Eden that the earlier negotiations with the Laniel government concerning the possible inter-nationalization of the war must be deemed to have lapsed. The US Secretary of State also agreed with the thesis that partition was a more acceptable solution in the case of Vietnam than immediate nationwide elections, the first time an authoritative American spokesperson had been prepared to comment favourably on either alternative in conversation with the British.[62] By the conclusion of their talks on 29 June, the two sides had agreed on a seven-point document to be presented to Mendès-France containing the terms of a negotiated settlement in

Indochina which both Britain and the United States would be prepared to 'respect'. These included the integrity and independence of Laos and Cambodia and the preservation of 'at least the southern half of Vietnam'.[63] This was virtually identical to the proposals put forward in the Foreign Office brief for Geneva the previous March. Agreement was also reached on the establishment of a joint Anglo-American study group meeting in Washington, which would examine the steps which would be necessary with regard to a collective security pact for South-East Asia.[64] The old tensions soon re-emerged, however. At the first meeting of the study group on 7 July, Bedell Smith admitted that the United States still believed that there was little chance of a satisfactory settlement at Geneva and had therefore been concentrating on the problem of collective security. Indeed, three days later the Americans produced a draft treaty. This document was not at all to Eden's liking. He complained that the area to be covered by the proposed pact was 'undesirably vague' and went 'far beyond the understanding which we reached in Washingon'. At the same time, he objected to a specific reference in another part of the draft to 'Communist subversion and infiltration'[65].

On 13 July the Foreign Secretary reported from Paris that 'Dulles cut a sorry figure' in his discussions with him and Mendès-France when the Secretary of State tried to explain a decision that the Americans should not be present at the concluding stages of the Geneva conference. 'He kept trying to insinuate', wrote Eden, 'that Mendès-France . . . would abandon the seven points . . . and that internal American politics made it impossible for him to underwrite any settlement.' Both Eden and Mendès strove to convince Dulles that the United States *must* be represented, if only to demonstrate Western solidarity, and the Secretary of State eventually agreed to reconsider.[66] It was in fact the case, as Eden had told Dulles, that 'we were on the knife edge [at Geneva] with an even chance of getting the sort of agreement we all wanted'. On 18 July Chou En-lai broke the deadlock over the composition of the body which would supervise the various cease-fire agreements by proposing India, Canada and Poland. Two days later Mendès-France and the Viet Minh delegate announced that agreement had been reached on a line of partition in Vietnam (the 17th parallel) and that nationwide elections, which the Viet Minh had wanted to hold as soon as possible, had been postponed until July 1956. The detailed agreements for Laos, Cambodia and Vietnam were signed on 21 July 1954. The United States did not associate itself formally with the outcome of the conference, but Bedell Smith did make a unilateral declaration in which he took note of what had been agreed and pledged that the Americans would not disturb the settlement by the threat or use of force.[67] In the absence of adequate documentation from the communist side, it is of course impossible to assess the extent to which British policy facilitated the successful conclusion of the Geneva agreements on Indochina, although it seems safe to assert that its influence was positive rather than negative. The documents leave absolutely no room for doubt that Eden genuinely wanted a settlement and that he did all he possibly could to obtain one. He told his Cabinet colleagues on 23 July that it must be assumed that when elections were held in Vietnam the communists would win them. In Laos and Cambodia, however, the existing regimes were more soundly based and should therefore be able to survive.

> The essence of the settlement [he concluded] was that Laos and Cambodia should remain as an independent and neutral buffer between China and Siam. It was therefore essential that the United States should not seek to establish any military influence in these two States. Any attempt to do so was bound to provoke some counter-move by China.[68]

The crisis over Indochina in 1954 had highlighted tensions in Anglo-American relations which had been evident for some time, and which went well beyond any personal antagonism between Eden and Dulles: at least since the outbreak of the Korean War, British governments had been deeply concerned at what they saw as a lack of political sophistication and 'trigger-happiness' in American policy, especially in the Far East, a region where Britain had little to gain and much to lose from any major conflict (particularly if this involved China or meant the use of nuclear weapons). The temporary resolution of Anglo-American differences, exemplified by the signature on 8 September 1954 of the Manila Treaty, which established the South-East Asian Treaty Organisation (SEATO), unfortunately failed to solve the long-term problems of the area. Indeed, in the case of Indochina, it can be argued that it made them worse. Although Laos and Cambodia, as well as South Vietnam, were excluded from actual membership of the new alliance, they were accorded its protection by a special protocol. To the Chinese this was a clear violation of their neutral status, which had been agreed at Geneva. It is impossible to say what would have happened if Laos and Cambodia had been genuinely neutralized at Geneva, as Eden argued they were, but it is clear that American policy in the area – including the establishment of SEATO – helped to undermine this as much as the regional imperialism of the Vietnamese communists.[76]

Notes

1. PRO, CAB 134/669, SAC (49) 17.
2. FRUS *1950*, VI (Washington, DC, 1976), 747.
3. CAB 134/670, SAC (50) 3.
4. CAB 134/669, SAC (49) 8th.
5. Kenneth Younger Papers, Scott minute, 4 April 1950. By kind permission of Lady Younger.
6. CAB 131/12, D (52) 2nd.
7. *Ibid.*
8. CAB 131/13, D (53) 13th.
9. CAB 128/26 (19 Feb. 1953).
10. PRO, DEFE 11/95, JP (53) 79. I owe the last three references to Joanne de Pennington.
11. PRO, PREM 11/645.
12. *Ibid.*
13. PRO, FO 371/106750/17.
14. A. Eden, *Full Circle* (1960), 87.
15. PREM 11/618.
16. FO 371/112047/19.
17. FO 371/112047/26.
18. FO 371/112047/27.
19. PREM 11/645.
20. FO 371/112049/103; FO 371/112050/135.
21. PREM 11/645.
22. *Ibid.*
23. *Ibid.*
24. *Ibid.* The ANZUS treaty was concluded in 1951 by America, Australia and New Zealand. Britain deeply resented its exclusion.
25. *FRUS, 1954–4*, XIII (Washington, DC, 1984), 1238–41.
26. PREM 11/645; CAB 128/27 (7 April 1954); CAB 129/68 (7 April 1954).
27. FO 371/112052/202.
28. *Ibid.*
29. PREM 11/645.
30. FO 371/112054/252.
31. *FRUS 1952–4*, XIII. 1322.

32. FO 371/112053/232.
33. *Ibid.*
34. E. Shuckburgh, *Descent to Suez: Diaries, 1951–6* (1986), 189.
35. FO 371/112054/279: *FRUS 1952–4*, XIII, 1362–3.
36. FO 371/112055/280, 281, 283.
37. FO 371/112055/305.
38. Shuckburgh, *Diaries*, 171–2.
39. FO 371/112056/314.
40. Shuckburgh, *Diaries*, 172.
41. *Ibid.*, 172, 174; CAB 129/68 (27 April); FO 371/112056/321.
42. FO 371/112056/321.
43. CAB 129/68 (27 April).
44. PREM 11/645; DEFE 4/70, COS (54) 47th.
45. PREM 11/645.
46. FO 371/112066/555/
47. FO 371/112085/104840 (a printed collection of documents on the Geneva conference), documents 56, 58, 61; Shuckburgh, *Diaries*, 186.
48. FO 371/111863/46; Shuckburgh, *Diaries*, 187.
49. FO 371/112085/104840, doc. 57; Shuckburgh, *Diaries*, 187–92, 198.
50. *FRUS, 1952–4*, XIII, 728–9, 737, 742, 1522–5.
51. FO 371/112065/540, 543.
52. CAB 128/27 (24 May); FO 371/112067/561.
53. PREM 11/666.
54. *Ibid.*; FO 371/111864/65; Eden, *Full Circle*, 127.
55. CAB 128/27 (5 June).
56. FO 371/112085/104840, doc. 123.
57. *FRUS, 1952–4*, XIII, 1083–5; and see J. Cable, *The Geneva Conference of 1954 on Indochina* (1986), 93.
58. DEFE 4/70 (8 June); FO 371/111864/90, 97.
59. FO 371/112085/104840, docs 127–9.
60. *Ibid.*, doc. 138.
61. CAB 129/69 (22 June); PREM 11/649.
62. FO 371/112075/792.
63. Eden, *Full Circle*, 132–3.
64. *FRUS 1952–4*, XIII, 580–2.
65. FO 371/111867/170; FO 371/111868/178.
66. FO 371/112085/104840, doc. 172.
67. *Ibid.*, docs 173, 190; Eden, *Full Circle*, 141–2.
68. CAB 128/27 (23 July).
69. This essay is a conflation of two chapters from L.S. Kaplan, D. Artaud and M.R. Rubin (eds.), *From Dienbienphu to Saigon: Franco-American Co-operation and Conflict, 1954–5* (Wilmington, Delaware, 1989).

Select Bibliography

D. Acheson, *Present at the Creation* (1970).

K. Adenauer, *Memoirs, 1945–53* (1966).

S. E. Ambrose, *Eisenhower: The President* (2 vols, New York, 1983–4).

E. Barker, *Britain in a Divided Europe* (1971).

G. Barraclough and R. F. Wall, *Survey of International Affairs, 1955–6* (1960).

C. Bell, *Survey of International Affairs, 1954* (1957).

M. Beloff, *New Dimensions in Foreign Policy* (1961).

N. Beloff, *Transit of Britain* (1972).

B. J. Bernstein, 'The struggle over the Korean armistice', in B.Cumings, ed., *Child of Conflict: The Korean-American Relationship, 1943–1953* (1983).

G. Berridge, *Economic Power in Anglo-South African Diplomacy* (1981).

R. Bullen, 'Great Britain, the U.S. and the Indian armistice resolution on the Korean War, November 1952', in I. Nish (ed.), *Aspects of Anglo-Korean Relations* (1984).

D. E. Butler, *The British General Election of 1951* (1952).

P. Calvocoressi, *Survey of International Affairs, 1951, 1952 and 1953* (1954–6).

D. Carlton, *Anthony Eden: A Biography* (1981).

J. Colville, *The Fringes of Power: Downing Street Diaries, 1939–55* (1985).

R. Divine, *Eisenhower and the Cold War* (1981).

A. Eden, *Full Circle* (1960).

D. Eisenhower, *Mandate for Change, 1953–6* (1963).

R. H. Ferrell, ed., *The Eisenhower Diaries* (1981).

— ed., *The Diary of James C. Hagerty* (Bloomington, Ind., 1983).

D. Folliot, ed., *Documents on International Affairs, 1951, 1952, 1953 and 1954* (1954–7).

J. Frankel, *British Foreign Policy* (1975).

N. Frankland, *Documents on International Affairs, 1955* (1958).

E. Fursdon, *The European Defence Community* (1980).

J. Garner, *The Commonwealth Office, 1925–68* (1978).

L. Gerson, *John Foster Dulles* (New York, 1967).

Lord Gladwyn, *The Memoirs of Lord Gladwyn* (1972).

P. Gore-Booth, *With Great Truth and Respect* (1974).

M. Gowing, *Independence and Deterrence: Britain and Atomic Energy, 1945–52* (2 vols, 1974).

W. Hayter, *The Kremlin and the Embassy* (1966).

— *A Double Life* (1974).

N. Henderson, *The Private Office* (1985).

A. Howard, *'RAB': The Life of R. A. Butler* (1987).

R. R. James, *Anthony Eden* (1986).

Earl of Kilmuir, *Political Adventure* (1964).

I. Kirkpatrick, *The Inner Circle* (1959).

S. Lloyd, *Suez, 1956* (1978).

G. McDermott, *The Eden Legacy* (1969).

I. McDonald, *A Man of the Times* (1976).

R. McGheehan, *The German Rearmament Question* (1971).

H. Macmillan, *Tides of Fortune, 1945–55* (1969).

R. Massigli, *Une comédie des erreurs* (Paris, 1978).

Lord Moran, *Winston Churchill: The Struggle for Survival, 1940–65* (1966).

J. Morgan, ed., *The Backbench Diaries of Richard Crossman* (1981).

F. S. Northedge, *Descent from Power* (1974).

A. Nutting, *Europe Will Not Wait* (1960).

L. Pearson, *Memoirs: The International years, 1948–57* (Toronto, 1974).

H. Pelling, *Winston Churchill* (1974).

A. Schlaim *et al.*, *British Foreign Secretaries since 1945* (1977).

A. Seldon, *Churchill's Indian Summer: The Conservative Government, 1951–55* (1981).

E. Shuckburgh, *Descent to Suez: Diaries, 1951–6* (1986).

P. H. Spaak, *The Continuing Battle* (1971).

D. Stikker, *Men of Responsibility* (1966).

C. Sulzberger, *A Long Row of Candles* (1969).

H. S. Truman, *Years of Trial and Hope* (1956).

N. J. Wheeler, 'British nuclear weapons and Anglo-American relations, 1945–54', *International Affairs*, 62, 1986.

J. Wheeler-Bennett, *Action This Day* (1968).

J. W. Young, 'Churchill's "No" to Europe: the rejection of European union by Churchill's post-war government, 1951–52', *Historical Journal*, 28, 1985.

— 'Churchill, the Russians and the Western alliance: the three-power conference at Bermuda, December 1953', *English Historical Review*, 101, 1986.
— 'Britain's Latin American dilemma: the overthrow of "communist" Guatemala', *International History Review*, 8, 1986.

Index